AN INTRODUCTION TO POLITICS

AN INTRODUCTION TO POLITICS

by

ROGER H. SOLTAU

Sometime Scholar of Pembroke College, Oxford ;
Professor of Political Science in the American
University of Beirut

LONGMANS, GREEN AND CO
LONDON • NEW YORK • TORONTO

LONGMANS, GREEN AND CO LTD
6 & 7 CLIFFORD STREET LONDON W 1
ALSO AT MELBOURNE AND CAPE TOWN
LONGMANS, GREEN AND CO INC
55 FIFTH AVENUE NEW YORK 3
LONGMANS, GREEN AND CO
215 VICTORIA STREET TORONTO 1
ORIENT LONGMANS LTD
BOMBAY CALCUTTA MADRAS

First published 1951

PRINTED IN GREAT BRITAIN AT
THE UNIVERSITY PRESS
ABERDEEN

PREFACE

THIS book was originally planned for use in an Introductory
Course in the American University of Beirut; it also served
as the basis for a similar course given in the London School
of Economics in 1945-46; I think that it might have a wider
use for similar study either in other universities or in Adult
classes. It assumes no previous knowledge of the subject, but
only such acquaintance with general history as will enable the
reader to understand simple allusions.

I have decided, in consultation with my publishers, that
in view of the fullness of the table of contents and the
bibliography there is no need for an Index.

My thanks are due to my assistants in Beirut, Mrs. Pamela
Lockett Barakat and Messrs. Albawi, Tueni and Zuwiyyah;
to Messrs. Sydney Herbert and Ieuan John, my colleagues
in the University College of Wales, Aberystwith, during the
two sessions I spent on its staff, for kindly reading through
the manuscript and indicating points for clarification; and
especially, as always, to my wife for constant encouragement,
assistance in the revision of the text and valuable suggestions
as to the treatment of a number of questions.

ROGER H. SOLTAU

BEIRUT, *October*, 1950.

CONTENTS

CHAPTER I

WHAT IS IT ALL ABOUT?

'What is man but a question? He is here for that—for asking honest, bold questions and humbly waiting for answers. Not asking boldly enough—and giving oneself flattering answers, that is the source of all error.'

—Rachel van Hagen (eighteenth-century feminist).[1]

'Things are what they are, and their consequences are what they will be—so why wish to be deceived?'

—Bishop Butler.

1. WHAT IS 'POLITICS'?

POLITICAL Science is the science or study of Politics. *But what is Politics?* Literally, it is everything that concerns or belongs to the 'Polis', or City, or better, community, since the 'City' is no longer the unit of common life.

Does this mean that when we speak of 'Politics' we really mean *all* that affects our common life? The answer is 'no', because although there is, as we shall see, no aspect of our common life which may not, sometimes and somehow, become political, the term is reserved for those common affairs which are under the direction of an authority or agency managing or controlling these affairs on behalf of, and in the name of, the community. This agency or authority we call the *State*.

A political activity is thus an activity of a community exercised through and under the state, and what is political and what is not has therefore varied. For many centuries religion was a political matter since the state made certain forms of it compulsory and others illegal; now there is only (we believe) one state in the world (Hedjaz) whose citizens must all be of the same religion; there are several states whose rulers must by law belong to one particular faith (Great Britain, Syria, Spain, the Scandinavian monarchies); one state officially discourages religion and denies its exercise to all its officials

---

[1] Quoted by Mary Beard, 'Rise of Women', p. 477.

(Russia); there are states in the Arab world where parliamentary representation is closely connected with religious affiliation, and lately two new states have emerged (India and Pakistan) based on the dominance of their majority religion. But in most countries nowadays religion is no longer a matter of state concern and no encouragement is officially given to any particular faith.

Education again may be under state control, as in France and Russia, etc., and in that case educational problems take on political aspects: appointments, programmes may be decided on other than purely educational grounds. Again, the matter of state intervention in economic life has taken many forms, from almost total non-interference to strict regulation, as in the days when the state fixed the kind of dress that could be worn by different classes of the people (these 'sumptuary laws', as they are called, were frequent in the Middle Ages), or decreed in what particular towns were particular kinds of materials to be manufactured (as in the France of the *ancien régime*), or ordered persons to be buried in woollen shrouds so as to encourage the woollen industry (as in seventeenth-century England). Police, the administration of justice, the coining of money, the right to levy armies and to make war, which we are accustomed to think of as powers solely exercised by the state, were largely in private hands in the days of medieval feudalism. Almost everything was 'political' in Nazi Germany, where 'whatever was not compulsory was forbidden' as has been wittily said, and almost everything is 'political' in contemporary Russia. On the other hand the sphere of politics has rarely been as restricted as in the England of the eighteenth and early nineteenth century, where it was often difficult to get the state to act at all.

'Politics' and 'political' are therefore terms which vary from time to time and place to place, and in theory there is no department of our collective life which may not become 'political' by being brought under state direction. But in all contemporary societies, there is, at any given time, a clear distinction between what is political and what is not, although the state's share may greatly differ in kind and extent.

It follows from all this that, even taking the narrowest possible definition, *politics is the concern of everybody with any sense of responsibility*, for everybody is affected. The qualities of the rules or laws we live under, their fairness and good sense, the effectiveness of their enforcement, the purity of our judicial system, the good management of public finance—both in the way the money is collected and the way it is spent, the honesty of officials, the maintenance of adequate standards of hygiene, the avoidance of war and the adequacy of our defence; these and many others are questions to which no one should be indifferent. And our modern democratic systems are based on the old principle, that 'what concerns all should be approved by all'.

The Problem of Indifference.—How is it then that so many people almost pride themselves on 'not being interested in politics'?

Lack of imagination is certainly one answer. There are people who cannot look beyond their noses, and cannot realise how closely their welfare is bound up with state policy. Their number is fast diminishing however; those whose memory goes back to the early years of this century will remember the widespread indifference of English opinion to Foreign Affairs up to 1914 and the difference made by the First World War: nobody could help seeing, after that, how vital were the problems of war and peace to everybody. Others would say that in a modern state the citizen can directly do so little; of what use is one single vote and one lone opinion? True, but little is better than nothing; and the ordinary citizen can do more than he thinks through the innumerable groups and organisations which do so much to express the views and exert the influence, of the ordinary individual.

More serious is the opinion that so much of political life is 'unreal'; that elections, parliamentary debates, parties are all largely puppet-shows, the real power being behind the scenes, outside our control. We shall discuss this later at greater length. Here it is enough to say that, admitting the view to have *some* basis in fact, is it not better that all active citizens should get together and reduce this 'hidden control' to a minimum and oppose its worst manifestations by an intelligent organised public opinion?

In fact, the alternative to a wide interest in politics is leaving them to irresponsible groups, to ambitious and often unscrupulous bosses. It is possible to imagine, in pure theory, the effective management of public affairs by an enlightened despot, or by a small disinterested governing class; but history shows how rarely the despot is enlightened, or the governing class disinterested. There are undoubted defects in the rule of the many, and it is everybody's right to prefer the rule of the one or of the few; but such a preference will find it hard to justify itself by historical precedent, whether of Roman emperors, Venetian aristocracies, or modern dictators. Better let all interested in the results take their share, however small, in matters of common concern.

To quote the hero of a contemporary novel, 'Politics were damned important. The smaller and the more entangled and the more bloody the world got, the more important they were. Politics were himself and Carla (his fiancée) multiplied a billion times—two billion people instead of two, struggling to find a way of living together and not being successful about it.'[1]

Politics is therefore everybody's business, and it is with that conviction that this book is being written. It is good that the reader should be frankly informed of the author's viewpoint—or bias—and we shall not attempt to hide our belief in what are commonly called 'democratic' forms of government as opposed to 'authoritarian' or 'autocratic'; as we see it, the goodness of a state is largely proportional to the scope given to individual responsibility, to the widespread development of a civic sense, to the opportunities given to the ordinary man. We know of no other acceptable standards.

The State as the Subject of Study.—Political Science, then, is going to be the study of the state, its aims and purposes—the institutions by which those are going to be realised, its relations with its individual members and with other states, and also what men have thought, said, and written about all these questions. It has three essential aspects. The first is an analysis of *what is*, both in human nature and in its manifestations in political action; this may be called *descriptive*. The second is a study of what *has been* in the past, and may be called *historical*, and the third is an examination of what *ought to be* in the future, and may be called *ethical*.

It is, of course, evident that, properly studied, political

[1] Ullmann, 'The White Tower'.

science must call in the help of other sciences or branches of study. First and foremost it will need history—so closely related that, to some writers, history is really the past tense of a subject of which political science is the present. 'History is past politics and present politics future history', as Seeley said. Without going quite so far as to identify the two to that extent, we may say without hesitation that history is the most indispensable of all other disciplines to the political scientist. He will also need psychology in his analysis of human nature, his raw material; he will need philosophy, ethics and religion, by which to form the standards to which political action should conform: he will need economics for an understanding of the interference of the state in that domain, and of the conditions of collective prosperity. He will also need an unprejudiced mind for much of his subject-matter is highly controversial and easily arouses violent passions that inhibit reason. And more than all, will he need sound common sense, keen powers of observation, and—a sense of humour.

It is a great enterprise, and its successful undertaking requires, as Professor Hocking calls it, 'a sense of the destiny of the human mass' and a 'clear view of man's place in the world'.

2. IS THE STUDY OF POLITICS A 'SCIENCE'?

Before going any further we must, however, face a number of problems. The first concerns the very name of our study: are we right in calling it 'Political Science'? Is the term 'Science' a correct description?

Our answer to the question will naturally depend on the meaning we give to the words 'Science' and 'scientific'. Of course, all serious study must be 'scientific' in the sense that all conclusions must be based on ascertainable facts, and research carried out with the minimum of prejudice and emotion, with the maximum of rational enquiry and deduction. But if we imply by the term 'Science' the obtaining of mathematically predictable results, such as can be obtained in a laboratory, politics cannot be a 'Science', for it is dealing with people, not things; it is the art of getting men to live together and co-operate in matters of common interest.

'The Politician', says Hocking (and to a large extent the political scientist also), 'is the man who deliberately faces both the certainty that men must live together, and the endless uncertainties on what terms they can live together, and also takes upon himself the task of proposing the terms, and of transforming the unsuccessful human group into the successful.'

Absence of Exact Results.—In this sphere of human relationships mathematically accurate answers are unobtainable. For one thing, you can never quite tell what man will do in any given circumstances, and for another, there never are two identical sets of circumstances, creating identical human situations.

All the scientific study of politics can achieve is a number of strictly limited conclusions. 'It can obtain first of all fairly exact results about certain definite and concrete problems such as mortality, disease, crime, literacy, development of economic life, production, trade, currency; secondly it can formulate some rough laws about large-scale and long-term social and political movements'[1] (but very rough at best). Beyond that it can scarcely go, and we agree with Mr. Spender that 'belief in the existence of a science from which rules and principles may be deduced for the government of mankind seems to be one of the most disastrous of the many political myths of recent years'.[2]

This being so, we confess that to term our study 'Political Science' is misleading, and the term 'Politics' or 'Government' seems to us preferable. But the term 'Political Science' is so widely used that we cannot altogether avoid it, and must be content to warn the student to use it with due caution. 'Is there such a thing as a Science of Politics?' asks the French philosopher, Taine. And he answers, 'There is at all events a body of positive lessons which, in matters political, lend precision to discussion, guide judgement, and diminish the elements of speculation, exaggeration and error'.

[1] See Burnham, 'The Machiavellians', for an expansion of the point.
[2] 'In the last two centuries it has become fashionable for political thinkers to regard politics as a science to be mastered by the same methods and discussed in the same terms as any natural science. It is Mr. Morgenthau's thesis, (in his 'Scientific Man versus Power Politics') that the habit is responsible for the social and political disasters which have befallen Europe and the dangers that confront her.' (*Times Literary Supplement*, June 21, 1947).

We are concerned then with the behaviour of men in political groups. This must include both their ideas, emotions, and desires, and the institutions in which these are expressed. Our domain is the human personality, manifesting itself in one sphere of its innumerable activities, the organisation of collective life. Political science or theory thus first came into existence when man began to think about this collective life and to will its continuation and its transformation, when, says Lindsay, 'in some concrete situation men began arguing that the nature of the state required that such and such a thing be done'.

3. SOME PROBLEMS IN THE STUDY OF POLITICS

We may now turn to some of the specific problems that face the student at the very beginning of his work.

Inadequate Terminology.—The first problem concerns not so much the subject itself as our instruments of study. Whereas the natural sciences have a uniform technical vocabulary, we have not. If the doctor speaks of the sciatic nerve, the chemist of a catalyst, the physicist of atomic weight, their hearers know exactly what is meant by those terms. But let a political scientist speak of Democracy, Communism, Imperialism, Monarchy, Republic, and every one of his audience is free to place on these his own personal interpretation, and does so, with confusion worse confounded. Further, every period tends to produce new terms, to be used indiscriminately on all and sundry occasions, with the inevitable loss of any precise meaning. Planning, Isolationism, Independence, Propaganda, Reconstruction, Rehabilitation—what *exactly* do these words imply?

One of the primary needs of political science is thus the development, not to say creation, of an adequate and precise terminology, with words of recognised meaning, so that it will become impossible to confuse issues by the indiscriminate use of 'terms of all work'. But today that is probably asking for too much!

Apparent Ease of Subject.—Turning now to the specific difficulties to be faced, we first meet the paradox that whereas in some studies the greatest problems originate from their intrinsic hardness, ultra-technical character and remoteness from everyday concerns, political science is faced by the contrary obstacles that it seems too easy. Everybody thinks he knows everything about politics; its content is concrete and near at hand; every newspaper is full of it and it is discussed wherever people meet.

Of course, if everybody who talks about it really did know, there would be no problem. All subjects have their specialists, to whom ordinary people give a respectful hearing. But in politics, fools rush in where angels fear to tread. There is no question, however complex, to which thousands are not ready with their answers. Foreign Affairs, the Loan, Housing, the Veto, the Budget, the future of the Empire—those responsible for ultimate decisions are bombarded with advice and suggestions. 'Armchair strategy' has its peace-time counterpart, in what the French call 'la politique du Café du Commerce', where the amateur politician lays down the law. And what a babel of discordant voices, of cheap advice and hasty suggestions, the ignorant shouting of the man in the street! Such a nuisance to the student, such a disturbance to the politician! If only we could be left to our serious business, whether of study or of administration, how much simpler it would all be!

Would it really? What would we think of a doctor who would not allow the patient to describe his symptoms because it disturbed him? This unwanted advice, these ignorant suggestions, those easy solutions, are all part of the problem, politics being precisely the study of how men behave politically, of what they like and dislike, of what they feel and think about their collective life.

A Living Subject-Matter.—This initial difficulty, of the apparent ease of political study letting loose the amateur in all his hordes, leads us to what is in fact the central problem of political science, namely that you are not dealing with abstract issues or inanimate matter, but with living persons. Like the doctor, you *must* allow the patient to speak, you must listen, and take all he says into consideration. Politics is precisely the adjustment of countless individual, ordinary lives, which are the raw material out of which states are made. It is, of course, this livingness of the material that gives political science both its fascination and its complexity. Mishandle your material and it will let you know it in no obscure terms, from a popular demonstration to a lost election and sometimes to a revolution. The most essential lesson for the student is to translate into terms of living human activity and feeling the formal institutions and policies which he is studying. Kings and ministers are living persons, with their likes and dislikes, their prejudices, their flashes of intuitive genius, their lamentable mistakes—each of which may spell ruin or success to their country, misery or happiness to its members. A parliament is not an abstract unit but a congress of some hundreds of men and women of all kinds, intelligent and stupid, disinterested and selfish, honest and corrupt, young and old, carrying into politics their individual characteristics, strengths and weaknesses, capable of being moved to noble decisions and to ignoble. (And those decisions again spell sometimes life and death, always more or less well-being or power for somebody.) A small change in a tariff or tax, a slight alteration in the land laws—all these are going to affect everyday lives, probably some for good and others for evil. 'And the best I can hope for', says the politician, 'is that the sum total of people pleased will be greater than that of the displeased.'

And it is so difficult to know beforehand *what* is going to please whom! Man is so incalculable; his reactions so unexpected! You never can tell which of the innumerable aspects of his personality will be dominant at any particular time. Shall I appeal to his capacity for self-sacrifice or to his love for comfort? To his instinct for a quiet life or to his lust for power? One day he clamours for freedom; the next day he puts his neck under the foot of a Napoleon or of a Hitler (It was the same crowd that cried both 'Hosanna!' and 'Crucify!').

All Political Issues are Personal.—But if the pressure of elections, and other manifestations of public opinion, help to remind the politician that he is dealing with living people and not with abstract tendencies, remembrance of this cardinal truth is much harder for the student of politics or, for that matter, of history. It is a constant effort of will and imagination to clothe with flesh and blood the dry bones of institutions and laws. That is one of many reasons why the student should do his utmost to see men actually at work, to be present at sittings of Parliament and municipal councils and to visualise processes

I *

he reads of in his text-books. It will not necessarily increase
his respect for them—but of what value is a respect based on
illusion? In the same way the keen student will lose no opportunity of discussing current issues with as many people as he
can, of the most widely differing elements of society; only
thus can he gauge the incidence of those issues on individual
lives and incidentally the degree of interest and intelligence
shown by the rank and file. The writer has never forgotten the
acute and prophetic criticism of the Anglo-Japanese alliance
made by two working men in a London suburban carriage at
the time of its conclusion over forty years ago. But he has also
heard a lot of political nonsense in suburban railway carriages!

If the student clearly grasps the importance of this translation of political issues into terms of individual lives, he will
be readier to face the next problem, namely their relevance to
moral and ethical standards. For, to the politician making his
calculation of majorities and minorities, comes the moralist,
reminding him that his decisions must be not only popular
but just; 'You can please thousands by an injustice to one'.
And in such a case, it is the one that counts. That is, in political
science results must be not only quantitatively accurate but
qualitatively congruent to certain values. The problem of
politics, as Leacock says, is that of 'the unsolved riddle of
social justice', and its basic principle is that justice can never be
established by injustice to one single individual.

The Problem of Values.—But what is 'justice'? This question
brings us into the heart of our subject, that human behaviour
is based on 'values' which it is our duty to define and defend.
From the times when Plato and Aristotle equated the good
citizen with the good man, men have debated the meaning
of the term 'good' and wondered how far the 'goodness' of
individuals was the same as the 'goodness' of collectivities.
We are not endeavouring to answer the question here and now,
but only pointing out that the search for the just is no less
essential in politics than the search for the practical, precisely
because the raw material of politics is the moral personalities
of live people. If they are leaders, or even mere agents of the
government, they must justify their actions, not only to their
own conscience but to the moral judgement of the world;
this is the great lesson of the German trials. If they are mere

subjects, then the reminder comes that every one of them has his life to live, and that far from its being expedient that one should die for the people (save by his own free will), 'if anyone caused one of these little ones to stumble it were better for him that a millstone were placed round his neck and that he should be cast into the sea'.

The search for justice is, of course, slow and fumbling; men's ideas of what is just do not always agree; but the student of politics will not lose courage or allow himself to believe that his search for right is a mere will-o'-the-wisp and that the 'riddle of social justice' is not only unsolved but insoluble.

The Problem of Change.—Yet another difficulty for the student, itself inherent in the live character of his material, is that, like all living matter, it is always changing and never keeps still. No country is today what it was yesterday or what it will be tomorrow, any more than I am myself the same on two consecutive days. Body, mind, experience, personality are undergoing perpetual modification. We say sometimes, after some great event or shock, that so and so 'was never the same man again', and the same is true of collectivities. There is no country in the world that will ever be 'the same again' after the two world wars. Hence the need to be on one's guard against formulae that express a fixed or static state of things.

Politics are in fact a process, a perpetual becoming. We are not watching a picture, but a film, sometimes in very slow motion, sometimes going past at breathless speed. To judge the speed of the film is in fact one of the tasks of the political scientist, and one of those in which lamentable errors can be committed. The fear of this will protect him against two recurrent dangers. Remembering, in the first place, that all judgements on a changing scene and its actors must be tentative and temporary, he will be careful to limit them in time, and to avoid giving permanence to characterisations which, while perhaps accurate at one time, would be ludicrous at another. And especially will he refrain from prophesying, remembering that the unexpected does happen, though not always. 'Man, that unknown', as Carrel called him, is apt to make a fool of the prophet. The student must never forget that he can never

expect to 'know' and depend on his material as a chemist or
a geologist knows and depends on his. 'There are two words
in medicine that you must never use', said a Professor of
Medicine to his pupils;'they are "Always" and "Never" '—
and the same applies to political science.

The Apparent and the Real.—A further complication may be
described as the contrast between theory and practice. When
we have elaborately analysed a series of institutions and their
connections, described with minute clearness and apparent
accuracy the working of a political system, we shall have only
described a façade, something visible from the outside. We
shall not have pictured the real inner working of the machine—
'who gets what, when, and how?' as Professor Laswell asks
in a well-known book. Who pulls the strings? What are the
real secret powers behind the throne, Press, Finance, Civil
Service, Grey Eminences?

An eloquent picture of the subjection of government to the
bombardment of group interests is drawn in the 'Grain Growers
Guide for Western Canada' of 1913, under the heading of
'Dont's for Grain Growers'.—'Don't agitate for lower tariff
duties, because you will offend the Canadian manufacturers'
association. Don't agitate for lower freight rates, because you
will offend our three great railway companies. Don't agitate
for cheaper money, because you will offend the bankers'
association. Don't complain about the high price of lumber,
because you will offend the lumbermen's association. Don't
complain about the high rate of interest you pay on mortgages,
because you will offend the loan and mortgage companies.
Don't advocate co-operative stores, because you will offend
the retail merchants' association. Don't advocate honest
politicians, because you will offend both the government and
the parties.'[1]

The Mystery of Human Decision.—And finally, studying
as we do the actions and decisions of men in certain aspects
of their common life, we shall not often know why they act
and decide thus. What makes a man a Conservative, another
a Socialist? What makes them change their minds—if they do?
We can answer in vague general terms but in each case the
choice is an individual one, and each man carries his secret.

[1] Quoted in the *American Political Science Quarterly*, 1923, p. 639.

When the challenges of Christianity, of Islam, of the Reformation faced the men of the time, each one individually had to decide between the acceptance of the new faith or loyalty to the old. For what reasons did thousands of obscure people rally to the one or remain faithful to the other, often at the peril of their lives? Why was the French Revolution hailed on the one hand, and condemned on the other, by people of apparently similar backgrounds, interests and prejudices? We do not know. And this ignorance transferred from the past to the present, remains the constant complication of our study. If our raw material be as was quoted, 'the facts of human nature', then we have to admit from the start that our raw material is capable of great vagaries and presents in its behaviour many unsolved enigmas.

4. HOW TO MEET THESE PROBLEMS

'And what about it all?' asks the student. 'You have enumerated some of the difficulties I shall have to face; have you any positive suggestions to offer about the best way of meeting them?'

Realising our Limitations.—Taking for granted the open mind, the humble spirit, the readiness for more knowledge, we might first mention the need to realise that we stand at a particular point in space and time. Although most problems tend nowadays to take an appearance of geographical universality, we must bear in mind that their particular forms still vary considerably, and that, therefore, their interest and importance is relative. There are other forms of civilised government than the western parliamentary system. Many people believe that democracy has not yet found its appropriate institutions. And our surveys of comparative government could with advantage cast their nets somewhat further afield.

Need for the Humble Mind.—As regards time, the essential duty of the political scientist is to remember that wisdom will not necessarily die with him. In common with the historian (and is there any essential difference between the two?) he finds it easy enough to look backwards but very difficult to look forward. He can scarcely visualise a world that will function without him. And yet, unless we are to despair of man, we must go on hoping that our present follies and crimes are but some of the infantile diseases of mankind; that the few thousand years of recorded history are only the prelude to many more thousands of years of greater wisdom, deeper sensitiveness to the sufferings of others, greater reluctance to profit at the expense of our fellow-men.

The Personal Test.—Having tried to look beyond his geographical and chronological environment, the political scientist will endeavour to test every system and every policy by its effects on individual human lives. He will reject the theory that the immediate good of the people of today can be sacrificed to an alleged good of those of tomorrow, and demand no sacrifices that cannot be related to the welfare—moral as well as material—of those from whom it is expected. He will especially refuse to admit that it can be right to make of men and women mere means to ends in which they do not share.

However coldly scientific he must be in his analysis of the collective life of mankind, he will remember that in the last resort he is nearer in his work to the physician than to the physicist.[1] Much of his field of study, not to say all, is concerned with the sufferings and imperfections of mankind and with the attempts made to relieve these. He will be merciful in his judgements, ready to credit good intentions, yet stern towards any wrongs that appear as regressions from already accepted standards, not as perhaps inevitable stages in evolution. And above all, he must show towards his 'raw material' the patience and the sympathy that come from an understanding of its weaknesses, its contradictions, its mistakes because, after all, those weaknesses, contradictions, and mistakes are his own. Being himself a man, he is himself part of that raw material which he is studying. 'Homo sum et nihil humanum a me alienum puto.'

[1] In an article entitled 'Are the Social Scientists Backward?' Professor Kemmerer enumerates 'five conditions under which the social scientists must work and which would drive a physical scientist frantic. He can make few experiments; he cannot measure results accurately; he cannot control the conditions surrounding the experiments; he is often expected to get quick results with slow moving economic forces, and he must work with people, not inanimate objects.' (*Bulletin of the American Association of University Professors*, January, 1949.)

CHAPTER II

THE LAND AND ITS PEOPLE

THERE can be no community without people to form one, and no common life without some definite piece of territory in which to make that particular experiment in collective living. Land and population must therefore be the starting-point of any study of man in his organised groups.

I. THE TERRITORY OF THE STATE

All Land Belongs to Some State.—If you open an atlas, you will see that the whole surface of the earth, and some of the sea as well, is divided up among those units that we call states. Just as every person belongs to a state, so does every square yard of earth, and the boundaries that mark off the states are of the utmost importance, political, economic, social. There is no state without its proper territory, large or small, and no territory that is not part of some state, large or small. And as far as we personally are concerned, it is connection with a particular territory that normally creates our membership of a state. You are a citizen because you were born there, or because your father was born there—or because, though born elsewhere you have taken up your permanent residence there and obtained citizenship by naturalisation. Your fellow-citizens, with few exceptions, are your fellow-residents, and it is this sharing of the same territory that creates most of your common interests.

What are the relations of the state to its land? Note first of all that in most countries the land does not now belong to the state but is the private property of its citizens. The one great exception to this rule is, of course, Communist Russia, but in primitive times it was a common thing for the land to be the collective property of the community. Traces of this can still be found where 'common land' exists in some rural communities; for instance, some English villages own bits of common land, municipalities often own parks and promenades, and all roads are the property of some public authority. The state may sometimes buy land for some special purpose, but it will pay for it like any other purchaser.[1] Mines are often state property, as they are now in Great Britain. The state may also make rules about the way land shall or shall not be used, and in rare cases take land away where it is not being properly developed.

The State's Monopoly of Power Within its Own Territory.— But if the state claims no ownership of land, it does claim the monopoly of authority inside its boundaries. The extent of that authority may be great or small according to the type of state, but great or small it cannot be shared with anybody else, especially not with any other state. (That is one meaning of the term 'sovereign', so frequently used in political science, and to which we shall return.) None of its members within its borders owes any obedience to another state, and even if they are foreign residents they cannot plead the orders of their own state as a reason for not obeying those of the state in which they are now living; if they did, they would soon be expelled.

But if the state admits no rival within its own territory, it follows that it has no authority outside it. It was one of the grievances against Nazi Germany that it tried to exercise over its citizens abroad a control going far beyond the general protection of interests recognised by the ordinary rules of international intercourse; in fact, it tried to do this still when they had actually acquired a new citizenship by naturalisation and had therefore legally abandoned all allegiance to the Reich.

If a state has sole authority over all its territories, that authority is not necessarily exercised everywhere in the same way. King George VI rules in Great Britain and in his 'Crown Colonies' through Cabinet and Parliament in Westminster; and in the Dominions through the Cabinet and Parliament of each of these. Many states have overseas dependencies which may have some self-government or none at all. Some states are absolutely limited to their own bare territory; except that

---

[1] In many countries the state owns land acquired for public purpose. In England, Crown Lands are mostly former royal property, ceded to the state by the King in exchange for a yearly payment on the Civil List. But the King is also a private landowner, with the same rights and duties as any of his subjects.

ships and embassies are always held to be the territory of the state that owns them.

Acquisition of Territory.—This variety of authority is closely connected with the fact that states have acquired their territories in several different ways. Most states have grown around an original kind of 'core' or nucleus; Wessex for England, the country between Seine and Loire rivers for France, the old mark of Brandenburg for Prussia, the Atlantic seaboard for the United States, and expansion has come usually by conquest. Much as we may condemn conquest by our modern standards, the fact remains that its consequences have to be accepted, otherwise scarcely one state would continue to exist. Is there a single state which is now under the same control as a thousand years ago? Territories have changed hands times without number with little or no protest; the first real revolt against acquisition by conquest (the partition of Poland) is not two centuries old. On the matter of conquest nobody can afford to cast the first stone.

More peaceful methods of acquisition have been marriages, exchange, purchase and cession. The French state was partly built up by judicious marriages of kings with heiresses to large domains, and Austria did much the same. 'While others conquer you espouse', was her motto. Exchange is rare, but that is how Lorraine became French in 1766, and how Prussia in 1890 obtained Heligoland from Britain in exchange for Zanzibar. It was by purchase that the United States obtained Louisiana from the French and Florida from the Spaniards, while Cyprus was ceded to Britain by Turkey in 1878 in gratitude for diplomatic support in the Russo-Turkish war.

2. THE FRONTIERS OF THE STATE

Frontiers and Treaties.—Every change in the ownership of a piece of territory is registered in a public treaty, so that all the existing frontiers in the world today are the creation of some treaty, recent or old. The English Channel, for instance, only became our recognised frontier by the treaty of 1662 by which Charles II sold Dunkirk back to the French, thus confirming our final abandonment of any claims to lands in France. The frontiers of that country with Spain go back to the treaty of the Pyrenees (1659), with Belgium to the treaty of Vienna (1814) which detached from France territories conquered during the Revolutionary period, with Germany to the treaty of Versailles (1919), with Italy to the treaty of 1947, and so on. An excellent exercise is to take an atlas and see how one can indicate the corresponding treaty for each major frontier.

'Good' and 'Bad' Frontiers.—Frontiers are, therefore, most important, historically and politically. A 'good' frontier must have certain definite qualities; it must give security; and yet not be too much of a barrier; it must be acceptable to both parties according to some recognised principle or interest. It follows that a frontier may be 'bad' in one way and 'good' in another. The old boundary between Germany and Czechoslovakia was 'good' for the geographical security of the latter, but 'bad' by leaving three million Germans on the wrong side. The Alps and Pyrenees are practically perfect frontiers in every way. So are the Channel and any very broad sea. But note that for five centuries the Channel was *not* the boundary between England and France; since from the Norman conquest of 1066 to the loss of Calais by Queen Mary in 1558 England had at least a foothold on the continent, which she had again later during the eighty-odd years that she held Heligoland[1] (1807-90) while the Channel Islands are much nearer to France than to England.

Rivers have often been taken as boundaries because they are so clearly marked but only a very broad river makes a good line of defence, and it rarely forms a linguistic or cultural barrier. Many frontiers are purely artificial; from the North Sea to the Ural mountains there is not one boundary that was originally more than a haphazard line, though many of those lines became real frontiers after a number of years. There is no suggestion for instance, of revising the boundary between Belgium and France, though this is a mere line drawn through the former Spanish Netherlands corresponding to the advance of the armies of Louis XIV. It was a mere military accident that Tournai, Brussels, Malines, Antwerp even, did not fall to him; and the frontier does not correspond even now to that of the French language. It is also a military accident

---

[1] Heligoland is of course an island, but so near the continent as to be strategically a part of it.

that during the same reign France did not reach the Rhine north of Alsace and include German-speaking territories that would presumably have become as French in sentiments as Alsace further south. In the same way, the boundaries between Lebanon, Syria and Palestine are purely artificial lines, the result of Anglo-French bargaining over what had been Arab land under Turkish rule, and of Zionist military success.

Common Life Creates Common Interests.—The fact is that common life under one rule creates common interests and consciousness, and custom and inertia have preserved for many years many unsatisfactory frontiers. It is only in recent times that the rising tide of nationalism has burst many old divisions and tried to substitute new ones based on the principles of nationality.

One thing is clear, that the so-called 'natural frontiers' which have been the will-o'-the-wisp of many diplomacies are so few that only rarely can policies be based on them. Frontiers are nearly always a human creation, and second-rate at best from most points of view. And one is inclined to say that the best thing to do with frontiers, since you can't abolish them, is at least to make them as insignificant as possible. In the days of passport-less travel, of free migration, and unrestricted movement of currencies, we were much less conscious of them than now. A return to those happier days, and an abolition of customs, could practically eliminate the frontier as far as movement and settlement is concerned, and collective security, if ever established, could remove the danger of a poor strategic frontier. And one could continue dreaming thus.

3. THE SIZE AND LOCATION OF THE STATE

Large and Small States.—Passing now from the frontiers to the territories within them, we are at once struck by the great contrast in the respective sizes of states, as between tiny Monaco (four square miles) and huge Russia (ten and a half million square miles, i.e. over two million times larger). But the question of size cannot be separated from that of shape. France and Chile have the same area (just over a quarter of a million square miles) but Chile is all length and France an almost perfect hexagon. The same contrast between

length and breadth is seen in Norway and Czechoslovakia,
and creates many problems of defence, of internal communications and control, and of homogeneity.

Space and Power.—And so the question arises 'Is space
power?' And the inevitable answer is, that taken by itself
space is of little significance. Canada and Brazil have a larger
area than the United States, but their population is much
smaller because so much of their areas has been, so far, of
little value to man (new economic and technical processes might
change this of course). Thousands of square miles of desert,
or of wild mountain, or of snow and ice are no great asset
except as a barrier against possible invaders, while some small
states have attained great prosperity and reached the highest
levels of civilisation.

Nevertheless space is power in so far as it helps defence
and in so far as small areas are more open to attack. Small
states have suffered many more vicissitudes in history than
large; unless, like Switzerland, they are protected by more
powerful neighbours, or stand well away from the roads of
expansion, like Portugal, their life is always precarious, as is
shown by the history of the Netherlands and of the countries
along the Danube valley. No wonder that the small states
rallied round the League of Nations and its promises of collective security, and are still suffering from the disillusion of the
last ten years. In a word, as long as power remains a primary
factor in international politics states must either be large or
make no attempt to play an important political role.

Importance of Location.—Location, in fact, matters far more
than actual size. To begin with, all world powers have been
in middle latitudes, and certain types of climate definitely
exclude certain zones from political importance. Here again
technical advance may help by better modes of artificial heating
or air conditioning; irrigation has done wonders and may
yet do more. But it is difficult to visualise powerful communities in the Arctic regions, or the Sahara desert, or in the
Himalayas.

Again, access to the sea has always been an asset, so has
nearness to strategic points such as straits, isthmuses, islands on
main ocean routes, important mountain passes. Proximity to
some of these may have caused political difficulties by the

competition of rival claimants but may have always been economically profitable.

Finally, the possibility of establishing good internal communications by road or river helps cohesion and good government, although these may also help the advance of invading armies, while poor roads across mountains, while impeding internal administration, also impede aggression. The fact is that there are few physical features which may not at one time be an asset and at another a hindrance; insular isolation has probably been an unlimited gain to Britain but it has not helped Ireland.

Natural Resources.—The possession of certain natural resources matters as much as location. A country's capacity to grow enough food for its population by having enough cultivable land in proportion to the population is the most obvious; dependence on the foreigner for food creates problems which are only too evident in our day. The growth of towns, by diminishing the amount of land available for cultivation, and increasing the number of mouths to feed, has seriously aggravated the problem. Minerals are also important ; the possession of coal made modern England, that of oil is revolutionising the Middle East, and the United States would not be where they are now without their large and varied mineral deposits. In the same way the future of Russia as a great power depends largely on her capacity to develop her mineral supplies. And we need spend no time in discussing the significance of wool and rubber in world politics, remembering always that modern technique can often compensate for the lack of natural raw material.

In some cases the whim of nature has given certain countries advantages or disadvantages about which nothing can be done. Spain, Syria, and Palestine, cannot become great industrial powers any more than England can become once more a grain-exporting country. Purely continental states and maritime states are bound to have different policies. But it is amazing what man can do against great handicaps and here again modern technique has destroyed many obstacles that once were considered final.

4. GEOGRAPHY AND GOVERNMENT

Government and Security.—How far do geographical circumstances influence the form of government? It is evident that the lesser the security, the stronger the government should be. If Great Britain has led the way in representative institutions guaranteeing considerable freedom, if the United States have been able to adopt democratic government with a widely scattered authority, they can thank the Channel and the Atlantic for that. The collapse of Poland at the end of the eighteenth century was largely due to her refusal to do away with a constitution which ignored her lack of natural defence, and by legalising anarchy left her helpless before covetous neighbours. Just as war establishes a temporary dictatorship in the most democratic state, so perpetual insecurity demands a government permanently able to rally and control all the resources of the country. Certain circumstances may also create a need for strong government in one particular branch of the common life: countries depending on an elaborate system of irrigation cannot leave this to the vagaries of the individual, and centralised water-control becomes essential. A young pioneer state needing to develop all its natural resources will have to control strictly its exports and imports.

Geopolitics.—Many of the topics just dealt with form a part of a new study to which the Germans gave the name 'Geo-Politics',[1] the politics of the soil, or how far do conditions of physical geography determine political life, and especially relations between states. In one sense the subject is as old as political science, and Aristotle had some wise things to say about it; in modern times Montesquieu laid the foundations of a more scientific approach. But contemporary geopolitics has at its disposal a much greater technical knowledge and a broader field of historical experience.

'Geopolitics', to quote its chief German exponent Haushofer, 'demonstrates the dependence of all political developments on the permanent reality of the soil'; it is 'the doctrine of the earth relations of political units, of the

[1] The real founder of the new science was Professor Mackinder of Oxford, whose 'Democratic Ideals and Reality', published before the First World War, forms the basis of all future study in that field. But the book was unnoticed at the time and was resurrected by Nazi geographers.

relationship between space and politics'. It proclaims the 'spatial requirements' of every state, its necessary 'living-room'; it is, as another geopolitician calls it, 'the geographical conscience of the state'.

As used by the Nazis it was only an instrument to defend German expansionism and deny the right of any other people to whatever happened to conflict with its desires; but properly used it is of course invaluable; its main use is to remind us of certain factors that cannot be changed at will and must in-fluence politics to the end of time. States will never achieve perfect equality in all things, any more than individuals; their character will always be intimately bound up with the particular earth conditions that nature gave them.

Man and Nature.—As long as these geographical con-siderations are kept in their proper place as forming one essential factor in the life of the state, geopolitics is valuable. But geographical considerations are not the only factor, and are not even an unchanging one; inventions can alter geographical advantages; the aeroplane destroys the protection of natural frontiers; streams too swift for navigation, and worthless fifty years ago, are now all important for the electric power which the French call 'white coal' and if oil has not superseded coal as completely as was once expected, it has nevertheless greatly diminished its importance and made its possession less sig-nificant. And most important of all, man can always try and re-dress the inequalities of nature. Tunnels have been pierced through mountains; irrigation and artificial fertilisers have revolutionised agriculture; exchange has generalised access to all the essentials of life. And there is no saying what technique will not have accomplished by the end of this century; it may of course have destroyed civilisation but it may have solved numerous problems which have so far baffled us. The essential thing is to reject all theories of geographical determinism: it is man that matters, and it is to the human element that we now turn.

5. POPULATION: THE PROBLEM OF QUANTITY

Just as when studying territory we had to consider its two aspects, its size and its value, so in population. First, how big a population, both in itself and in relation to the size of the territory ? Secondly, what kind of a population is it? How fitted to tackle the problems of its particular state? And in each case we shall have to relate quantity and quality to the two-fold needs of each state, external and internal.

* * * * *

Density of Population.—There are small and big states in population as in territory. Russia and the United States head both lists as regards bigness. But there is in most cases a sharp contrast between size of population and size of territory; Canada is immense in territory, small in population; Great Britain is the reverse, more than four times the population, about a fortieth of the area.

The ratio between size of territory and of population, or 'Population Density', is expressed by a figure indicating the average number of inhabitants per square mile. Using such figures Canada gets a density of 3; Brazil, also a huge thinly populated country, has 12. At the other end of the scale comes Belgium with 700, the Netherlands with well over 600, Great Britain with nearly 500, Japan, Italy and (pre-war) Germany are some way behind with round about 300. France and Norway have about 200. Russia and India with 90, U.S.A with 36, bring us back to the countries with low density. Here are, therefore, great inequalities, both absolute and relative.

Density Problems.—Population numbers have to be related to three factors: amount of supplies available, standard of living expected, and needs of defence and production. The amount of supplies depends of course on the net extent of cultivable land or of raw materials available; but it also depends on possibilities of transport: a breakdown in this, as recent events show, may be equivalent to famine for all regions not food-growing, and to low industrial production because raw materials cannot be brought to the factory or goods removed from the factory to the market; while scarcity in food-producing countries or difficulties in world-transport will create serious problems in food-importing countries. A population that is not too large in normal times may well exceed the resources of the country when all is abnormal.

No less important is the level of standard of life expected. There is an abyss between the requirements of an American worker and of an Indian peasant, and even within Western Europe between an English and an Italian factory hand. Obviously a low-standard population needs less space and fewer supplies. This variation in standard is partly climatic, but is also largely a matter of custom and tradition, and varies in various departments of life. The French bourgeois is more particular about his food and much less about his material comfort than the Englishman of the same social class.

Finally come the needs of the community. A country open to invasion must have men for defence, while one secure from attack can dispense with a big army. Large-scale industrial production requires an abundant supply of labour. A country of extensive agricultural estates needs proportionately fewer workers on the land than one of small farms.

Over-population.—The question arises, whether one can really speak of 'over-population'. It is obvious that there is no such thing as absolute over-population; it is all a matter of relativeness to certain factors. A country is over-populated if it fails to maintain its normal population in the standard of life which this population normally expects.

If a country complains of being over-populated, it must follow one of four policies: either put up with a very low standard of life, bordering often on starvation (e.g. India); or increase its home-grown food supplies; or again produce goods which it can sell abroad and so buy extra food and other necessities; or finally diminish its population, either by birth restriction or by the emigration of its 'surplus' inhabitants.

The countries driven by necessity to the adoption of the first course are of course greatly to be pitied. The lowness of their subsistence levels, is due to a very dense population[1] pressing on (usually) badly farmed land coupled with poor health and vitality, and with inadequate industrial production. Britain and Belgium are typical of the third category—and on a smaller scale Switzerland. Enormous exports enable them to keep their people at a high level of comfort, and all goes well so long as the demand for their goods continues to be adequate. But any widespread economic depression is apt to cause

[1] India's average density is not very high, but its population is concentrated on the plains leaving thousands of square miles of barren hill country sparsely populated.

unemployment and distress. These countries may of course try and expand their food production, but this is inevitably limited by the fertility and extent of the soil, and it is certain that never could those two countries feed their present population. Consequently any permanent diminution in the demand for their goods would drive them either to a lowering of their standards of life or to a deliberate diminution of population by lowering the birth-rate or by emigration.

Emigration.—Now emigration can be of two kinds. It can be to foreign countries; in that case the economic problem may be solved but at the cost of the permanent loss to the emigrant country of numbers of citizens. Or it may be to lands under the country's flag, colonies or other dependencies, in which case there is direct economic gain and slight political loss. But in fact colonies have never taken large numbers of settlers. The total non-native or immigrant population of the colonial world is very small, and its removal from its home countries does not solve in any way the problem of over-population there. The emigration to German, Italian or Japanese colonies has never represented more than a fraction of the normal yearly increase of the population in the metropolis. And the same applies to dependencies of all countries.

If we single out Germany, Italy and Japan, it is because those three countries were especially responsible not only for raising the cry of over-population and their need for more 'living-space'—but also for actual policies of territorial expansion under colour of providing outlets for their peoples. But how poor was that pretext is shown precisely by the fact that they had made so little use of the dependencies they already controlled, and that this later expansion was to a large extent towards lands already well-filled. The 'lebensraum' cry was merely one of political domination, not one of genuine economic distress. And it may be observed that on sheer density figures Belgium, the Netherlands and Britain had a better claim; the fact that Britain retains such a high density in spite of the large extent of her empire shows how little territorial expansion is a solution for that particular problem. In any case, the world has now set its face against direct territorial expansion, for whatever motive, and it seems clear that this remedy for alleged over-population is now definitely ruled out. There only remain the other three solutions: diminution, industrialisation and increase of food supplies.

Increased Food Supplies.—To take the last first, it is a fact that the world's potential food output is practically unlimited. It is said that in the United States not half of the food produced reaches the consumer, and even then there is much waste. If all land were fully used with extensive methods, there would be enough food not only for the world's present population but for many more.

But . . . there are several buts! It would require a world-authority to organise and control production, direct all land to its best use, prevent waste, secure the necessary labour, manage the necessary transport. Further, it would have to see that everybody needing food should be able to get it—that is, able to afford it. That means a world guarantee of adequate employment and wages, in other words a world economic government. The new World Food Organisation may be its embryo, but it is advisory rather than executive or coercive. At least one may hope that never again will 'surplus' food be deliberately destroyed, or the growing of food officially discouraged, as in the days of the great depression in America.

Countries in fact can only increase their own food supplies by more intensive cultivation of their own soil, to which there is an ultimate limit; when they have reached this limit they must get it from outside, and pay for it by their industrial production.

Exporting for Food Purchasing Abroad.—The limitations of this second way of dealing with population problems are also evident. Goods produced must be sold. That means that the cost of their production must not exceed that of these countries' products, allowing for freight, ease of transport, etc. Now it is practically impossible for certain countries to compete on world markets because of their lack of essential raw materials. Having to import these at great cost, their prices will always be higher. Better technique and selling organisation may some-times offset these disadvantages but not often. No amount of human resourcefulness can make Iraq or central Africa industrial rivals to Belgium. There are countries for whom industrialisation is ruled out; the utmost they could hope for would be to meet their own domestic needs at the cost of high prices, thus keeping their imports for absolutely inescapable needs.

And even industrialised countries are in a precarious position with depression and unemployment always round the corner if something goes wrong with the delicate mechanism of the world exchange system. Not indeed that world demands are not large enough to keep all world industry busy, even just trying to meet unsatisfied essential needs (still crucial enough in all conscience), after which the ever-rising standard of life will make new demands. But, as in the case of food, this could not happen without a world agency for controlling industrial production and distribution, and this still seems to be out of our reach.

Decline of Population.—Industrialisation is therefore far from being the sure and infallible solution of population problems. We therefore come to the last remedy suggested, actual diminution of population. Now this is already taking place. The practically universal fall in the birth-rate is a matter of constant discussion, and the fall in the death-rate is not yet an adequate compensation. After all, it is obvious that the population of a country will be finally determined by the number of children actually born to every married couple; even if everybody married, a minimum of two children, per family, each of whom married and had two children, would be necessary to maintain the population at its present level; and since some people do not marry, and since some married people are childless the minimum rate is three per couple, any country with a smaller reproduction rate is seeing its population diminish and ultimately solving in that way its population problem.

The situation, however, has certain consequences which must not be overlooked. First, it affects almost exclusively the prosperous communities of Europe and America, not the really overpopulated areas of India and China where a high birth-rate still maintains a steady increase of population in spite of a high infantile death-rate. The remedy, if it be a remedy, is only being applied in the wrong place. Next, lower birth- and death-rates send up the average age of a population, an increasing proportion of which is over instead of under forty. This means that many are past their best working days and have yet to be fed. Hygiene, good food and medical science will probably prolong working capacity, but again there is a limit to this; a country should have large numbers of strong young people, and a low birth-rate coupled with a low death-rate deprives it of these necessary productional forces.

There is also always a possibility that diminution of population may go too far, or in the wrong direction. It is lamentable, for instance, to see rural depopulation and urban over-population as in France. Nor is it snobbery to regret that the diminishing birth-rate should be mainly among those sections of the population able to maintain high standards of health and education; until levels of hygiene and culture are raised as they should be, an overpreponderance of lower standards is to be deplored. Finally diminution can go too far and permanently reduce the population level below the needs of the country for defence or industry; 'empty cradles' were a major cause of the French defeat in 1940.

What may be called an 'unplanned' decrease of population is therefore full of danger and yet it is difficult to talk of a 'planned' population. Governments may, of course, try and encourage a higher birth-rate by giving some material advantages to large families; but the essential factor is usually housing, which is largely a matter of private enterprise and therefore of profit, not of common need. No educational facilities or tax exemptions will avail against the primary need of shelter; a material campaign for more children must be accompanied by a national control of housing, not only of house building but of house distribution.

6. POPULATION: THE PROBLEM OF QUALITY

But behind all these quantitative factors lie the qualitative elements referred to earlier. Populations cannot be reckoned altogether in mathematical terms; the kind of people they are matters not less than their number.

The quality of a population would seem to depend on four main factors: its cultural level, its physical level, its integration and its stability.

Cultural Levels.—Under cultural level we would include: native intelligence, education, capacity for organisation, readiness to work. That the average intelligence of collectivities as of individuals varies seems certain; that it is distinct from education is equally certain. Illiteracy in not necessarily stupidity; on the contrary it seems to develop observation and memory; though obviously at the same level of intelligence an educated person is better than an illiterate one. Therefore a people naturally intelligent, technically trained, able to think independently, is of far greater value to its state than one lacking all these, and will be able to use those mental advantages for the better development of natural resources, for the overcoming of handicaps and exploitation of opportunities. History for example knows no instance of a naturally stupid seafaring people.

Capacities for work and organisation are closely connected with these others and with each other. A collectively lazy people will never succeed, nor will one incapable of combined effort and planning. The successful people will combine personal initiative with discipline and compliance with law and planning; they will believe in education and in all forms of cultural development.

Physical Levels.—In the second place a good population will be healthy. Disease diminishes intelligence, capacity for work, energy and vitality; it makes for poor production, laziness, lethargy. No country can afford to neglect the physical welfare of its people.

Unity and Security.—Thirdly comes integration. We mean by this that it will approach unity and homogeneity; it will not allow religious or political differences to destroy its capacity for concerted action; it will command general loyalty by respecting everybody's convictions and rights. It follows that nothing weakens a people so much as irreconcilable minorities, whether religious or national; while the amalgamation into the community of new elements is usually to be welcomed, alien elements that refuse assimilation and insist on remaining separate cannot be carried in large numbers.

Finally a 'good' population will be one in which good institutions will develop contentment—for instance, the absence of extreme inequalities of wealth, education and social prestige, the encouragement of those types of social and economic organisation that make for stability such as a large farmer-owner class as opposed to a rural proletariate. If it be true that nothing breeds restlessness and discontent like a sense of insecurity and inferiority, a wise state will provide guarantees against the one and eliminate all that encourages the other.

Is There an 'Ideal' Population?—It is only when we consider together the qualitative and the quantitative factors that we can face our last question, namely, is there a best or ideal population for a particular state at a particular time, or, as economists call it, an 'optimum' population? The answer is probably yes, but discovering the correct number is a difficult matter. We may say that it is the result of an elaborate formula which would include all the qualitative and quantitative elements mentioned in relation to the needs of the country and the standard of living desired. We would probably have to add the general condition of the world as influencing everything else. If we knew all these we might be able to hazard a guess, but it would only be a guess.

The difficulty of determining such an optimum shows how difficult a thing it is for a country to have a so-called 'population policy'. Quite apart from the delicacy of what is after all a very personal question, it is only rarely that a country can be sure of what it needs. Even then it takes many years for any policy to show its results, and the consequences either of increase or of decrease are hard to calculate. One is tempted to think of Belgium and the British Isles as over-populated; but unless reduction only affected the productively unimportant elements of the population a change might easily be for the worse. A decrease in the number of producers without one in the number of idle mouths would not improve matters.

The only certain facts are that there are still large areas of the world that call for development and that world prosperity and happiness are probably best secured by the encouragement of the free movement of men. But this also requires a degree of co-operation between states, or of widespread single control, which still seems utopian to generations brought up on passports and other restrictions. Imperfect as it was, nineteenth-century life savours sometimes of a lost golden age!

CHAPTER III

SOCIETY AND THE STATE

I. THE THREEFOLD BASIS OF COMMUNITY LIFE

THE life of man in communities is rooted in three fundamental realities about human nature. The first, that man cannot live alone. The second, that every man is different from every other. The third, that man likes to have his own way and impose his will on his fellow-men. Society meets man's need for companionship; the state solves the problems created by man's conflicts with man.

Man is a Social Animal.—There can be no life worth living without association. This, the beginning of all 'social' study, is the meaning of Aristotle's famous phrase, 'Man is a political animal'. He was not thinking so much of elaborately organised political groups as of man's unfitness for solitary existence. No one can live for long unto himself; solitary life is 'nasty, brutish and short', as the philosopher Hobbes said some two thousand years later, and common life appears, in some way or other, as far back as human records go.

You can say, with Professor Hocking, that 'the joining function is inherent in man', or with Hume that 'in all creatures that prey on others there appears a remarkable desire of company which associates men together'. What makes this desired 'joining' or company-seeking is the realisation by each man of the essential similarity of others to himself, in spite of superficial differences. He knows that his instincts, his likes and dislikes, his way of thinking are sufficiently the same to make co-operation possible and profitable; without this knowledge he could never be sure of being understood and of understanding others; he must feel that he and they are driving at the same things.

Co-operation.—A psychological and spiritual desire for companionship, of man with woman and children in the family, of men and women together in daily life outside— that is the starting point of community life. We need many

32

things from each other; our minds are hungry for the exchange of ideas, for the enrichment of our personal experience by sharing in that of others. But mere life cannot remain for long without definite objects and the desire soon manifests itself to get certain things done. Now, in order to act together there must be some kind of organisation, some co-operation of people trying to do the same things, in what sociologists call 'functional' institutions, groups formed, more or less consciously, for a common purpose. When such groups appear on any scale, a human society or community has been born.

Individualism.—There is, however, another side to the picture. If man were nothing but a co-operative person, common life would involve no problems. But man's co-operative and group-forming instinct is checked and thwarted by his individualism. He may be incomplete by himself, but he is also himself first and foremost. Every man is unique and has only one life to live; he suffers alone and no one can share his pain, not even his nearest and dearest. He has his individual desires, appetites, ambitions, his will to live, and wants his social life to be both the expression of those desires and the instrument by which he will realise them. Nor must we say with easy optimism that this egoism and individualism are superficial faults, to be cured by reason and experience. They have their roots in the essence of human nature, in the need for each of us to defend his life against death and time, in a word, in man's instinct of self-preservation. And this instinct, this will-to-live, and to do so in his own way, becomes in practice the attempt made by man to impose his own will, or as we say, 'to have his own way'. This is the instinctive desire for power.

2. THE PROBLEM OF POWER

What is Power?—It has been defined by Tawney as 'The craving to be a cause, to see things and men move in the fulfilment of our own will; the capacity of an individual or group to modify the conduct of others in a manner which he desires, and to prevent his own conduct from being modified in a manner he does not desire. It must not be confused with authority. 'Authority', as Maritain remarks, ' is the *right* to direct and command, to be listened to and obeyed; power is the *force* that enables one to compel obedience.' The gangster has power without authority, Socrates had authority without power; in a well-ordered community the two will go together.

Power is thus the capacity to make one's will prevail over that of others, even against these other wills, and the desire to exercise it seems to be inherent in the nature of man. It manifests the instinctive feeling that control of resources and therefore of other lives helps survival; we all want a place in the sun, and as large a place as possible. This instinctive urge, like all other instinctive urges, must be kept under control, but it cannot be suppressed, and it is in fact a condition of all creative work. It is an expression of vitality, both of body and of mind, an assertion of the self which is, after all, our one point of contact with the universe.

Power is a Relation between Men.—Whether checked or unchecked, selfish or unselfish, power is a relation between men brought into contact with one another by some form of common purpose or activity, a relation of ruler and ruled, of command and of obedience. It follows that practically all men are both the users and the victims of power; [1] rare is the man who never gives orders to anyone and never receives an order from anyone. Community life is in fact a huge network of combinations of power. Man is made up of desires and 'every desire is a force, making or marring, weakening or strengthening, the structure and function of the society of which he is a part. These desires are the social forces which make society move; it is from the combination and harmonising of those desires that human purposes are realised. Even in its crudest form, it contains initiative and the power of unification, necessary to create a social whole and give it capacity for action.'

Power is, therefore, necessary to organised life. It is, as Bertrand Russell says, the fundamental concept in social science; it is to social science what energy is to physics, that without which nothing would ever happen. It can take many forms, and is of course not limited to direct physical coercion.

---

[1] Or, to use technical terms, the *objects* and *subjects* of power.

It can work by inducement, by reward or punishment; it can be the mental predominance of one mind and will over another, bending it to its own purposes without the other being really conscious of it. It can be the influence and prestige of wealth, of birth, of success. It can be moral authority, rooted in certainty and courage. It can be the economic power of him who holds the key to production and to the livelihood of thousands. It can be the power of the priest and of the magician, the technical skill of the doctor, the love of a mother. 'Soul-force' coming from an intense spiritual vitality, from the prestige of a saintly life, is power no less than that of the soldier or policeman because it overcomes without physical coercion. It *is* coercion because its wielder is imposing his own desires on one who is not morally convinced but yields to something stronger than his own will or inner conviction. Further, power need not be actually exercised; its potential use is usually quite enough. An unarmed policeman may dispel a crowd, a handful of soldiers quell a riot without firing a shot. The mere fear of hurting someone's feelings may be a stronger deterrent than the possibility of prison. Power is in the last resort a mysterious essence, and more a concern of the psychologist than of the political scientist.

The Morality of Power.—Is power evil in itself and is the mere desire for it evil? Only a disciple of Tolstoy or of Nietzsche can answer by a plain yes or no. It is totally evil, says the Tolstoyan, because it is independent of right and morality, and involves forcing a free man to act against that free will which alone gives value to what he does. He that takes up the sword shall perish by the sword, the imposition of will on another is in all cases a wrong; better suffer oneself than resist by force. 'The use of power', says Niebuhr, 'is due to the force of sin, to our tendency to regard ourselves as more important than anyone else, and to view all problems from the view point of our own interest.'

Such an attitude is an obvious reaction against the glorification of force as such, when Nietzsche writes that 'all that enhances the feeling of power, the will to power, and power itself in man is good; all that proceeds from weakness bad. Happiness is the feeling that power is increasing, that resistance

has been overcome.' It reminds one that power is a contradiction to brotherhood, to willing co-operation, and that
there is no connection between the successful use of physical
force and the rightness of a cause; victory is no guarantee of
justice, and we must deny to power any inherent authority
just because it can do things. Might is not Right, and we agree
with Alain, the French philosopher, that 'we must cling to
this fundamental and precious idea, that never can any force
decide a matter of right. This is the starting point of all freedom, of all equality, of all real civilisation.'

But to say this is not to agree with the Tolstoyan and to
say that might is never right; it is simply to assert that power
is in itself neutral, an instrument that can be wrongly and
rightly used. Like everything in the universe it must justify
itself. 'It is an error', writes Niebuhr, 'that violence is a natural
and inevitable expression of ill-will, and non-violence of
good-will, so that violence is always evil and non-violence
always good. All group relations require some coercion.'
This is not to deny that power is dangerous, and there is
much truth in the saying that all men having power should
be distrusted. The exercise of power goes to the head of most
men:

> Man, proud man!
> Drest in a little brief authority—
> Most ignorant of what he's most assured,
> His glassy essence—like an angry ape,
> Plays such fantastic tricks before high heaven,
> As makes the angels weep.

These words are as true as when Shakespeare wrote them,
and no precautions will altogether guard against the misuse
of power, for if power is helpless for evil it will also be helpless
for good; and history has much to say of the evils caused by
weak authority.

Claimants for Power.—There are in a modern society
many claimants for power. Apart from ambitious individuals
with dictatorial tendencies, out for any occasion of self-
assertion,[1] we find innumerable organised groups jealous of

---

[1] 'These stars you see overhead at night, those vast worlds which we can
never reach . . . I would annex the planets if I could. I often think of that.
It makes me sad to see them so clear and so far away.' Cecil Rhodes quoted by
Morgenthau, 'Scientific Man versus Power Politics'.

preserving old powers and obtaining new ones. The family is still in many countries a formidable power-group, able to impose its will not only on its members but on society by its influence and control of strategic posts in the state. In militarist societies the army or navy is another such—Imperial Germany and Japan are obvious examples. Churches are still, in some countries, the state's competitors for a power derived from their claimed superior spiritual authority; in most Roman Catholic and Moslem countries the state has in fact to share power with organised religion. But far more important, because more universal, are the economic forces that exercise a real though unofficial power. They take various forms. At one time the land-owning class was all-powerful. Now organised Labour in its trade unions can paralyse all social life by ceasing work, and a general strike ushered in the Bolshevist revolution in 1917; Labour also commands many votes and can go a long way to influencing the policy of the party it supports, especially when that party is in office. On the other side, the Employers, organised in corporations, federations, chambers of commerce, can be no less power-ful. The German industrialist-economist-statesman Walther Rathenau once said that the economic life of Europe was controlled by 300 individuals, and it was alleged that 200 families really ruled the French Third Republic. In the United States, the Commission on Industrial Relations reported that six financial groups controlled two and a half million wage-earners, or nearly half a million per group and such control inevitably entails the kind of power referred to by President Taft when he said, 'The time was, and we all know it, when in many of the directorates of the great corporations of the country orders for the delivery of delegates in a convention, and of members of the legislature for purposes of corporate control were issued with the same confidence in their ful-filment as an order for the delivery of machinery'.

The State as the Regulator of Power.—Society must, there-fore, set up some agency to which it will entrust the power of controlling and regulating the manner and degree in which power will be used in the collective life. This agency is the state, which by its monopoly of effective coercion decides how other social agencies may be allowed to use their own

potentialities for coercion. In other terms the state decides
how power shall be exercised within society by individuals by
groups, or by the state itself, according to the fundamental
purposes pursued by that particular community, in harmony
with its conception of justice. Law is in fact the sanctioning
and regulating of the use of power.

This regulating of the use of power is essential because
everybody wants to use what power he has and, as Laski
says, 'Men move differently to the attainment of conflicting
desires; a coercive authority is therefore necessary to define
the terms on which that movement may legitimately proceed,
to lay down the rules of permissible social behaviour'.

The choice in fact is not between the power of the state
and no power, but which of several potentially force-
brandishing groups do we prefer to have dominant. The power
of the state should have the advantage of being publicly
exercised according to certain definite and recognised principles, and this on behalf of the whole community and not for
some section thereof.

The State's Use of Power.—In what situations is the exercise
of power by the state necessary? Primarily whenever conflict
arises between individuals or between groups; and such conflicts
come whenever there is a lack of balance and equilibrium, in
other terms, whenever such individuals and groups are
misusing the power they possess inherently by their nature
or function. Over-dominance, an attempt to use others for
one's own purposes, to behave as if one alone constituted the
whole of society—this calls for some checking power, and a
well-organised state will provide for those over-assertive
temperaments, for the ambitious, for the natural leaders, the
scope they need in which to satisfy their nature without
injury to others or to themselves, along lines of socially
creative activity.

There is, however, another and no less important reason for
the necessity of state authority over and above the spontaneous
free action of social groups, and it was well expressed by
Lincoln. 'Government', he said, 'is a combination of the people
of a country to effect certain objects by joint efforts. The
legitimate object of government is to do for the people
what needs to be done but which they cannot do by them-

selves at all, or do so well for themselves.' 'But', he goes on to say, 'most of these objects spring from the injustices of men.'[1] In these words he links together the two essential aspects of the necessity and activity of the state, the controlling and checking of the anti-social elements in man, and the organising and integrating of these processes that are beyond the free and spontaneous activities of social groups, whether local or functional. Its work may take many forms, but will always fall, if closely examined, into one of those two categories. Under the first heading, it will hold the individual in check whenever he tries to impose his will on his fellows, and acts as if they existed to serve his personal purposes, whether in their property or in their lives; under the second it will decide what needs to be done by collective action, and therefore will both undertake tasks which are beyond the voluntary efforts of a limited number, and decide between the rival desires (all perhaps good, but mutually exclusive) of people wanting either different things or the same things done in a different way.

The State's Claim to Power.—It may in fact be reasonably argued that the state has its own rights as the agent of the community, and that these rights include those powers which are necessary to its essential functions. Without these powers it could not prevent the anti-social acts of individuals or groups, nor harness individual energies and resources to collective purposes. But it must be added that its tendency is and always has been to take as much power as possible, irrespective of its relation to any particular purpose. This is natural enough. People who exercise power enjoy it and want more. They tend to consider that the essential function of the people is to obey, and the masses are no longer those on whose behalf and for whose benefit power has to be wielded; they exist for the sake of power, and to make its exercise and enjoyment possible; they become its raw material, as it were, the 'Administered ones', as French officials call it. Instead of means to an end, power and its maintenance

[1] It would perhaps scarcely be true to say today that *most* state activities spring from human injustice. The scope of state action has been greatly enlarged since Lincoln's day, and includes many domains of which he could have no idea, and which spring from man's co-operative not from his individualistic instincts.

become ends in themselves. The voluntary abandonment of power is in fact one of the rarest events in history.[1] Genuinely free abdications can be counted on one's fingers, and deliberate resignations from high office are few indeed. Desire for power and the keeping and increasing of it are among the most fundamental realities of politics.

Left to themselves, states and their agents would steadily enlarge their authority in quantity and scope, leaving less and less to individual freedom and initiative. 'Its so much simpler and more efficient that way', they plead; 'Give us a blank cheque and see what marvels we can do for you.' Hence Lincoln's famous phrase about eternal vigilance being the price of liberty.

The 'Morbidity' of Power.—The truth is that, whoever wields it, and however justified its use may be, power has its diseases, its 'morbidity', as Merriam puts it. And the first of those diseases is the extreme difficulty of exercising power in moderation and reason.

> O it is excellent
> To have a giant's strength, but it is tyrannous
> To use it like a giant.

and few can refrain from not using it so if they have it. The others listed by Merriam are a poor social functioning of the system, inadequate civic cohesion, weak personnel, defective techniques, law and ideologies.

These are all obvious enough but another weakness not noted by Merriam may be added, namely that the lust for power is often to be found among the weak rather than the strong. 'It is the expression of the inability of the individual self to stand alone and live, a desperate attempt to gain a secondary strength where genuine strength is lacking.' And Fromm in his 'Fear of Freedom', goes on to say that destructive tendencies which are one form of the lust for power come from the same source: 'They too are rooted in the unbearableness of individual powerlessness and isolation. I can escape the feeling of my own powerlessness in comparison with the world outside myself by destroying it. The destruction of the

---

[1] 'The great men of the world being invested with the power thereof, cannot be imagined to eclipse themselves or their own pomp, unless by the violent interposition of the people's spirits who are most sensible of their own burdens and most forward in seeking relief' (John Ward, 1649).

world is the last, almost desperate attempt to save myself
from being crushed by it.'

Power is also perpetually confronted by the resistance which
its very existence provokes, from jealous other institutional
agencies of all kinds, from those dissatisfied with its results, who
either grumble without organising themselves or form
organised opposition groups. In fact it will largely show its
real qualities by the way in which it handles those opposing
forces.

How to keep Power.—Given those difficulties from within
and without, the maintaining of power is no easy task.
Perhaps its best support comes from the fact that in spite of all
tendencies to opposition the instinct of man is to obey rather
than to resist, to say 'yes' rather than 'no'. Apart from this,
the successful wielding of power is made up of many elements.
An intimate knowledge of other power groups is essential,
of their mutual relationships, their loyalties, their ideologies.
An understanding of popular psychology, of how to win and
hold support, by rewards to helpers, by forms and ceremonies,
is no less necessary, together with the development of the
ideology necessary to evoke the loyalty of the particular
community, and above all, moderation in the use of power,
the avoidance of too much outward show, the knowledge of
how to offer leadership without domination. It is disregard
of those essentials that has brought down apparently well-
established political systems.

It may be said in conclusion that the less the state uses
actual coercing power, the better it will normally be for all
concerned. Its work is best carried on by prestige relying on
the habitual self-control of the citizens. Education may in
the long run give better results than domination, and like
all human undertakings the use of power is known by its
fruits. If social desires are generally satisfied, if an orderly,
free life is possible to the great mass of citizens, power is
obviously being well used.

3. DISTINCT PURPOSES OF SOCIETY AND STATE

The important thing at this point is to keep in mind the
essential distinctness of state and society. Their geographical

2 *

areas may be the same, though certain social activities will probably be closely linked to those of other communities;[1] their membership may be identical, but they are distinct in origins, aims and functions. Society is natural and instinctive, the state is the creation of will and reason. 'The organisation of the state is not *all* social organisation', as McIver says, 'the ends for which the state stands are not *all* the ends which humanity seeks, and quite obviously the ways in which the state pursues its objects are only *some* of the ways in which, within society, men strive for the objects of their desire.'

Life in Society.—It is primarily in society that we live and move and have our being. Take a walk in the main streets of your town and see how many of its activities are social rather than political. Shops, factories, clubs, churches, many schools are the spontaneous creation of free human activities.[2] They exist because some private persons, at some time or other, decided to establish this particular industry, to open that shop, to found some school, to start an association for charitable or propaganda purposes. Of course at intervals a police station, a constable on duty, a passing soldier, traffic control signs, a Town Hall will remind you of the authority which, in the freest country, lays down certain conditions under which those free activities may be run, and which protects them from unwarranted interference from rivals or mischief-makers. But economic, cultural, religious, professional, recreational or other groups are based on the free initiative of persons who are members of a society before they are citizens of a state.

The State and Social Groups.—We shall study later the problem of the relation of the state to those social activities and organisations. There have been many solutions offered, none wholly satisfactory. All we want to do here is to insist on the existence of the problem, due to the fact of the distinction between state and society. If they are considered identical, there is of course no problem; but the moment you admit their separate identities, as one must in any community based on any degree of freedom, the difficulty at once arises.

We must therefore look upon the state as a force or

---

[1] Churches, for instance, are practicaly always associated with sister churches abroad.

[2] Some schools of course are the creation of the state.

organisation within society but distinct from it. Society is *(1s)*
anterior to the state and has never been wholly superseded by
it, not even in Nazi Germany or Communist Russia. Which
activities will remain social as distinct from political will
vary from country to country and time to time; this forms,
in fact, one of the major problems of political science. It is
true that on the whole the historical tendency has been for the
state to grow at the expense of society, because of the increasing
need for central control; but society remains primary in
origin and importance and the state is its creation and agent and
therefore its subordinate. The disappearance of the state would
not necessarily mean chaos or anarchy; spontaneous social
activity might very well meet emergencies until a new state
emerged. (This would naturally be truer of communities
where the social element had always been strong, as in England
or America, than of others such as Germany where the people
had for many centuries looked to the state for direction
in all things.)

This capacity of social agencies to rise to new challenges
is a sign of collective health, and it may be well to remember
that the state, as we know it, is of comparatively recent
origin. Assuming man's life on earth to go back some fifty
thousand years—a low estimate—some four-fifths of this
life has been spent without the state, since the earliest states
sufficiently established to have left any record are not older
than ten thousand years. Stateless societies have been the rule
rather than the exception, and until recently survivals were
still to be found among Indian tribes in America and in some
South Sea islands. Those communities lived without any
central authority; there was no conception of common rules;
'law' was simply a traditional form of behaviour, and any
aggrieved individual settled the matter in his own way.
In some societies indeed magicians or committees of elders
exercised some form of control, but in the main those people
lived, as Lord puts it, 'peaceably and comfortably without
politics, and there was nothing in their life to indicate that
political order would ever grow out of it'.

The Purpose of the State.—Whatever be the tasks of the
state, it is clear that they can only be carried out according
to certain principles, embodying a common purpose or way

of life for all members of the community. Every state must represent some such purpose, and no two states have ever been identical in their aims. The problem of what constitutes the proper purposes of a state really takes us to the very heart of political science, for it is really the problem of the proper relative spheres of authority and freedom. We shall leave it for fuller treatment later, and content ourselves now with raising some broad and general issues.

To say that the state exists to promote the welfare of its members is of course meaningless unless you define welfare. Obviously no state would exist in order to make its people unhappy! Most thinkers would agree that the state must maintain internal order, develop prosperity, and defend the people against the aggression of other states, but every one of those terms, 'internal order', 'prosperity' and 'defence' is open to many interpretations.

State Purposes in History.—There have been many different views of what constituted the proper purpose of a state. Some have frankly made power their chief aim and subordinated to this both the personal freedom and the cultural development of their members. Ancient Sparta, modern Prussia, Napoleonic France, Fascist Italy, are obvious examples. This power need not necessarily be military; the economic self-sufficiency which makes a state independent of external supplies is but another aspect of the same policy. When Henry VII made of England a definitely protectionist country, 'he bowed the ancient policy of this realm', says Lord Bacon, 'from consideration of plenty to considerations of power'. And no state can altogether neglect the latter; if it be not powerful enough to hold its own, its existence will be precarious, unless it can depend on the support of some powerful friends, like Switzerland, Belgium or Portugal. But a distinction can be made between power limited to self-preservation and power exerted on others, either brutally for its own sake or under cover of some less ignoble purpose.

Some states have claimed to represent a certain type of civilisation and to have been entrusted with what they called a mission in the world. Ancient Israel is the obvious instance, Revolutionary France and Communist Russia are others. Unfortunately the cultural mission is often accompanied by a belief in the use of force for its extension, and 'vocational' or 'messianic' states have often used their soldiers as their chief missionaries.

The Ancient Greeks, on the other hand, saw in the state the necessary agent for the moral and intellectual, more than the material development of its members, the forming of the perfect man. As a rule this noble ideal was vitiated by the belief that the good citizen had to conform to one single pattern laid down for him, so that it was not always easy to distinguish between Plato's ideal of the good and just man and later totalitarian ideas of the standardised citizen. It is certainly unfair to Plato to couple his name with that of modern dictators, from whose aims and methods he would have recoiled with horror, but it cannot be denied that his philosophy seems to imply that only in the state can man really be himself, and it is only a step from this to the conclusion that the state must be an end in itself, irrespective of any other function or purpose.

Varying Views of State Purposes.—'The state has no deter- minate function in a larger community, but is itself the supreme community, the guardian of a whole world', says the English philosopher Bosanquet. 'The moral relations presuppose an organised life, but such life is only within the state and not in the relations between the state and other communities.' And in this the Englishman is only echoing the German Fichte, who had written some three-quarters of a century earlier that ' the purpose of the State is to direct all individual powers for the life of the species and to urge them into it. It is a compulsion-organisation.' And so, for these thinkers and their followers, whatever helps the state is good, whatever hinders it is bad; its own existence is its only function and justification. Such a state claims the right to a monopoly of all forces within its borders including the censorship of opinions and the regulation of personal ways of life, so that it has been wittily and rightly remarked that in such a state 'whatever is not compulsory is forbidden, and whatever is not forbidden is compulsory'.

At the other extreme stands the school of thought whose only test of state action is its utility in relation to a broadly conceived general welfare. These 'utilitarians', from Bentham,

170 years ago, to Cole and Laski today, distrust the state and its possible tyranny, and want to keep out of its clutches the largest possible part of the life of its citizens. But while Bentham had no belief in the state's right or ability to control economic life, the younger 'Neo-Utilitarians' are mostly Socialists, and see in the non-interventionism of the older *laissez-faire* an absence of system that leaves the individual worker and consumer at the mercy of the profit-making employer and producer. They would, in other words, while distrusting the state as an agent of coercion in thought, see in it a necessary instrument for the correction of natural and social inequalities. Lastly comes Communism, approaching the problem from the sole angle of the liberation of the workers from the uncertainties and hardships of the prevailing systems of economic production under private control. It endeavours to place the whole productive and distributive machine under a state which becomes the only employer of labour and the only large-scale seller, having for its chief purpose the complete control of the community's economic life. Soviet Russia is without any doubt a new type of state which only later times will judge according to the results of its policies.

We may finally quote this definition, placed by the representatives of the United States before the United Nations Commission for the drawing-up of an International Bill of Human Rights. 'The state is created by the people, for the promotion of their welfare and the protection of their mutual rights. Everyone has the right to a fair and equal opportunity to advance his own physical, economic, spiritual and cultural well-being, and to share the benefits of civilisation. It is the duty of the state, in accordance with the maximum use of its resources, and with due regard for the liberties of the individual, to promote this purpose by legislation or by other appropriate means.' In our opinion this definition cannot be seriously improved upon. Its insistence on the state as the 'creation of the people' reduces it to its proper position as subordinate to society in origin and purpose and rightly strips it of any sacred or hallowed status, 'of any mystic sanctity or authority which would place it above morality or free it from the Law by which wrong-doing brings its own retribution in the lowering of character'. (Hobhouse.)

4. STATE, JUSTICE AND MORALITY

Can the State be Neutral?—People often speak as if the state could 'arbitrate' between conflicting parties. It is of course evident that many disputes arise in which neither the state as such nor its agents as individuals have the slightest interest, and in such cases its machinery will be used in a perfectly neutral manner, in accordance with recognised principles of decision. But it is quite another matter if the point at issue involves any concept or institution which forms an essential part of the life and thought of the community. Advocacy of capitalism in a Communist state, direct attacks on property in a capitalist state, criticisms of hallowed beliefs and revered age-old institutions can scarcely be judged in a detached spirit. The state was hardly an impartial arbiter in the struggle for recognition of the early trade unions, or in the attempts at survival of oppressed national minorities, or in the fight for a democratic franchise; in these it was both party and judge. And this is equally true of the modern state if the principles on which it rests are seriously challenged.

The State must Appear Just.—We said in the Introduction that one of the problems of Political Science was that the state must be judged not only quantitatively on the efficiency of its achievements, but also qualitatively on their harmony with certain ethical or moral values. The state in other words must act in conformity with certain standards of justice. We shall raise later on, when dealing with law, the problem of the existence of eternal or universal principles of abstract justice; it is enough to say now that the action of the state must in the long run, *appear* just to the majority of its members. 'The act of government, can be described in one aspect as the art of making men and women think that the world they inhabit obeys in some degree their own ideas of justice.'[1] People will not indefinitely tolerate what they think unjust; it must be presented to them, however deceitfully, as right. History is of course full of theories put forward to justify injustice; but the very existence of such theories, however specious, witness to the need in the human mind for harmonising our actions with some ethical principles.

[1] J. L. and B. Hammond, 'The Age of the Chartists'.

The establishment of justice has been in fact, almost universally recognised as one of the essential purposes of any state; differences of opinion have been more in the methods than in the aims. Practically everybody agrees, in theory at least, that the state must encourage right-doing and discourage wrong-doing, and that its own actions must be subjected to ethical tests. But it is also clear that the morality of the state will never be ahead of that of its members. It will be, as Ward says, 'as good as society will let it be'. The reforms it will carry out, the moral and spiritual welfare it will develop will represent its members' conceptions of necessary reform and desired welfare.

The State and Morality.—It follows that the state does not in any sense create morality or define its standards. No action becomes moral because it is done or endorsed by the state, nor immoral because it is officially prohibited or discouraged. State morality will be what its members make it, and will always represent a middle course, neither as high as the levels of the élite, nor as low as those of people with no moral sense. It is futile for the former to demand from the state the enforcement of their personal standards, such as the prohibition of divorce or alcoholic drinks; experience shows that nothing can be enforced for long that does not meet with general approval. It is equally futile for extremists at the other end to demand the abolition of all those restrictions that try and protect the rank and file from certain forms of what public opinion calls evil: control of dangerous drugs, for instance, enforcement of certain minimal conditions of decency in public performances etc. Of course, here as elsewhere, the exact drawing of the line between morality and narrow-minded prudery is not always easy, and stupid mistakes are inevitable. It would seem, however, that a jury of twelve ordinary citizens, if capable of deciding of a man's guilt in a murder trial, should be able to decide what the community will tolerate in the moral sphere. All one can ask of the state is, to quote Ward again, 'to enable men to do right along lines agreed to as right'.

Is the State an 'Organism'?—Another question that must be answered is whether one can speak of the state as an 'organism', a kind of live body with its independent birth, life, growth, diseases and final death. It is very tempting to do so, just as it is tempting and convenient to 'personify' the state. Let us, however, ask first of all what are the distinctive marks of an organism. There are six of these, says Professor Hocking:

1. It is an identifiable group of parts, exchanging matter and energy.
2. It has a character as a whole expressed on every part.
3. It persists as a whole and is aided to persist by what each part does.
4. Its function is expressed in terms of purpose rather than mechanism.
5. It ultimately fails in conserving activity and has a definite life cycle.
6. It persists in the life of its children.

This being so, we may say with Hocking, that 'the state has marks of an organic character to a higher degree than any lesser group' especially as regards 'the independence of its parts, division of labour and assimilation of its members into the whole', but 'it is not a fully realised organism'. It is not true that every part, i.e. every citizen, has a character impressed on him as a member of the state, nor that all its parts exchange matter and energy, nor is there any proof of states having definite life cycles.

This means that the organic analogy gives but little help in our study. It has also the danger of making us forget one of our basic truths, that there is no such thing as state or society apart from the individuals that compose them. Whatever happens to the state happens to its members, to living people, not to an abstract entity, and we must be on our guard against the fallacies involved in speaking of the character, policy, vices and virtues of any particular country. Its policy is made by its leaders, its virtues and vices are those of its citizens; it cannot suffer, or be punished or rewarded except in the person of those who belong to it at that particular time. Never must we think of the state apart from its human elements.

Conclusion on State Characteristics.—The state is then what holds society together; it restrains, commands, organises. In so doing it must inevitably possess certain distinguishing features. It must be monopolistic, inclusive, compelling and permanent. Monopolistic, because there cannot be at the same time more than one fundamental purpose, more than one way of common living; a house divided against itself cannot stand, and within its own sphere the state can brook no rival.

Inclusive, because it cannot leave anybody outside its scope without reducing to nothing its efforts towards the realisation of that common life. Compelling, because co-operation in the state's aims and activities cannot be left to the private decision of the individual, so that membership of the state and conformity to its rules is involuntary. Man is born a member of a state and cannot disown this membership; naturalisation only means exchanging one membership for another.[1] Finally the state is permanent, because no time limit is placed on its activities and existence. No change of rules or form of government alters its continuity. This fact, to which we shall return more than once, lies at the basis of our system of international relations, the rule being that each political system inherits its predecessor's obligations, such as debts and treaties. The same principle, for that matter, also prevail in internal affairs; all laws made by one régime continue to be valid under the next, until formally repealed. States in fact act under the expectation of indefinite continuation, never making any allowances for the possibility of their disappearance.

[1] The cruelty of our modern world has reduced some unfortunate individuals to statelessness, but this is, we trust, a passing tragedy.

CHAPTER IV

THE STATE IN HISTORY

WE have seen how Society and State grew out of the needs and nature of man, and in some ways the question of origins could be left there. As students we are bound, however, to go somewhat deeper into the problem and see what History actually has to tell us on the subject.

I. THE ORIGINS OF THE STATE

Probable Origins in Family.—We may as well confess at once that we know very little indeed about it all. 'The question of exact political origins is unanswerable in the present state of knowledge' says Professor F. H. Hankins,[1] and anything that is advanced is largely, if not entirely, guess-work. It seems, however, safe to hazard that the family, being the most primitive of all human groups, must form the starting-point of any enquiry of this kind. 'In the family, the primary social unit', says McIver, 'there are always present the curbs and controls that constitute the essence of government . . . which is the continuation by the more inclusive society of a process of regulation that is already highly developed within the family. The same necessities that create the family create also regulation. . . . Here is government in miniature, and already government of a quite elaborate character.' It begins with marriage and inheritance, controls the simple family economy, carries on the family worship, organises defence, arranges hunting and pasture, sees after the upkeep of water-springs, of shelter, of supplies.

It is easy to see how families spread, joining on with other families for certain common interests, until groups emerged in which the original common kinship had become forgotten.

---

[1] Quoted by Maxey in the introduction to his 'Political Philosophies'. This introduction is perhaps the best and the simplest brief statement of this difficult question.

When this stage was reached the unit based on blood relationship had given place to the tribe. This may have traditions of a common descent and of a common religion derived from the worship of common ancestors, but the mark of the tribe is neither kinship nor religion; it is a common obedience to a recognised chief or leader, thanks to whose authority the group can act together in matters that are beyond the scope of individual or family.

Property and Defence.—Two factors contributed especially to this expansion. The first is the change from a nomadic life, dependent mainly on pasture, to agriculture and settlement on a definite piece of territory. This led to the replacement of the bond of kinship to that of life in common in a given place; it also created the need for an authority able to define and to enforce the respective rights of individuals to a share of the land within the territory of the group. In other words, the state appears as bound up with the development of property—first of land, then in other forms of wealth gradually created—and with the problems which property involves: theft, inheritance, the exchange of goods produced in excess of strictly individual needs, the inequalities created by differences of wealth.

It may be said, in fact, that property created the state. An attack on property was more than a private affair; it was an undermining of the whole social and political system, an offence against the established order. 'Where there is no property', writes Adam Smith, 'or at least no more than exceeds the value of two or three days' labour, civil government is not so necessary.'

The part played by defence is no less important. More than anything else it required unified leadership; and the problem must have arisen very early in the life of organised communities. We need not discuss here whether man has a strong fighting instinct; there is ample evidence that many human societies were, and are, by nature quiet and peaceful.[1] But the instinct of survival is the most deeply rooted of all instincts, and struggles for food supplies, fertile lands, food pasture must have been frequent. Hence the early need in many

---

[1] See Kropotkin's 'Mutual Aid', for many instances of natural co-operativeness.

societies for some kind of military organisation and leadership, for aggression, on the part of those who saw the
possibility of exploiting the economic resources of some
neighbouring tribes, for defence on the part of those
weaker ones.

Desire for Domination of Group over Group.—Any form of
struggle or war creates a relationship of victor and van-
quished, i.e. a relation of power and submission. War, conquest
and obedience must have been essential factors in the amalgamation of families into clans, of clans into tribes, and of
tribes into the larger units that become states. It may almost
be said that the state originated when a victorious tribe
subjugated instead of destroying its defeated rivals, and
established itself as its dominant governing minority, while
the peasant who could not flee remained to develop the land
for the victors. In the same way, loot and piracy were the
foundations of what became maritime states. Struggle and
warfare are therefore historically a most important element
in state-formation, and it is certain that the union of two groups
even by force, develops after a while common interests, out
of which is born a sense of unity.[1]

The desire for domination, political and economic, is
therefore one of the most important factors, perhaps *the*
most important single factor in the development of the state.
Our modern dislike of violence may regret this but we must
remember that it may have been the only alternative to something worse. An organised state, however brutal, is better than
plunder and insecurity, and the only choice was presumably
between disorderly force and force with an element of order.
'Frontier justice' may be rough and ready, but it is better than
no justice at all.

Confused Process of Growth.—Much of this which we present
as a regular process was of course very slow and confused.
As Gettell says, 'When human life in general reached a
certain general point, and came under certain general influences, some form of organised authority, more or less
political, resulted, and numerous states arose by process

[1] The complete identification of Alsace and Lorraine with France in 1792,
a bare hundred years after their annexations, is a good instance. The same
became true of Nice and Savoy after 1860.

similar only to its main features'. Especially did it take a long time for the distinctive political authority of the state to become disentangled from numerous other forms of social control. Military leadership was probably the first to become clearly differentiated, then the settlement of important disputes in which the stability of the whole group was involved. The distinction we now make so carefully between the state and society is of comparatively recent origin. The sanctions of religion, were, for instance, often more serious than those of the law, and the magicians who controlled them more powerful than any agent of the political authority. The power of the father over wife and children (and usually slaves) remained absolute in many societies side by side with the existing legal system. We see in fact through the centuries a double process at work, one by which the state takes over powers hitherto enjoyed by society, and the other by which it abandons to society powers it no longer needs. It has given up in most cases its connections with the family, with the ownership of land, with religion; it has taken increasing control of cultural and of economic life. We must remember also that the various stages here separated were in fact overlapping—as are indeed all stages of every kind in human development.

We thus see emerging from the ill-defined and confused authority of primitive societies various differentiated organs of control with differentiated functions, out of which appears clearly the contrast between rulers and ruled and between various aspects of the common life, the political and the non-political. The state may therefore be said to be both natural and artificial. It is natural in origins, in the instinctive forces which are necessary to any growth or action; it is artificial in its development. 'There is', says Bowman, 'some critical stage at which spontaneous and instinctive development gives place to the deliberate creative action, either of some man or of the community as a whole.' The primitive forces of kinship, religion, need for food, and defence, become the tool, as it were, of active minds *willing* something coherent and organised and usually *imposing their wills* on individuals in the group and on other groups.

2. LEADERSHIP, FORCE, RELIGION AND CONTRACT

Leadership.—The way in which certain men can, as we say, 'impose their wills' on others lies at the very root of politics. Physical prowess does not go very far as an explanation, for the strongest man in a group can be overpowered by the concerted action of a few. It is rather the possession of two certain qualities, different, but closely related, which we may call 'authority' and 'leadership', both being easier to recognise than to explain or define. Why does an insignificant puny fellow keep in perfect order, without cane or imposition, a class of unruly children who reduce to helpless despair a six-foot athlete? One has the 'gift of discipline' denied to the other. Why in a committee can certain quiet, unobtrusive people invariably get their own way, while apparently far more influential and important members passively endorse all their recommendations? Why are certain statesmen outstanding when others, with no less legal power, achieve little? Why a Gladstone, a Briand, a Stresemann, a Feisal on the one hand and a host of nonentities on the other? Why will men follow some to the most dangerous hazards, to the most demanding sacrifices? 'Blood, sweat and tears', said Churchill, and a hundred years earlier, Garibaldi had promised to his followers 'hunger and forced marches'.

Can we explain all this? Obviously some of the elements of authority and leadership can be analysed, such as willpower, clear vision, imagination, understanding of the common man, courage, perseverance. But when all is said and done there remains an elusive 'something', which just makes all the difference between the Churchill and the average run of prime ministers.

Leaders as State Builders.—We stress this because history seems to point to authoritative leadership as the starting-point of every new stage and advance, whether good or bad, whether Alexander, or Mohammed, or Luther, or Napoleon, or Hitler, or Lenin, or countless others. The leader of course does not stand alone or aloof; he must represent the dominant tendencies of his day; he cannot be too much ahead of his troops, or be too different from the rank and file. But he has that 'something' which makes him stand out, and gets him recognised and accepted, so that under his guidance some fresh advance is made and new heights of achievement are reached.[1]

We shall return to this question when we discuss present-day problems; here it is enough to stress the fact that the inspiration of a great leader must be at the origin of many political societies, and that the legends of founders and law-givers are certainly rooted in reality. But for the study of primitive groups we shall turn for our analogies away from our advanced societies to those more spontaneous groups which we find among children. 'Boy-gangs', with their un-disputed leaders, their elaborate rules and conventions which the leader himself must obey, surely take us back to the earliest forms of political association, around a chief who became a focus and inspirer of common action, and an object of loyalty and devotion, and yet whose rule was controlled and checked by innumerable taboos and conventions which even he dare not disobey. And we may perhaps add that there is still a good deal of the gang spirit in modern politics.

Rational Explanation of State Origins.—Another way of approaching the problem of origins is to see whether any prin-ciple of development can account for the facts as we know them and give a satisfactory clue to the true permanent nature of the state—'a rational attempt to justify the nature of authority', as Gettell puts it. Such a method looks back to the past as a confirmation of the present, usually by fastening on one phenomenon of the past and making of it the clue and justi-fication of the present. However small or great the element of historical fact these theories contain, they have a value that may be described as psychological or ethical, in stressing some essential feature either of the state's origins which may shed light on the present, or of the state's present nature which sheds light on its essential function.

---

[1] A Welsh legend, which has given its motto to Bangor University College, gives a striking picture of true leadership as opposed to mere domination. The story is that a chieftain and his men, escaping from a pursuing enemy, reached a ravine too broad to be crossed by any ordinary method—and safety lay on the other side. The chief was a man of gigantic height; throwing himself arms foremost across the chasm, he could just reach the other side. Then, taking a grip of some tree, he told his men to walk across his extended body and all reached safety. The motto derived from this legend is: 'He who would be King, let him be a Bridge'. And the true leader is he who can lead his followers to realisations that might have been outside their unaided reach.

State Origins and Force.—The champions of force as the ultimate basis of the state are historically justified in so far as force did play, as we saw, a considerable part in the formation of the state. But they insist that force is not only *a* historical factor but is *the* present essential feature of the state; that states were born of force only, that power is their justification and *raison d'être*, and that the maintenance and extension of power within and without is the state's sole aim, justifying whatever means may be necessary to achieve it. This, which we may call the Prussian theory of the state, is in fact extremely old; and its propounders can point to the fact that the oldest states we know were essentially empires based on force, 'plunderbunds', as Lord calls them.

Although we recoil from this theory of the state, we should not forget that, whenever control is imposed by any group on any other, we justify that theory by which power is its own justification. Colonisation, for instance, may be defended by numerous arguments, and may be proved, in the long run, to have benefited the colonised, but it is nevertheless an assertion of superior force. Wherever a small state is obliged to adapt its policy to that of a more powerful one, we get another expression of the same tendency. This over-insistence on the part played by power in state origins is in fact only a reminder of the part played by power now.

State Origins and Religion.—The same is true to a great extent of religion as the essential bond and basis of the state; there are some who would make unity of worship the test of citizenship, identify the laws of the state with those of the dominant church, and give ecclesiastical rule the final word. Theocracy, as it is sometimes called, was indeed a stage in the development of many states, and traces of it have remained in history in the theory of the Divine Right of Kings, a doctrine found in many communities, of which the Emperor of Japan was the last representative, since the disappearance of the three empires of Russia, Austria, and Germany. We also see it in the attempts made at various times to make of one creed the official creed of the state. In this sense Spain, and Saudi Arabia are perhaps the only theocratic states extant, though the division of India on religious lines is a return to the identification of state with religion. And in a slightly different form, its identification with a particular ideology is a legacy of theocracy, strange as this might seem to a Nazi or a Communist. Other survivals are the religious coronation of kings, some of our liturgical phraseologies,[1] and the still half-consciously lingering view of law and of state commands as something sacred. The whole tradition of the divine origins of political power dies hard.

State Origins and Human Nature.—The theory that the state is natural, again historically true up to a point, has inspired many thinkers, from the Greeks onwards, to claim for the state a certain finality that puts it above any other form of association or group. Only in the state can man be himself or realise his true nature and the state is therefore entitled to include and control the whole of his life; against this all-pervasive state man has no claims to put forward.

This insistence on the natural or spontaneous element in state origins is of course urged against all those who would make of the state a human creation for human convenience. It is essentially the denial of any utilitarian view; it reduces or ignores the part played by human wills, desires and interests, anything that would weaken the final and compelling character of authority. It has been extensively used to justify every form of autocracy, even though the Greek originators of the theory always qualified this by saying that the state was natural in so far as it was necessary for the *good* life.

State Origins and Contract.—The struggle persists, however, between those who believe the state was made for man, and those who hold that man was made for the state.

But of all attempts to justify a certain view of the state by its origins, the most important, both in history and in essential significance is the consent or contract theory. Here more than anywhere else must we distinguish between historical and psychological truth. The 'contractualist' holds that the state originated in a deliberate decision of men. In order to avoid the evils of isolation they organised themselves on a political basis, resolving to abandon their individual freedom of action to a common authority in exchange for its protection. This 'contract' theory has many forms into which we need

---

[1] As for instance, whenever Romans xiii is read as a lesson in church, 'All powers that be are ordained of God'.

not go now; it is obviously absolutely unhistorical, since it assumes on the part of primitive man a political wisdom, self-control and other virtues that were to be painfully acquired throughout the ages.

But the contract theory, however unhistorical, has the advantage of giving us perhaps the only sound assumption on which to build and maintain any system of political relationships. It insists upon the fundamental truth that no stable state can exist without the consent of its members, that it is they, and they only, who make the state, that there is no state either before or without them, that the state has no authority except that given to it by them; that the relation of government to governed is essentially one of contract or bargain, obedience being conditional on the state fulfilling its own part, i.e. doing all it is entitled to do by its 'charter', and no more. However unscientific the contract theories, they nevertheless offer the the only alternative to the exaltation of the state at the expense of its members. We must build our political systems *as if* a contract had actually been made; it is the only salvation from authoritarianism, the only foundation for any assertion of 'individual' rights.

3. THE EVOLUTION OF THE STATE: ANCIENT TIMES

The search for historical origins, however interesting to the scholar, is of small help to us in the solution of our own problems. The distant past is so remote and dim that it sheds but little light on the present and much less on the future. We must now pass on to see how, once constituted in its earliest forms, the state evolved in those periods of history near enough to have left us ascertainable records. We can trace with fair accuracy the evolution of various forms and patterns of states; there has been of course no single uniform evolution, and very different types have coexisted, and coexist now.

Earliest State Forms.—The earliest states we know were built up along the great rivers of the middle lattitudes— Nile, Euphrates, Tigris, Indus, Ganges, Yellow River, Yang Tse. These fertile valleys were naturally the earliest sources of surplus wealth, and this was accumulated in cities that became centres of commercial exchange and of administration.

These states tended to expand upwards, as it were, away from the mouths of rivers (often unnavigable) into the interior until mountain or desert was reached. They were essentially power and property states, built on wealth and military force; they attracted the jealousy of nomadic tribes beyond or of each other, and had little stability, the conqueror being conquered in his turn; sometimes the breakup came from inside by the revolt of some subordinate official, who either made his province into an independent state or actually overthrew and replaced his sovereign lord. Expansion by annexation, then disruption and re-constitution, either from within or by conquest from the outside, were the normal processes that marked those early empires.

But if they were politically unstable they were socially stable because they were based on that most stabilising force, agriculture. The peasant does not move, does not welcome change, is indifferent to political vicissitudes as long as he is guaranteed a minimum of security in the cultivation of the soil. 'The peasant', says McIver, 'is perhaps the most permanent, the most conservative of all social conditions. He seeks above all things establishment, the customary way, provided it is not beyond measure intolerable. He is not inclined to question or disturb the order of things. The forces of nature convey to him that sense of ineluctable, abiding yet capricious power which reflects itself in submission to authority. For him the distance between God and the king is one of degree. The peasant is therefore in harmony with the class power of the land empire.'

The permanency of the essential social and economic framework is marked by the development of those institutions that separate the real state from the still primitive tribe; law replaces tradition and custom; organised armies are an important element, and warfare goes with elaborate rules of international intercourse.

Oriental Empires.—It must not of course be assumed that those states were primitive and barbarous. Most people know about the scientific knowledge of Babylonians and Egyptians, their division of time, their mathematical calculations. The code of Hammurabi regulated with detailed common sense almost every imaginable aspect of life, and reveals a highly-organised, prosperous society, with a carefully worked out hierarchy of functions. The Sumerians are said to have established rotation of office, annual appointments and election by secret ballot.

The Oriental type of empire, based on slavery, legal or disguised, and on the tax collector represents probably the way in which a great part of the world has been governed until modern times. The short-lived maritime states of the Eastern Mediterranean, the Roman empire, and later Europe to the West of Russia provide the only important exceptions; outside of these we have no records of any other type, except where the more primitive tribal system survived as in Africa and some Pacific islands. When we criticise it for its tyranny, its hardness, its warlikeness, we must remember first that its autocracy was limited in practice by custom, tradition and religion, next that it kept large areas of the world in comparative order and quiet; finally, that none of its members ever dreamt of anything else. Famine, excessive taxation, the misbehaviour of particular officials might cause local revolts but the long centuries of its predominance show that, under the circumstances of those days it was on the whole adequate to its function. That of course is not to say that many of those empires did not outlive their utility, but the fact of having lasted a little too long does not destroy their past contribution to human development.[1]

From the point of view of the student of politics, those empires offer, however, little interest. Few of them evolved any significant institutions that would repay study,[2] and they were all characterised by an internal inertia amounting to something like paralysis. They might wage successful wars and expand, or be defeated and decrease, but there was little or no change in their political, social and economic structure, little growth in their cultural life. Their ultimate collapse before the more dynamic forces of Western Europe was their inevitable end.

The States of the West.—It is thus a very limited part of the world which produced types of government that were different

[1] China, India, the Arab and Turkish empires, Russia, and much of central and South America were all for centuries parts of such empire states.

[2] Except perhaps for the admirable Chinese civil service built from time immemorial on competitive examination.

and capable of change or adaptation and which calls for the
attention of the political scientist. This world was originally
that of the Aegean and Eastern Mediterranean Seas, where
communities developed on somewhat different and varied lines,
all based, however, on regarding the sea as a highway instead
of a barrier. We know very little of the people who established
the maritime states of Troy, Crete, Mycenae, a great deal
more of the Phoenicians of the Eastern Mediterranean coast,
and still more of the tiny city states of the Greek mainland
and islands.

These maritime states, however different in many ways,
in origins, culture, and civilisation, had nevertheless certain
common characteristics. They all arose out of trade, either
as carriers for the product of inland states, or as pirates and
dealers in loot—often as both. They were small, being concentrated on harbours with some hinterland, and were therefore easy to defend; they expanded not by conquest of large
areas but by the establishment of trading outposts or colonies.
They had mobility and adaptability; their wealth was in their
ships and their brains; their cities were, like all harbours, the
meeting places of varied people, markets not only for goods
but also for ideas; their life required technical skill, alertness,
quickness of mind. These qualities and the circumstances of
their life gave them an influence quite out of proportion to
their numbers or to the extent of their possessions; and it is no
accident that one of the greatest, perhaps *the* greatest, invention
of the human mind, the alphabet, should have come from those
adventurous seafarers.

Greek City States.—It is also with one of these that the
study of political science may be said to begin, for the Greek
city states seem to have been the first communities to have
given conscious thought to the problems of politics. We say
'seem' because, for all we know, the ancient empires may have
produced political thought of the highest order, but if they did
no records of it have survived.[1] The Greeks, therefore,
deservedly or not, are to us the pioneers in our field of study;
although their political institutions were probably not unique,
and would in all likelihood have been found in other cities of

[1] It is difficult to believe that such a code as Hammurabi's does not represent
the fruit of much thought as to the nature of the state.

the Aegean and Eastern Mediterranean sea-boards; for the circumstances which led to the formation of those self-governing communities were much the same for them all—nearness to the sea, tiny islands or narrow valleys, preventing any widespread, unified control and making easy the maintenance of independence.

The Greek city state represents therefore not so much something new as the most fully developed instance of a way of life and government of which records have come to us; and is the only one we know representing a deliberately conceived and thought-out philosophy of human collective life.

What those city states offer us is a number of small units independent of any external control and having evolved within their limits systems of government based not on the personal authority of one leader but on the common wills and personal participation of their individual members, who are no longer subjects but citizens. It was probably the very smallness of these units that enabled them to become self-governing. The contacts between government and governed were too close, the problems too immediate, for the people involved not to have tried to manage their own affairs instead of leaving them to some more or less responsible chieftain. The development of this spirit is not easy to trace in history; all we do know that the Greeks soon developed a hearty contempt for absolute hereditary rule, or 'tyranny' as they called it.

Greek Citizenship.—It is then on all citizens that fell responsibility for the business of the community. 'He that has good advice to give to the city, let him come forward and speak'; so does Euripides the dramatist summarise this duty of citizenship.

We must not forget that the Greek idea of citizenship was limited and exclusive. Slaves were of course barred as were 'foreigners', i.e. residents who were not themselves sons of citizens born in the city. Naturalisation was unknown; it may be said that there remained a strong element of the old concept of common descent. But if the citizen class was limited, it really ruled, electing all its officials, carrying on itself the work of legislation and of justice, and being really collectively responsible for the city's policy.

But while citizenship was exclusive in numbers, the scope

of its activities in the name of the state was not. It was on the contrary 'an all-inclusive partnership in every aspect of human existence, in all science, in all art, in every virtue and in all perfection', as Burke was to express it some twenty-two centuries later. But this broad inclusiveness made the Greeks neglect one of the most essential of political problems, that of clearly defining the functions of the state and separating it from those of other social agencies. 'The failure to distinguish the state from the community', says McIver, 'left Athenian liberty itself a monument broken and defaced. The all-inclusive state, whether its dimensions are those of the city or nation, cannot draw the line between law and custom, between enforcement and spontaneity, between the conditions of order and those of culture. So long as the theory is accepted that the state is omni-competent, there will be confusion and suppressions. . . . Under such a theory no form of life is safe, no religion, no opinion, unless its adherents control the government. So the very diversity which enriches a civilisation when recognised as existing of right, creates under the principle of the "universal partnership" those violent and factious oppositions which on the contrary destroy it.'

Was it all a Failure?—Nor must we forget, in our admiration for the Greek political experiment, how shortlived it was. After having maintained a precarious independence against Persia the city states were swallowed up in the Macedonian empire before it absorbed in its turn Persia and the whole Middle East.

It looked, in fact, as if the Greek 'democratic' experiment had been a complete failure leaving behind no legacy and no heirs. No-one would guess that during the very process of its disappearance two writers had embodied its philosophy and speculation in imperishable works, which were to form the basis of all future study of politics, and that a large body of plays and historical writing had made available for all future generations the experience of Greek political life. It is this survival that is perhaps the greatest miracle of 'the glory that was Greece'.

With the victories of Philip and Alexander the world was thus back again at the stage of the despotic empire, more cultured and enlightened, but the same in all essentials;

geographically it was still limited to Asia and the European fringe of the Eastern Mediterranean, and it looked as if the world had just undergone one of the greatest 'as-you-weres' in history. And then appeared a new political phenomenon, destined both to open new horizons and to save and transmit to posterity the essential elements of the order now about to disappear. This new phenomenon was the development of Rome.

The Roman City State.—Rome was originally just one of the numerous little states which had been born in Italy, in much the same way and for the same geographical reasons as in Greece. But although these had some commercial relations with Greece, they remained agricultural and isolated until Rome began to expand, first in Italy then outside.

The original Rome was a 'Republic' having got rid of its early rulers or kings just as the Greeks had expelled their 'tyrants'.[1] Here also appeared a citizen class charged with the management of the city's affairs. But Rome never became a democracy on the Athenian model because one of its assemblies, the Senate, making itself partly hereditary and partly self-recruiting, managed to keep the reality of power, even largely manipulating the nominally popular elections of consuls and other officials. It would therefore be more correct to call Rome an aristocratic oligarchy than a democracy, until the time when the Senate virtually abdicated before the 'strong man' of the day, at first a successful soldier—Marius, Sulla, and finally Caesar, whose nephew Augustus established a practically hereditary autocracy.

The contribution to politics of Rome as a city state and a republic is, therefore, negligible, except perhaps to show how democratic forms can be completely neutralised by an aristocratic or autocratic reality. Rome may be said to have taught later dictators that the way to establish tyranny is not by the outright destruction of free institutions, thus creating conflict, opposition and resistance, but by gradually and secretly emptying them of all effective power while respecting their outward forms, a lesson well learnt by the two Napoleons, by Mussolini and by Hitler.

[1] 'Rex' remained a term of abuse in Rome, in imperial as well as in republican days.

3

The Roman Empire.—Incalculably more important was the contribution of Rome as the capital of an empire. There was first of all the enlargement of the known political world by the inclusion of France, Spain, England, Western Germany, North Africa. The Mediterranean became a Roman lake, the English Channel merely an exceptionally broad river of the Roman world; Alps and Pyrenees ceased to be boundaries.

In the second place come some of the methods by which that empire was controlled, namely the use of loyal local chieftains, acting as Roman agents, the respect for local customs and rules where they did not conflict with any vital Roman principle, and for all essentials the establishment of one single system of Roman Law. This varied according to status from slave to free non-citizen and up to full citizen, but seems at least to have been rigidly applied and gave to the concept of Law a majesty hitherto unknown. Further, the granting of full Roman citizenship to any loyal member of the empire, whatever his national origins, gave to all citizens thus honoured a direct interest in the maintenance of the Roman system.

And thirdly, though this is not directly political, we may mention the provision of an effective police, of excellent roads, of easy communications by ship, horse and coach, the establishment of free trade over a vast area, which included practically all the civilised world of the time; all this gave the Roman empire in its heyday a prosperity and a grandeur hitherto unknown, and some would add, scarcely known since.

The Weaknesses of the Imperial System.—That is not to say that everything was perfect in Rome, far from it. Slavery was cruel and religious persecution frequent in the first three centuries of the Christian era; many emperors were irresponsible despots, and although this irresponsible despotism rarely went beyond the borders of Italy and was compatible with good government in the provinces, the administration was often weak; bureaucracy was unenterprising, afraid for its job, mistrusting the peoples whose life it controlled. Taxation was heavy and unscientific; military expenditure was too high. The various parts of the empire were not sufficiently linked together; their one bond was direct dependence on Rome herself, and there was not enough democracy in the local units. Rome, in fact, missed several opportunities, the formation of a great civil service, the building of a real federation, and the creation of the representative system.[1] Only in the development of municipal autonomy did she make anything permanent in the way of institutions.

In a word, the weakness of the system was that it remained too Roman, too centralised, too much dominated by the desires and interests of Rome, too dependent on the personality of the emperor of the day. Rome had political genius up to a point but lacked creative inventiveness. With more wisdom and power of adaptation, her empire might well have endured; it had no rivals (the Barbarian 'invasions' were just as much internal disintegration as external aggression and could easily have been repulsed by better organisation and cohesion); it had assimilated Christianity and turned this possible enemy into an ally, an act of the highest statesmanship on the part of the state, if not perhaps on that of the Church. There was nothing inevitable in its fall, any more than in any other historical event.

4. THE EVOLUTION OF THE STATE : THE MIDDLE AGES

The Byzantine Empire.—With Rome disappeared the last attempt at an empire comprising the virtual entirety of the civilised world, and the last hope of unity. In the Eastern part of it, it is true, no problem arose: the empire had been virtually cut into two over a century before, and the heir of the Caesars who ruled in Byzantium continued the imperial autocratic tradition; his successors, first the Arabs, then the Turks, introduced no new principle of government. Not until the end of the First World War did most of the former Eastern empire know anything but an irresponsible tyranny, which sapped their populations of any independence of spirit or initiative and bequeathed to them an inheritance of mis-government, inefficiency and corruption—a heavy burden which the newly independent states which have emerged from the former Ottoman empire are painfully endeavouring to shake off today.

[1] Rome nearly invented printing. Movable types were used to stamp lead water pipes. But slaves as copyists were too numerous and too cheap to create a demand for reproduction of books on a large scale.

The Western half of the empire had a very different destiny. The collapse of Roman rule brought about a disintegration so complete, that the innumerable fragments into which the Western world broke up were scarcely states; 'Once more', says McIver, 'the state had to be rebuilt within a primitive society.'

Western Feudalism.—The foundation on which this rebuilding was slowly and painfully carried out was the one remaining concrete reality in all the chaos and confusion, namely the land: the authority of a landowner over his slaves and tenants. Within his lands he could keep order and maintain a minimum of economic activity and coherent existence. Each district had its lord, who ruled over it as a miniature king, delegating his authority to his chief tenants in return for certain personal services, mainly military, and for financial dues.

It is this association of political power with land control that is the essential principle of what is commonly called the 'Feudal System'. The word 'system' is, however, too precise; feudalism was more a civilisation, a form of society, than an elaborate political or economic or social organisation. Politically, it is simply government by a territorial aristocracy filling the vacancy created by the collapse of any central power. The fact of controlling a definite area of land replaced any abstract 'right' to govern because such control was immediate and inescapable; in that sense might was right.

Then, gradually the state *was* rebuilt. Powerful lords subdued less powerful ones, and small kingdoms emerged, becoming gradually larger and stronger by successful conquest or lucky marriages, and by the consolidation of an authority that was generally welcomed by the masses, if not by the more important lords whose powers were gradually limited by the new monarchs. Thus, emerged France (a much smaller country than now), England, a number of little units in Germany and central Europe forming a loose federation under the leadership of an elected head termed the Holy Roman Emperor, and these together with numerous other small states, many of them city states, made a new political map of the Western world. The state had been rebuilt.

The Medieval Church.—Political necessity was not, however, the sole agent in this rebuilding. No less effective was the unifying influence of the Church. By giving Europe one worship, one culture, one law in many departments of life, one language of civilised intercourse, the Church held together for centuries the broken fragments of Roman rule and directly helped in the rebuilding of rival political forces which were ultimately to prove stronger than the unifying forces of religion.

But the participation of the Church in the work of political reconstruction raised an entirely new problem, that of the relation of Church and state. It was a new problem because it could not arise as long as religion was simply the worship of the deities special to and protecting each particular state. The Church, whether people or clergy, could not possibly develop interests or policies conflicting with those of the state.

The situation changed with the coming of Christianity, partly because, being a universal religion, it was no longer limited by any state frontiers, partly because the Church professed loyalties higher than those to the state—to God, and more immediately to the Pope. She claimed, therefore, in her affairs an independence which was something new. Had it been possible to draw a clear line between her spiritual concerns with souls and the secular concerns of the state, with bodies, some kind of working compromise might have been achieved. But on the one hand the Church, as a property owner (and therefore as a participant in justice and administration), was an important element in the secular order, not to speak of her claim to control her clergy even in the most mundane matters; and on the other hand the state could not dismiss as purely 'spiritual' such practical matters as marriage and inheritance, or accept as 'crimes' whatever acts the Church chose to condemn as such.

The struggle between secular and spiritual authority dominates medieval history and ended, in spite of many partial victories for the Church, in the final success of the state. The causes of this are many and complex and cannot be fully discussed here ;[1] it is enough to say that once state power had again become re-established and re-unified, it could brook

---

[1] An excellent account will be found in H. W. C. Davis' 'Mediaeval Europe' (Home University Library).

no rival and insisted on imposing on the Church within its
borders those controls which it considered necessary; even in
the most Catholic of countries, such as Spain, Portugal and
France, the last word in any conflict, whether over finance, or
law, or ecclesiastical appointments even, rested with the
sovereign, however piously he might be termed His Catholic
Majesty in Spain, His most Faithful Majesty in Portugal and
His most Christian Majesty in France. The Protestant Churches,
which sprang out of the Reformation, were as a rule even more
subject to the state; in fact, only where it was persecuted
and outlawed, as Protestantism in France, or Catholicism in
England did any Church achieve real spiritual independence
from the state. The present position of the problem we shall
consider later.

The Medieval State.—The problem of Church and state
was the first legacy of the Middle Ages to modern times.
The second was a principle, that of the limited nature of
monarchical authority, expressed in an institution, that of
representation.

The new political states were not at first autocracies of the
Oriental or Roman types. They inevitably carried with them
the principle on which was built the feudal order from which
they were born, that of reciprocal contract, and the obedience
yielded to the new kings was by no means the unlimited
subservience given to an Eastern despot. And if the kings
had tried to demand it, they would have been met with the
answer that above the state was the Church, and that to her
rulers alone could final authority belong.

The Middle Ages, in fact, had no idea of a legally unlimited
will, autocratic and absolute. This came out most clearly
in the limitations of state power in matters of finance. Never
could a king just seize the property of his subjects as if it were
his own. It had to be obtained by proper forms, either by the
legal process of confiscation for certain offences, or by some
process of voluntary yielding for common purposes. Finance
acted, in fact, both as a unifying influence and as a limitation
on the unifying power. As the business of government grew
more complex, the need for a greater revenue arose, and this
made kings increasingly anxious to enlarge their dominions
and thereby their wealth in money and men. But increased

revenue could only be obtained by increased taxation, and this was checked by the human reluctance to part with money. Further, the more the king claimed, the more anxious were subjects to see that this was spent on objects of which they approved.

Out of the king's need for money, of the subjects' disinclination to give it, and of their intention to see how, once given, it was spent, came the great contribution of the Middle Ages to political practice, *Representative Assemblies.*

Who invented Representation?—The Church probably, in the election of representatives by the local houses of certain monastic orders to a central council or chapter. But there are traces of the systems in Anglo-Saxon tribal organisation, and it seems to have been used in municipal affairs long before it was applied to a whole state. The question of origins, however, is one for the historian. All that concerns us is the appearance in many states of assemblies—diets, estates, parliaments—claiming to represent various classes and groups of the population for deliberation, consultation and granting of supplies.

Finance was not, in other words, the only question which made representation necessary. Not being autocrats, and often lacking the actual physical force to compel obedience, medieval kings were obliged to consult those among their subjects whose co-operation was necessary to get anything done on a large scale. Hence the calling of lords and bishops in councils, and the gradual enlargement of the classes consulted as the life of the state grew more complex, especially as commerce developed and with it a wealthy merchant class. So gradually not lords and bishops only, but representatives of the smaller gentry, or of business interests in the towns and of the monasteries and lower clergy are drawn in.

The problem, it should be remembered, is not so much that of choice of representatives, or choice of classes to be represented; it is that the electors should agree to be bound by those they have elected, so that the decision of the assembly should really be that of the whole people represented. This took some time; there are many cases of representatives being disavowed when they got home to their constituents, especially when the amount of taxation granted seemed to these excessive. So we find kings insisting that representatives must come with clearly worded binding authority from their electors.[1] And so gradually representation became established, because it was the only common-sense solution of the problem as to how a government is to keep in touch with the governed, and to know that it is not putting on them intolerable burdens.

Most medieval monarchies and city states had some kind of representative assembly. But the fate of these assemblies varied. The French Estates General and the Spanish Cortes in particular failed to make themselves indispensable by exercising adequate control over taxation; lacking the authority with which to meet national crises, they were called less and less frequently and ultimately ceased to meet. In some cases the assemblies lost all really representative character and became mere agencies of some small governing class or group; this often happened in the commercial city states of Germany and Italy. Only in Britain did parliaments not only survive but ultimately take to themselves the reality of power. By that time, however, the Middle Ages were over.

Medieval Problems.—But although the Middle Ages bequeathed the modern practice of representation, their problems were largely removed from ours.

'The Middle Ages', wrote Bryce in his 'Holy Roman Empire', 'were, as compared with the age that preceded and the ages that followed, essentially unpolitical. Ideas as familiar to the commonwealths of antiquity as to ourselves, ideas of the common good as the object of the State, of the rights of the people, of the comparative merits of various forms of government, were, to those generations, though such ideas often found an unconscious expression in practical expedients, in their speculative forms little known, and to most men incomprehensible. Feudalism was the one great secular institution to which those times gave birth, and feudalism was a social and legal system, only indirectly and by consequence a political one. Yet the human mind, so far from being idle, was in certain directions never more active; nor was it possible for it to remain without general conceptions regarding the relations

---

[1] A representative must not be confused with a delegate. The latter is given definite instructions as to how to speak and vote, and dare not depart from his orders; the representative is free to act, according to his judgement and conscience, in the best interests of the whole community.

of men to each other in this world. Such conceptions were neither made an expression of the actual present state of things, nor scientifically determined by an induction from the past; they were partly inherited from the imperial scheme of law and government that had preceded, partly evolved from the principles of that metaphysical theology which was ripening into scholasticism. Now the two great ideas which expiring antiquity bequeathed to the ages that followed were those of a world-monarchy and a world-religion.' The passing of those two great ideas, by the coming of the Reformation and the development of the modern sovereign state, marks the end of the medieval period.

5. THE EVOLUTION OF THE STATE: THE MODERN AGE

Emergence of the Modern State.—The modern state, which gradually superseded the feudal organisation, was characterised by the unquestioned supremacy of its central authority over all subjects and groups, a supremacy made necessary by the chaos following on long feudal wars. No over-mighty subject could any longer claim freedom from royal control in law or finance; no class could escape the royal judge or taxgatherer; Churches had to submit to the state's jurisdiction, or at least obtain state confirmation of their laws. And in relation to one another, each separate monarch was absolute and independent, knowing no limitation to his right to make war as he pleased, expand as he chose, behave towards his neighbour as a bird of prey, if he could.

Nationality.—The development of the national spirit is often mentioned as an important factor in this evolution, but nationality was a result as much as a cause of the forming of the modern state. It is true that to some extent common descent and language helped to bring people together. But common language did not bring about the unity of Britain till 1707, nor prevent its disruption by the secession of the United States in 1776 or of Ireland in 1922; it did not unite France either to Belgium or to the French-speaking cantons of Switzerland, nor make Swiss-German-speaking provinces into part of the German empire. It is probably truer to say that life under a common rule created a common feeling of nationality sprung

3 *

from common interests, leading to a common way of life and
to a desire to remain together separate from other groups of the
same kind. We must distinguish, in fact, between the feeling
of a common nationality as a consciousness of separateness, and
the insistence on living permanently together as an independent
nation; there was certainly a great deal of national feeling in the
France of Joan of Arc, but many Frenchmen cheerfully
accepted Henry V of England as their king. It was in fact a
long time before the national link was stronger than the
religious. Catholics and Protestants welcomed the help of
foreign fellow-believers in the wars of religion. There is no
evidence either that the provinces which frequently changed
hands in the sixteenth, seventeenth, and eighteenth centuries
minded very deeply; in fact, the Polish opposition to par-
titions and the war of American independence, practically
contemporary events, are perhaps the first manifestation of
desire of national independence and of sorrow at its loss.

The Coming of Democracy.—Just as the feudal state was
gradually superseded by the autocratic independent state, so the
latter in its turn was to make way for the modern so-called
democratic state, based on the doctrine of popular sovereignty
and on the revival of representative institutions. In both processes the evolution was slow and gradual, and there was, as
always, much overlapping and regression. But the general
trend of the nineteenth century is clear, and consists very
largely in the widespread re-adoption of the parliamentary
forms of government which had survived only in Britain.[1]

The doctrine of popular sovereignty was the child of two
parents, both of Genevese origins: the individualism of the
Protestant Calvinistic tradition, which had been the driving
force of the English civil wars in their assertion of parliamentary
supremacy, and Rousseau's preaching of the political equality
and sovereign rights of all men. By the end of the nineteenth
century the doctrine of popular rights and its application in the
supremacy of popular representative bodies had become
general in all states which claimed to be 'progressive' and
'civilised'.[2] The parliamentary state, whether republic or

[1] Lord suggests that this adoption was largely due to the victory at Water-
loo. Had France won, 'the oligarchic city state pattern which predominated
before in Europe might well have become the norm for Europe'.

[2] See chapter viii, 'The Democratic State'.

constitutional monarchy, appeared in fact as the normal culmination of centuries of political evolution. Later events were to show this was an illusion.

Evolution in State Action.—And now to conclude. We have travelled far from Oriental despotisms to the democratic modern state but the change has not been confined to outward forms, or to the principles on which they are based; it is no less marked in the kind of work which the state undertakes, and in the nature of its problems. This evolution has been marked by the steady shift in the emphasis of state activity from the political to the social and economic. If we take a normal year's work of the government of any modern country we find that most of the items in its programme would have been totally outside the scope of any medieval government; the education and protection of children, guarantees for workers in industry, cultural activities, upkeep of roads, elaborate national economic policies. None of these would have troubled the medieval lawmaker. On the other hand we take for granted the neutrality of the state in matters of religion and expression of opinion. And if the scope of state activity has both broadened and narrowed, it has also become far more complex. This, is of course the result of the increasing control of man over nature by fuller knowledge and more perfect technique. Just as life in itself is a less simple matter than it has ever been, so is the life of the state. This means in a word that the modern state, as an element in the whole of modern life, inevitably makes much greater demands on its members and depends far more on their sense of individual responsibility. Hence the increasing need for the guidance that political science tries to give to the ordinary citizen.

CHAPTER V

LAW AND SOVEREIGNTY

I. WHAT IS LAW AND WHY IS IT NECESSARY?

Life in Common Needs Rules.—No community can live without rules. In the most united family there must be established priorities in the use of bathroom and motor-car. Rules are necessary to ensure the minimun of uniformity, the behaviour in an expected manner, without which social life would be impossible, for as Bernard Shaw remarks 'life must be dictated and institutional activities must be determined and predictable'. The 'unregulated man', as Murchison calls him, 'has no social life. Dining-out, theatre-going, Church attendance, love-making, family life, education all have rules that must be kept.' Further, both individual and group must know what is the exact extent of their freedom of action and what limits are set to their activities, and when the inevitable differences arise between individuals, these must know according to what principles they will be settled finally. There are multiplicities of common undertakings, and there must be rules as to how these shall be run.

There are thus many departments of community life for which rules must be laid down. Put together they will represent 'a pattern of social behaviour sanctioned by public opinion and supported by the community'.

Social Rules.—Who will lay down those rules? It is evident that many will come from the groups within the community, made for their own members. Churches, trade unions, social groups and classes will all lay down patterns of behaviour of their own, and enforce them by their own sanctions— excommunications, expulsion, exclusion from certain advantages and circles. 'Hell, Coventry and the Poor House may be as effective as prison, gallows or tax', says Merriam. A civil marriage is equivalent to living in sin to a Catholic, and entails exclusion from the sacraments; what is innocent recreation on a holiday to some is Sabbath-breaking to Puritan or Orthodox Jew, and will get him into serious trouble with his community; to be seen wearing yellow boots with evening dress, or a made-up tie, will bar a man from many social circles. Of those rules, some are formal and deliberate, others are traditional customs; and within their limits they may be as formidable as any system that can be devised.

But there are limits. These rules only apply to the members of those groups and their sanctions only involve group membership and activities. Should the dictates of Church or trade union be resisted, expulsion is the only penalty; should one defy rules of social behaviour exclusion from the circles where these matter is the worst that can happen. There are other Churches, other economic associations, other classes where the rebel can find a welcome if he wishes and from whose shelter he can completely ignore the threats and denunciations of his former fellows. And anyway the group sanction would only have affected a part of his life, for group rules are limited in their scope no less than in their penalties, and in the numbers they will reach; they will only affect their members in their relations to other members and in a small portion of their lives. It is evident in other words that the rules of groups however powerful will not cover the whole of life's common unity. More rules will be needed of universal application; these it will be the business of the state to lay down, and these will be called laws.

Laws are the Rules of Life in the State.—A law is a rule of behaviour for the members of a state, the disregard of which meets with a penalty which will be enforced by the state's machinery of power. 'All law', says Kelsen, 'is in essence a system of compulsion; it seeks to bring about socially desired conditions by establishing as the consequence of untoward conduct on the part of the subject an act of coercion to be governed by such and such rules'.[1]

The state is more than law, but it is law; it makes law, and one may well define a state with Wilson as 'a people organised for law within a definite territory', for while the laws of the

---

[1] 'Without law there is no order, without order men are lost, not knowing where they go, or what they do. A system of ordered relationships is a primary condition of human life at every level.' (McIver.)

state do not operate outside the state there can only be one body of the law within it.

In other words, a law is a law because it is declared to be so by the state through the proper law-making organs, whether will of autocrat, act of Parliament, decision of Supreme Court. 'It is not the issuing of the law that makes the state a state; it is the force of the state that makes law law' as Hocking puts it.

Are we to make any difference between the laws of the state and the rules of the groups? It is evident that they have much in common. They can all compel the obedience of those whom they affect or punish disobedience by heavy penalties. They all represent the will of the community, in whole or in part, and depend for their effectiveness on its support. They are the result of evolution of opinion and must roughly correspond to it. As Ward says 'the force behind legal rules is the same reservoir of community activity which is involved in moral codes', and without that force no law or rules will be effective.

State Laws and Group Rules.—The differences between laws of the state and group rules are nevertheless fundamental. Laws are applicable to all without exception in identical circumstances; they claim to represent, however imperfectly, the whole of the community and not a part; and their sanctions belong to a special category, for they are enforceable by the courts and the whole machinery of justice. This last is the crucial point. Even where there is no question of a command or prohibition or punishment, the courts have their role— to decide on the validity of a will, to implement a contract, and even to decide the validity of group rules. Even Churches have had to appeal to the courts.

The breaker of a group rule may have to leave the group but he remains in fellowship with the community, in full enjoyment of his rights as a member. But a decision of the state courts may not be defied. Even if no command or prohibition be involved, disregard of a decision concerning a will,[1]

---

[1] Prof. Robson from whom we quote, points out in his 'Civilisation and the Growth of Law', that a law regulating the making of wills is not a command and need not be obeyed, since no one is compelled to make a will. But if one wants to make a valid will one must conform with the rules laid down, and disregard of these will lead to a legally enforced decision of the court putting aside the will and handing the property over to the natural heir. Surely this law must be 'obeyed'?

the formation of an industrial company, the claim to a house, involves penalties of the same kind as direct breach of a prohibition or disregard of a direct command, namely, imprisonment. Whatever distinctions we may make between various kinds of laws, and however much we tend to see in them mere expressions of common customs or desires, they are all in the last result enforceable by the state machinery of justice and whatever is not so enforceable is not law. All law, by whatever name we call it, or however classified, has but one function, to 'prescribe general conditions of human activity' (Ward). 'It represents the pooling of common experience' and 'legal structures and functions are organs of the community, prospective in character, aiming at facilitating certain types of action.' Its origin may lie back in ' the gradual emergence of various forms of co-operative practices and customary conduct which is the stuff from which the legal fabric is woven,' and its enforcement will depend on a general agreement to submit to common rules of conduct, without which no kind of co-operation is possible. It involves a settled state of affairs, a common consciousness of consent, and ordered unity.' [1]

It is also true that too much insistence has been placed on the 'command and prohibition aspect of law'. It does include these, but they are far from covering all the aspects of law. The way to make an effective will, the rules of inheritance, the mass of legislation that governs our economic life, all laws concerning private disputes—none of these is covered by the term of command and prohibition. But in the last resort it differs from customs, from traditions, from group rules in three ways—first by its origins. Law is law only if enacted by a law-making authority—legislative bodies, other bodies, duly authorised by these (by-laws of a railway company for instance), judicial interpretations that become law. It is definite, precise reference can be made, chapter and verse given. Secondly by the universality of its scope within the limits of the

---

[1] ' Rules must be reasonable and simple enough for any average person who wishes to do so to be able to understand their utility and their necessity. They must come from an authority which is not looked upon as either alien or hostile. They must be sufficiently stable, few in number, and general enough for them to be grasped as a whole once for all.'

(Simone Weil, 'l'Enracinement,' p. 17).

state, and thirdly, by its finality and manner of enforcement. Once the law has definitely and finally spoken there is no appeal except to force.

Varieties of Laws.—Laws are of various kinds and have different functions, though all have in common that they are made by and enforced by the state; but they fall into two main categories. Some are designed to prevent antisocial behaviour, to keep individual selfishnesses from getting into the way of each other; they represent what Ward calls 'the systematic enforced exclusion of certain kinds of action considered intolerable, the elimination of a certain type of conduct', the imposing of certain actions deemed necessary for the general welfare. Among the former are 'crimes', such as theft and murder; among the latter innumerable regulations of hygiene, road regulation, the sending of children to school. Other laws are the organisation of services concerned which cannot be left to individual initiative, the provision of education, national defence, industrial nationalisation, communications. Others again decide on what lines much of the common life shall be run, define the powers of the innumerable bodies which provide important services, regulate private affairs such as marriage, and lay down the principles on which disputes between individuals shall be settled. These laws may be said to state, and if necessary to enforce, certain agreed ways of acting. Opinions differ greatly of course as to what should be prohibited or ordered, what should be publicly administered and what left to private enterprise. But no one disputes the duty of the state to keep order, to protect what is recognised as private property, to organise defence and prohibit private warfare, to organise a system of peaceful settlement of disputes between citizens. The protection of private interests by public law is in fact a primary social necessity; the smallest football club could not exist without the legal protection of its funds; even the family needs law to define many aspects of its life, such as what constitutes coming of age and independence from parental control, the rights of bequest and inheritance, marriage and divorce.

Classification of Laws.—Laws are classified according to their character and scope; we call international laws those which regulate relations between states, public laws, those which regulate the relations of the individuals to the state, private laws those which lay down rules of behaviour as between one citizen and another. We distinguish between constitutional law which defines the powers of the state and of its agents, and lays down the rules according to which the machinery of the state will work, criminal law which deals with the breach of a law, and civil which deals with the settlement of disputes between individuals and groups; we may also separate general laws made by the law-making authority in the state, and fixing some general and permanent rule of conduct, and decrees which are the particular application of a general law at a particular time. A law, for instance, will lay down that Parliament is elected for five years by all men and women of the age of twenty-one and over; a decree will fix the date at which Parliament will be dissolved, on which elections will be held and on which the new Parliament shall meet within certain limits laid down in the law. A law will decide what are the qualifications for holding a certain position in the state, a decree will appoint a particular individual.

There is the same variety in the methods by which law is made and expressed, and the term itself covers many different institutions. In some countries, at various times, the law of the land has been expressed almost perfectly in a written code; Napoleonic France and the numerous systems modelled on its legislation are the chief examples in modern times. In other countries such as Great Britain and the United States interpretations and judicial decisions are just as important as actual enactments. And in all countries much law is only legalised custom.

Laws and the Courts.—But all laws, under whatever name, and whatever their form and content have this in common, that they will be recognised as such by the Courts of Justice appointed to administer them, and will therefore be enforced by the state's machinery. In the last resort law is what the judges declare to be the law according to their interpretation of the intentions of the law-making organs of the state. Should these organs disagree with this interpretation, they are free to change the law by a new one, according to whatever process is necessary to do so.

The last point is important; however independent we wish the judges to be, their decisions are themselves subject to the final word of the state, acting in accordance with the law governing the processes of state action. The British judiciary is probably as free as any in the world; it has not hesitated to proclaim as law principles and actions of great inconvenience to the government of the day; we may remember the repeated defeats of the British government in the Wilkes case or Lord Mansfield's majestic words concerning the negro servant, Somersett, whose status as a slave had become automatically changed to that of a free man by his having been brought to England by his master: '*Whatever inconveniences may follow from this decision*, I cannot say the case is allowed or approved by the law of England, and therefore the black must be discharged'.

But should the Parliament of the day have desired it, nothing could have prevented it from changing the law of England, and re-establishing slavery or Roman Catholicism, or anything else if both Houses of Parliament agreed and the King gave his assent, just as Habeas Corpus, and other cherished guarantees of British freedom have been suspended by Act of Parliament.

In the same way, the numerous laws and judicial decisions which established slavery as an integral part of the law of the United States of America, led, after a civil war, to a change in the law. Many years later, a constitutional amendment made Prohibition the law of the United States—and another abolished it soon after.

Thus in the last resort law is whatever the state declares it to be; it is essentially a department of politics like all state actions. Merriam rightly remarks that 'to say that the state has a monopoly of legality, is a slippery term; it is like saying that the political has a monopoly of the political', which is obvious.

2. LAW AND THE STATE

Relation of Law to the State.—We may hold that the state must be subject to the law, that law is supreme, and that this constitutes the normal difference between what we may call responsible and irresponsible power; we may multiply the agencies by which the responsibility of the agents of the state can be enforced—such machinery is much needed in England. We are rightly shocked when we see in certain countries the state manipulate the law to its advantage or frankly ignore it when inconvenient.[1] But the fact remains that the law is the creation of the state, that in the most completely democratic state a majority of citizens cannot be prevented from using its powers foolishly or tyrannically abrogating good laws and making bad under the influence of passion.[2] The only final guarantee against injustice is not the law but the moral sense and conscience of the ruler in a democracy, that of the citizens, in an autocracy, that of the monarch, in an oligarchy, that of the governing group. But in no case will the letter of laws stand for long as a protection against fanaticism, ignorance and passion. In fact, law must be looked upon as customs underlying the changing policies of governments rather than as expressions of the creative wills of legislative bodies.

When we say this we are not forgetting that the real issue is between arbitrary and constitutional government, between states that admit the supremacy of law and those that deny it. 'Shall we be ruled by law at all or only by arbitrary will?' asks Professor McIllwain in *Foreign Affairs* for January, 1936; and referring to a certain decision of the United States Supreme Court he adds, 'Reformers are naturally irritated when comprehensive plans of social betterment are thus wrecked, apparently on the rocks of mere legalism, but in their irritation they may be overlooking what the alternative means. When judges forget that their office is to declare the law, not to make it, it will be but a short further step to say, with the Nazis, that if no penal code applies directly, such an offence is to be punished according to that law, the underlying idea of which best fits it.'

Thus the only alternative to despotism is constitutionalism; call it mere legalism if you will, and let us admit to the full the

---

[1] 'Must I teach, therefore, henceforward that the supreme principle of the state is that whatever pleasest those in power is Law? As a man of honour I would cease to teach rather than sell to my audience for truth that which is a lie and a deceit.' (Judge Dahlmann, 1837.)

[2] 'England could never be ruined but by a Parliament.' (Blackstone.)

unfortunate obstructive delays that legalism sometimes involves. But let us not close our eyes to the choice involved.[1]

Legal Limits on Law-Making.—If law is the will of the state, if the state has a monopoly of law-making, and an order is a law because the state made it, the question arises: Can the state make any laws it likes? or must we say that only 'what the state has *legally* willed is law'? That reservation brings us to the heart of the problem of law, namely that one of its functions is precisely to say in what way the state's law-making power will be used, and in what way law will be created. This would seem to contradict what was said above, that it is the state that makes law, not law the state; but the contradiction is only apparent, for customs having the force of law were before the state, and the state only came into existence limited by these and by numerous traditions and ways of life.

Legal limitations on the state's power to make laws are the result of many forces—sometimes of the customs or traditions just mentioned, or sanctions of some elements within the state, or, putting it in another way, of the subjects or citizens (who are part of the state) imposing such limits on the government, their agent. The numerous laws which in England have laid down the rules according to which laws may be made, from the Bill of Rights of 1689 to the Parliament Act of 1911, and the numerous written constitutions of countries like the United States or France, are all actions of the citizens, through their representatives, defining and thereby limiting the law-making power of the state.

The constitutions which do this are therefore the ultimate guarantee of citizens against the arbitrary use of power by the agents of the state, as opposed to those countries in which the king's will was law. Nowhere is the political temperament of a people more clearly shown than in their constitutions—in their practical working, of course, rather than in their literal wording. What kind of power do they want exercised? What kind of laws do they desire?

Law and the Community's Sense of Right.—Law in fact will tend to express the common sense of right of a people at a particular time. 'This issues in general agreements regarding

---

[1] The state is a power not bound by law but relying on force. (Lenin.)

the value of both public and private interests, and this common agreement expresses itself in organs which clarify and make explicit the common judgements of right and also serve to maintain common interests'—Law thus represents 'an actually achieved valuation of interests', and this yields the standard by which conduct is judged. How is this 'common sense of right' achieved? This will evidently depend on many things. A common religion is the greatest help and violence of religious antagonisms, the greatest obstacle. 'That intangible complex of ideas which we call nationality' is obviously bound to express itself in law as in all other manifestations of the national spirit. But this raises many questions. How do communities arrive at certain common expressions of their outlook? What makes something seem right to one generation and wrong to the next? We do not know.

Relative Authority of Law.—Since law is merely the expression of a current dominant sense of right, and can be nothing more, it follows that it cannot claim for itself any higher authority than that of its makers. It will merely state the will of those that form the dominant part of the state at the time the law is made. In other words, since we attach no sacred character to the state, we shall attach none to its laws. If we see in the state a functional body, justified solely by its results, and only distinguished by its special powers, so laws will stand or fall by what they achieve for the welfare of the citizens.

Since therefore the state is a medley of imperfect men and women, and its government a smaller body of equally imperfect persons, moved by prejudice and private interests, often ignorant, often foolish, we shall not expect to find any special qualities in the laws they make. Laws are not the majestic utterances of perfect wisdom, much less divinely inspired ordinances; they are rules of behaviour made by the people who happen to be in power at the time, and represent their dominant interest.

'Law', says Laski, 'is the registration of that will in society which has known how to make itself effective; legal imperatives are a function of effective demand. They will correspond to the desires of those who know how to make their wishes felt at the centre of political power. From the welter of competing desires, some are selected for translation into legally imperative terms'; most systems of law have in fact justified a social order in which the many lived and worked for the benefit of the few.

Types of Present-day Laws.—Let us see what kinds of laws govern us now. Some merely enforce uniform action where uniformity is necessary, such as driving on one side of the road; others enjoin certain actions as socially necessary for the common welfare; all health and hygiene regulations would come under that heading. Others are expressions of a certain social ideal, as for instance compulsory education or freedom of religion and speech. Others are statements as to how certain necessary tasks which are beyond individual or group competence shall be organised, such as laws nationalising mines or setting up an electricity board. But most laws aim at preserving the present economic and social system, especially the safe-guarding of property. They are in fact the expression of a certain social order, prevailing at a particular time. It follows that the broader the political representation, the more likely laws are to represent the general interest and not those of a class. But perhaps economic equality is more important still, for 'legal imperatives are a function of effective demand', and while political enfranchisement has helped economic freedom, it could not come until men had enough importance as independent workers to be able to demand political recognition.

It follows that whatever it is, law is not an impartial arbiter. The state is not the guardian of law but only of a certain dominant conception of life, of which law is the expression. That dominant conception may be one particular system which it will defend against all attacks, or it may be a belief in free discussion of all systems, or, more usually, a somewhat confused mixture of the two

Justification of Law.—A law must therefore be judged by what it tries to do; 'its justification is to be found in terms of the ends it seeks to serve', and those are not necessarily immediately found in the terms of the law itself; motives are not always apparent, legislative bodies are often the tools of forces and interests carefully keeping off the political stage.

3. LAW AND JUSTICE

Law and the Community Sense of Right.—Law being the
expression of what a particular society thinks right, it follows
that law will be 'just' in so far as the society of which it is
the expression is just; it tries at least to realise some degree of
justice in its legal relations. A law may be profoundly unjust
in the eyes of some people, but not in the eyes of the great
majority, otherwise it would be unenforceable and sooner or
later disappear. Religious persecution only remained legal as
long as its justice was generally approved, as it was generally
in the sixteenth and seventeenth centuries, only appearing
unjust to a tiny enlightened minority. The Combination Acts
and other measures that crippled the organised activities of
workers, were not 'unjust' in the eyes of the legislators of
that day, whatever we think now. The same is true of those
appalling laws which punished by death the stealing of any
article worth five shillings, or which established judicial
torture; what was wrong was the level of the contemporary
sense of justice. Even now many generally accepted laws are
'unjust' in the eyes of some people; some sincerely believe
that compulsory education is an infringement of the sacred
rights of parents to bring up their children as they think best,
including the right to keep them illiterate.[1] Freedom of worship
has been denounced as being 'unjust' to the dominant religion, and so has the giving of preference to state schools as
'unjust' to private establishments. Nationalisation is now
attacked as 'unjust' to employers and capitalists. The Trade
Union Act of 1927 was declared 'unjust' by the unions, and
so was its repeal by the employers.

A law may rightly be termed 'unjust' from two standpoints. The first is from that of an ideal impersonal eternal
justice. But who is going to lay down its principles? Some see
it embodied in the teachings of a Church, others in the
teachings of a religion greater than any one Church; others
believe that the much-discussed *natural law* offers such
guidance.

Natural Law.—We agree with these last, and hold that the
recognition of natural law is an essential condition of the

---

[1] We heard a former Senior Wrangler and Professor of Mathematics
defend that view some forty years ago.

establishment in the world of any concept of objective justice.[1]
'Our courts', says Sir Frederick Pollock, the famous jurist,
'have to go on making a great deal of law, which is really
natural law, whether they know it or not, for they must
find a solution for every question which comes before
them, and general considerations of justice and convenience
must be relied on in default of positive authority.' It is
the tacit acknowledgement of this which lies behind the
trials of war criminals, for if there be no natural universal
principles of human behaviour, irrespective of time and place,
the trials are judicially and morally unjustifiable.

But if we accept natural law, then certain laws may well
be described as essentially and intrinsically unjust; we may
even go further and say that any state which does not base its
legalisation on natural law is in itself an unjust state and that all
its laws are ethically invalid. We could say this, for instance,
of the Fascist, Nazi and Bolshevist systems, which frankly
make law the servant of the state. Here are some extracts, for
instance, of the German Penal Code Amendment Law of
June 1935: 'Courts shall punish offences not punishable under
the Code, but deserving of punishment according to the
underlying idea of a penal code or according to healthy public
sentiment. . . . Service to the vital necessities of our people,
not to theories, is the ideal of the German guardian of law.
The German Academy of Law will develop the Aryan
conception of justice.' We know what this has meant: Dachau,
the gas-chambers, and 27,000 hostages shot in France alone.

Another definition would term unjust 'a law which is in
contradiction with the prevailing conceptions of justice on
which a particular state claims to be based'. For instance, it
may be argued that the law which in Switzerland limits the
suffrage to males is an unjust law, because Switzerland is based
on the recognition of full individual rights, so that the absence
of woman suffrage is an unethical anomaly. But the same
limitation, wise or unwise, is not 'unjust' in a state which
makes no pretence to equality of rights.

[1] 'Somehow or other men must be persuaded, if not of the truth of the
Christian religion, at least of a Divine order, a natural law, a common
standard above the human level, by reference to which all human conduct can
be judged.' (Prof. H. A. Smith, 'The Law of Nations, 1948', quoted in *The
Times Literary Supplement*, November, 1948.)

What is an 'Unjust' Law?—It is extremely important that this distinction be borne in mind. We are perpetually condemning by moral standards, without making it clear on what principles those standards are based. If there are no universally recognised eternal principles of behaviour, then the standards can only be what the conscience of a particular age will accept, and the law is only 'unjust' if it violates that particular conscience. It is therefore futile to condemn religious intolerance, or judicial torture, or slavery, unless, we can show that they ran counter to the conscience of that day—which they did not. In the same way we do not (if we are logical) condemn the anti-religious legislation of Soviet Russia, because the Russian people have never in their history acknowledged religious freedom as desirable. On the other hand, we condemn the anti-Jewish laws and the cruelty of Nazi Germany because the German conscience had risen to the level of accepting the doctrines of equal rights and high standards of behaviour in judicial and political affairs. The Nuremberg laws and the concentration camps were wrong in the eyes of those who worked them and therefore 'unjust' by prevailing—as well as by fundamental—standards. In the same way the imposition by Turkey of special taxes on non-Moslems is a violation of the professed democracy of Turkey, and therefore unjust, whereas the restricting in Syria of the headship of the state to Moslems is not unjust, since Syria is a professedly Moslem state. The whole point is whether the law is a regression from hitherto accepted standards, in a word, whether its framers really 'know better'. It should be added that a law may not be so much intrinsically unjust as be so unjustly administered as to become unjust in practice. In a country where some people can notoriously snap their fingers at the law because of their influential position, or where bribery will always secure immunity, then a law, which is just in itself becomes unjust. In fact in such a country there will rarely be such a thing as a really just law. Finally we should remember that an unjust law is not just any law that we happen to dislike.

Law and State Purposes.—The justification (not the abstract justice) of a law is therefore in the last resort a matter of its relation with the avowed purposes of the state that enacts it. If a particular law is in conflict with it, we may be able to get it altered; but if it is not, then there is little hope of any change in the law without a change in the purpose of the state, and this involves a change in the outlook of its members. Great Britain is now enacting legislation which will involve great changes in her economic and social structure, because such legislation is in harmony with the altered purposes of the state, as shown in the new point of view of the majority of its electorate; those nationalising measures could obviously never be brought forward with any hope of success as long as the majority still held to the principle of capitalism and free enterprise. In the same way although the Nazi system has been formally destroyed, no truly free system of government can be established in Germany until a majority of those who, actively or passively, supported National Socialism have changed their minds.

4. RESISTANCE TO LAW

Should One Resist an Unjust Law?—The problem of resistance to a bad law cannot be dealt with fully here as it needs a discussion of the limits of individual rights which will only come later. It is nevertheless impossible not to refer to it now.

We might begin with what is perhaps the conclusion, that resistance is never a *right*—it is either a crime or a duty.[1] If we admit that an unjust law should be resisted as hurtful, then no responsible person has any real option. Not to resist would be a betrayal of his conscience and of his community. Resistance is a loosening of the social bond, a break up of unity; it can never be entered upon frivolously or light-heartedly. It can never be just 'permissible', according to one's fancy.

Is it ever right to resist, and if it is, what kind of resistance is right? Few people would urge that any and every law must always be obeyed, and that duty to his country would have justified English Catholics and French Protestants to deny their conscience and conform according to the law. They refused to obey and took the consequences in suffering and death;

---

[1] See Thomas Hill Green's 'Principles of Political Obligation'.

no one can blame martyrs or call them bad citizens; the sin was on the side of the law-makers. Nevertheless, even the martyr's resistance is a grave business. Should everybody take the same attitude to laws they dislike, there would be an end of society. All that can be said is that, if the penalty for disobedience be heavy enough, disobedience will never be tried without good reason; and whoever deliberately risks his life is showing the highest kind of loyalty possible to an ideal and commands respect. And if the penalty be slight, it means that the state does not attach much importance to the observance of that particular rule; penalties are in direct relation to the social gravity of the offence.[1] In any case passive resistance is rarely immediately effective; the blood of the martyrs is indeed the seed of the Church, but the harvest is slow in coming and few martyrdoms have brought about any immediate change in the law.

Active resistance is different in so far as it involves inflicting violence as well as suffering it. It stands morally on another and less secure plane, and rebels do not command the same respect as martyrs, for rebellion is easier than martyrdom. But the final result is not very different. Revolt is only successful when it represents so many members of the community that the unjust law obviously did not represent its general desires. Violent resistance then became the only way of getting a majority will to prevail against a legal system that could not or would not change.

Some Suggested Tests.—Ultimately, of course, resistance is a subjective matter on which no one can lay down the law. But it may be possible to suggest a few fundamental principles of general applications. First, as we said, that disobedience to law—to any law—is a serious step, not to be lightly undertaken, and always with the question before one, 'What would happen if everyone acted as I am about to do now?', and especially, 'Would I approve of a similar resistance to a law of which I approve, by some one who felt about that one as I feel about the one I am proposing to disregard?'

Second, that we must not confuse an unjust law with one we merely dislike. Conscience is one thing, disliking is another.

[1] Not, of course, to its moral gravity. Forgery is punished more heavily than cruelty.

There is especially a great difference between a law requiring some kind of personal participation, such as military service, or religious worship, or compulsory joining of a party, or a law forbidding some personal service which we feel we must render, such as attending meetings wrongly forbidden, or reading books wrongly prohibited, or taking part in some unlawful propaganda, or finally a law requiring some financial payment. Refusal of personal service may be easier to justify than refusal to abstain from certain actions, and refusal to pay taxes is probably never justified, since paying money does not involve our personality.

Thirdly, if we do resist, it must be openly, as a deliberate public act to satisfy our own conscience. Underhand evasion of law is *never* right, for it has no moral value. The whole value of resistance is a call to public opinion, or appeal to the world, an appeal unto Caesar. The government must know it is being defied, so must the other citizens.

Fourthly, the exact purpose of resistance must be kept in mind. Are we trying to make the law unworkable by organised refusal to comply? That means in practice the coercion of the majority by an obstinate and convinced minority; it is the end of democratic government: it may be right, but it is dangerous. Or are we trying to call the attention of public opinion to an injustice, in the hope of winning over its support for a change in the law? That is good but is rarely successful. Or are we face to face with an urgent inner necessity and clearing our consciences, by a 'Come what may, I can do no other, God help me'? This happens but rarely, but it is by far away the most dependable case; for it can never be good for any society that any of its members should strain their consciences into forswearing themselves. The action is independent of any immediate result; it is irrelevant to success; it is the basis of all good life, the free action of a free conscience. But a state in which such attitudes become normally necessary is in a bad way.

Need for an Independent Attitude.—In all our upholding of the law from the point of view of the citizen, it should be remembered that supine passiveness is no guarantee of good government. The authorities should realise that the spirit of independence on which most states ultimately rest is never dead and might become active once more if challenged. 'Obedience to law is a duty, but, like all duties, it is not absolute but relative; it rests upon the supposition that the law emanates from a legitimate authority and is confined within just limits. No duty would bind us in regard to laws that would restrain our legitimate liberties, but which would also command us to act contrary to the eternal principles of justice and compassion', so wrote Benjamin Constant over a century ago and some fifty years earlier Jefferson had expressed this independence towards law in even stronger terms. 'God forbid', he wrote in 1786, 'that we should ever be twenty years without such a rebellion.' (A rising of farmers against excessive taxation.) 'What country can preserve its liberties if their rulers are not warned from time to time that their people preserve the spirit of resistance? . . . What signify a few lives lost in a century or two? The tree of liberty must be refreshed from time to time with the blood of partiots and tyrants. . . . The spirit of resistance to government is so valuable on certain occasions that I wish it be always kept alive. It will often be exercised when wrong, but better so than not exercised at all. I like a little rebellion now and them; it is like a storm in the atmosphere.' Few of us may be prepared to go quite as far but we must never forget that law was made for man, not man for the law.

Limits on the Effectiveness of Law.—We have stressed so far the importance of law as laying down the lines of expected and permissible behaviour in the name of the community. But it is equally true that the part played by law is only of relative importance in securing this behaviour. It would be completely misleading to imagine a community held down by bad laws which it detested and only obeyed because it must. No law, after all, would be enforceable without the general consent of the bulk of the people concerned. Resistance even by a small number is enough to make any law ineffective.[1] 'Governments', as Lindsay says, 'do not live by force or coercion but on their capital of confidence', which is derived from the citizens.

Laws are, as we saw, mere indications as to how the community wishes the various branches of its life and activity to be managed. It knows that rules are needed, and these rules

---

[1] We have seen it stated that ten per cent. of deserters would be enough to make any scheme of conscription unenforceable.

necessarily correspond to the general pattern of its existence and desires; it therefore accepts them and conforms to them without any feeling of compulsion, much less desire to resist. It sees in those laws the expression of its own will. Such laws scarcely need enforcing. And even the laws that have to be enforced are scarcely felt by the bulk of the community. Criminal laws, for instance, need only to be applied to a tiny fragment of the population; most people are honest by nature and instinct, not by law.[1]

The Value of Law.—The final value of law to the community would seem to be: first, to restrain a small number of un-socially minded, who would respect neither life, nor property, nor any of the common purposes of life, and are only kept in check by the fear of the policeman, and second, to work by suggestion and inhibition. Law accustoms one to what is the expected and desired behaviour, and makes conformity with it unconscious and automatic. It has in that sense a primarily educational rather than restraining value. As to the problem of the relation of law to morals, it is really part of the larger one of state and morals. It will be enough to say here that it is doubtful whether law can really be a moralising agent. It can, of course, forbid actions directly contrary to right behaviour, provided these can be unmistakably determined and classified, but it can scarcely force individuals to act rightly; all it can do in that direction is to provide encouragements to good and obstacles to evil. It can also guarantee protection to the doers of what public opinion calls right. But it all depends on agreement as to what we consider right.

5. WHAT DO WE MEAN BY 'SOVEREIGNTY'?

Origins of the Term.—The exercise of this final legal coercive power by the state is commonly called 'Sovereignty' and states are therefore described as 'Sovereign'. As first used in the sixteenth century the term was simply a statement of

[1] The increasing tendency to 'Black Market' offences might seem to challenge this statement. But the example of some countries shows that laws are helpless before any widespread determination not to respect rationing regulations. However, we are prepared to admit that we do not know how many potential criminals, ourselves included, might not be revealed to their own selves by the removal of all sanctions for their breach.

the fact that there must be an ultimate control, someone with the last word in any case of dispute, able to make final adjustments in the sharing of responsibility and power; and that the state, and no other social force, must exercise this final authority.

This idea is in itself very old both in theory and practice. 'Whatever the state appoints must be obeyed in everything, both small and great, just and unjust', says Creon in Sophocles's tragedy 'Antigone'. The respect for state authority, the finality of law is a commonplace in Plato and Aristotle. And long before the Greeks, the Oriental empires were built on the theoretical and practical basis of a state knowing no rival either at home or abroad.

The Middle Ages, it is true, knew nothing of the doctrine or practice of concentrated final authority. Their characteristic political form was its antithesis, feudalism, based on ideas of personal dependence and allegiance within many small groups, bound together in turn by other similar bonds of personal allegiance. In so far as any body claimed ultimate authority, this was the Church, not the state. 'The authority of feudalism and the belief in a law of God or nature superior to the human laws made impossible the modern idea of the unlimited and indivisible sovereignty of the state over all citizens.' (Ward.)

The anarchy of the wars of religion, in the sixteenth century, the end of religious unity, and of any hope of unified control under the Church called for the re-assertion of authority and this took place within well-limited territorial communities by the final emergence of the one power, which had gradually either destroyed or absorbed all possible rivals and intermediaries between himself and his subjects, including the Church. This was the monarch, head of the state. And so, as we saw in a previous chapter, the modern state emerged.

There stood now in each state a sovereign, in the sense of a definite organ or organisation within each territorial community, having final authority to define and pronounce the law therein, and having likewise final authority to adjust rivalries among all possible claimants to power.

Bodin and Hobbes.—The new reality of the supremacy of the state was given its philosophical justification by a Frenchman, Bodin, and an Englishman, Hobbes, each writing under the

influence of the civil and religious wars of his country, the
former at the beginning, and the latter in the middle of the
seventeenth century. They defended the need for one single
authority, against which no group or individual could raise
the objection of any earlier rights to autonomy or resistance.
Rights were what the state thought fit to grant, compatible
with the keeping of order and unity.

Bodin and Hobbes thought mainly of any assertions or
claims that would weaken political and religious unity. They
were rejecting the demands of religious minorities for toleration, of economic organisations like guilds and corporations,
of local authorities such as municipalities and provincial
bodies for some form of autonomy. There can only be one
power in the community, they urged; authority cannot be
limited, or divided and shared. The Middle Ages crashed in
confusion of conflicting claims to power; the monopoly
of power by the state was the only alternative to anarchy.

Sovereignty and the Absolute State.—Thus interpreted, the
new theory of sovereignty was merely a somewhat elaborate
way of stating a political and legal reality, the final supremacy
of the modern monarchical state. It was the philosophical
justification of absolutism, and of the single allegiance of
all citizens to an authority that must always be superior to that
of Church or local group. As Ward says, 'It clarified the situation at the birth of the modern state by facilitating and defending the emergence of the secular monarch from the welter
of feudal and religious ambiguities'.

'It is conceivable', Ward goes on to say, 'that the term
"Sovereignty" might have lapsed from political theory with
the disappearance of the absolute monarch. Forged as a
strong personal weapon in the hand of princes fighting for
power amid the chaos of a decaying feudalism, it had done
valiant service in the organisation of the modern state. The
modern state was now organised.'

The nineteenth century saw, however, this formal statement of ordinary practice transformed into a most complex
doctrine for the justification both of the absolutism and of the
omnicompetence of the state in its most extreme form.

Sovereignty and the Modern Democratic State.—The first
agent in this transformation was the French Revolution and the

philosophies which preceded it and brought it about. The state to which earlier thinkers ascribed legal sovereignty was largely a state that stood, as it were, outside the people— the French lawyers always in fact distinguished between the king and the subjects, or 'The Nation' as these were beginning to be called. In such a position the king was obliged to adapt the exercise of his powers to certain limitations due to tradition, custom, vested interests, local peculiarities, privileges—of Church, of important families, of municipal franchises, of corporations and particularly of a kind of unwritten law about certain things 'not being done'. The 'Sovereign' was indeed, very powerful and might know no legal and theoretical limits to his power, but in practice he was only a controlling agent, entrusted with wide powers for maintaining order and co-ordinating common activities and interests. The sovereign might claim to act on behalf of the people, but he was not the people.

The French Revolution made the people sovereign, and not only transferred to it all the attributes of the old monarchy of divine right but removed all its limitations, on the ground that the people, when governing itself, had no need to restrict its own authority. How could any group or individual claim power as against the whole people? Were they not part of the people? When the people legislated, every group and every individual was legislating for himself, since he was a participant in the sovereign power that was being exercised. To which argument one can only answer with Lord Acton: 'It is hard to be oppressed by a minority but it is worse to be oppressed by a majority. For from the absolute will of an entire people there is no appeal, no redemption, no refuge but treason.'

Nationalism.—The absolutism of the new 'democratic' state was reinforced by two new factors. One was nationalism, which added, as it were, the claims of the nation to those of the sovereign people; as a result the national state claimed not only unlimited authority at home over its members but also the right to expand abroad at the expense of others, each national state behaving as Wells said, 'as if it alone con-stituted humanity'.

The other factor was the enormous increase in the scope of state action which followed the Industrial Revolution,

4

and made of the state not only a policeman, an administrator, and a judge, but an organiser of economic life, an educator, an agent in practically every aspect of the collective existence. This meant an ever-increasing mass of legislation and a great increase in the importance of the state as supreme law-maker, thus reinforcing the dogma of sovereignty, by giving it a much wider field of application.

Rousseau.—All this was the translating into actual practice of the doctrines of popular sovereignty which had been expressed some thirty years before the French Revolution by Rousseau in his 'Social Contract'. He might indeed have made it a doctrine of individual freedom;[1] he made of it a vindication of a much more comprehensive state power than any previous thinker had offered since Plato. People and state having become one, the personality of the individual becomes merged with the social whole, and there is no longer any reason for maintaining any defence of the individual against the state; this last has become the perfect expression of the collective mind and soul, of which the citizen's mind and soul are but a part.

In other words, the will of the state is the will of the individual in so far as he has accepted this identification of himself with the community, and if he refuses, it shows he is pursuing selfish ends that deserve no consideration. His real self, his real will, is now part of the common or general will for the common good.

Hegel.—Still sketchy in Rousseau, this theory of the state was given its complete and coherent form by the German thinker, Hegel, who made it more definitely philosophical and metaphysical. 'The State', he said, 'is "perfected rationality", the eternal and necessary essence of spirit, the rational in itself and for itself, an absolute fixed end in itself.' In simpler terms, it amounted to the complete identification of society and state, to the insistence that only in and through the state does the individual receive what makes life worth living. Without it he is nothing, consequently the rights of the state are unlimited, not only legally as a matter of fact but morally as a matter of right, and he only lives in order to make his contribution to the common life in the state. The state on its

---

[1] As outlined in his earlier treatise on the causes of inequality but without the later identification of the state with the individual.

side is no longer the agent of society for some specific purposes and with clearly defined functions; 'It is', as the Hegelian, Bosanquet[1] says, 'itself the supreme community, the guardian of a whole world: organised moral life is only possible within the state, which becomes the source of morality and of all civilised existence.'

The implications of the doctrine and its criticism, will be seen more fully when we discuss the problem of freedom. This 'idealistic' theory of the state[2] obviously deprived the individual of any liberty to act or even think on his own, by identifying his freedom with the sole freedom of obeying the law that expressed the common purpose; it 'forced him to be free', in Rousseau's terms, by finding his freedom, not in following his own impulses but only in merging himself into the general will.

The General Will.—This theory of the state as Wilson points out; rests on three false (or at least questionable) hypotheses: first, that the actual[3] will of the individual is often contrary to his real will; second, that his real will is in fact the general will of society; third, that the general will is the will of the state, so that state and society are identical. Rousseau started out with a fact he had observed in the tiny democracies of his native Switzerland, that out of discussion that sincerely seeks to find a moral common good, a decision is often arrived at which is something more than the will of any one but is really a common decision, a blend of individual opinions adapted, adjusted, corrected, modified by the impact of each upon the other. This is also a common experience of religious groups with a common spiritual outlook and purpose:[4]

[1] Oxford teacher, author of 'The Philosophical Theory of the State', the classical exposition of Hegelianism in English. The most searching criticism of the Hegel-Bosanquet point of view is to be found in the earlier writings of the late Professor Laski on sovereignty.

[2] So-called because 'it takes the ideal of the universal as more real than the particular'—in other terms, it subordinates the particular individual to the state as representing the wider realm or universal.

[3] By 'actual' will, is meant the spontaneous personal will of the individual, unrelated to social needs and uncontrolled by his so-called 'higher' self; this self creates his 'real' or unselfish will, which wants primarily not his own advantage but the common social good.

[4] The Quakers, who do not believe in mere numerical majorities, come to no decision which is not accepted by what they call 'the sense of the meeting'. Lord Lindsay has this in mind, we believe, in his treatment of the subject in his 'Modern Democratic State'.

It is a true general will. But it has no relation to the modern state with its citizens numbered by millions, where decisions belong in fact to the small numbers who actually manage its affairs, whether in its assemblies or in its governmental offices.[1] It has no real common purpose,[2] not even in the material sphere, let alone in the moral and spiritual. The general will is a fiction, which is itself based on another fiction, the concept of the state as a real 'person' with a 'will' of its own, a 'moral and collective body', as Rousseau called it. Fictitious personifications are useful, inevitable even, but one must never forget that they are fictitious, a device of speech and no more, denoting the actions and policies of those who happen to control and represent particular collectivities—from football clubs to trade unions, Church, party or state. We are dealing with metaphor, not with realities.[3] The 'Will' of the state is the will of those who lead—at best the will of a majority, and it can only express concrete policies; moral purposes belong to individuals, who alone have a soul and a conscience.

The unreality of this elaborate justification of the ideal omnicompetent, omnipotent state was made all the greater by the fact that, side by side with the growing power and prestige of the national state, was a reverse movement tending to develop checks and controls on irresponsible power. A broad suffrage, popular elections, governments responsible to parliaments and to public opinion, assertions of individual rights, new developments of local liberties, freedom of press, meeting and association, all these were really incompatible with theories which were really forged for an autocratic irresponsible state. How confused was all this is shown by the fact that some genuine democrats used the theory of the general will to justify broad programmes of necessary social reforms and basic democracy.[4]

[1] It is significant that Rousseau always denied that representation was compatible with real democracy.

[2] Except perhaps in time of war or great general emergency. And even then there is usually an opposing minority.

[3] 'Do not confuse metaphor to describe decisions of people with common purpose, reached by discussion, with metaphor of "real person" which wills the advantage of any society for any purpose, with or without discussion.' (Lindsay, quoted by Carritt, 'Morals and Politics', p. 205.)

[4] In particular by T. H. Green, of Oxford, whose 'Principles of Political Obligation', already quoted on p. 90, is the classic of the school that may be described as liberal Hegelian.

6. THE DOCTRINE OF SOVEREIGNTY TODAY

Present-day Confusion.—It is evident that by this time the whole subject of sovereignty had become a hopeless confusion of a number of different issues and viewpoints. There was and still is, first of all, a confusion between what is and what some people would like the state to be. Extreme idealistic sovereignty is German in origin and tends to justify the state absolutism which has been the traditional policy of Prussia (Hegel was a Prussian), later to become totalitarianism in its Fascist, Nazi, and Communist forms.

Secondly there is confusion between ultimate decision and omnipotence. The referee in a football match arbitrates; he does not lead a side, kick goals himself and disallow all goals kicked by the other side, which is what the totalitarian state actually does, and is the ideal of many politicians in would-be democratic societies. How unpleasant to have to give an account of one's tenure of office! To have to answer awkward questions in Parliament! To justify oneself to one's constituency at every election! And yet the checks and balances of our democratic systems are not incompatible with orderly government and the clear and unmistakable assertions of authority.

Austin.—There is a third confusion between legal theory and political practice. It is mere commonsense that law must prevail and that only one law can be supreme, that there must be one final legal decision. This purely legal and formal aspect of sovereignty was stated a century ago by the English lawyer Austin, even though his famous definition is too formal and in parts ambiguous: 'The sovereign is the determinate superior who receives habitual obedience from the bulk of a given society'. The weak point in this definition is the assertion that sovereignty must lie inevitably and clearly with one permanent particular definite person. If we ask in fact where ultimate authority is to be found, we find there is not one single answer to the question; not only will it vary from country to country, but it will not be always the same in the same country, or point to one determined body. In Britain an Act of Parliament has the last word, but it can always be superseded by another Act, and the existing Parliament be set aside for a new one.

But sovereignty is in any case with the legislative power. In the United States, however, Acts of Congress are not sovereign, but are subject to the verdict of the Supreme Court, whose decision is final, and who may pronounce an Act to be unconstitutional. Legal sovereignty belongs in one sense to the judicial power, especially as judges cannot be removed nor additional judges appointed to secure a verdict favourable to the majority. In totalitarian states sovereignty will belong to the executive, since both judicial and legislative powers are subservient to it.

Legal and Political Sovereignty.—But these are legal concepts, expressing what in the last resort will be recognised as final by the courts. By its side has appeared another concept, that of political as distinguished from legal sovereignty. It is pointed out that in Britain behind an Act of Parliament are the voters, whose verdict can dismiss the Parliament and secure new policies; again, in the United States, the verdict of the Supreme Court can be upset by an amendment to the constitution, making constitutional what the court had declared to be unconstitutional—thus in both countries, as indeed in all democracies, political sovereignty lies with public opinion as expressed by the electorate. But again, the people themselves may be under the influence of particular individuals, or groups, or interests, and be so dominated by them in their voting that it becomes difficult to say where sovereignty really lies. And in a country where the government has complete control of all armed forces, it is doubtful whether the people would be able to assert sovereign power, even though the constitution was theoretically democratic and though the majority were against the government. Where has sovereignty lain in Russia since 1917, or in Germany between 1933 and 1945? The problem of the real location of political sovereignty has not yet been solved; it is perhaps enough to say that the legal sovereign is normally only the representative of the real sovereign power, which actually controls it, and that the location of that real sovereignty may differ in varying circumstances, 'That body is politically sovereign', says Dicey, 'the will of which is ultimately obeyed by the citizens of the state.'

There is a fourth confusion between actual authority and its source. It is one thing to say that all authority comes from the people, and another to say that the people actually govern. This they obviously cannot do; government can only be the action of a few. Rousseau sometimes sees this, as when he declared that representation was incompatible with popular sovereignty; this must be exercised directly, as in the tiny democracies of Switzerland. But he does not always make the distinction, and his disciples carried the confusion into the most extreme defence of the omnicompetent omnipotent sovereign 'popular' state, where sovereignty is in fact in the hands of the small number of men who make up the government.

There is lastly a confusion between the theory of government, both legal and political, and actual daily practice. All this elaborate argumentation about the seat of sovereignty overlooks the fact that the greater part of our social and political life 'rests more on custom and tradition than on reasoned analysis and conscious approval'. How often did a Roman father exercise his right of life and death over his children? Everyday life is a series of adjustments and compromises, many made out of habit; each part of the machine does its work, and much of this discussion really leads nowhere, and is, as Lindsay puts it, ambiguous and fertile in nonsense. In fact it is probably just as well not to raise too many legal issues. 'Political power may flow most smoothly when juristic exactness hibernates, when the question as to ultimate authority is not too sharply raised, when the crown remains, as it were, a fiction. Consistency may well be inconsistent with reality.' With these wise words of Professor Merriam's we entirely agree.

An Academic Matter.—Because of all those confusions it would be just as well if the term 'Sovereignty' could be dropped instead of being, as Ward puts it, 'twisted and tortured by a wide variety of interpretations. It is a notion', he adds, 'that has been carried over, out of the setting in which its historical function lay, with its implications of irresponsible absoluteness and inherent supremacy of law, to plague and befog contemporary thought with ideas of national exclusiveness, inherent rights, moral absolutism and legal omnipotence.'

But although the legal omnipotence which the term has involved has never existed, we need a term to express the fact that there must be, as Merriam puts it, 'a concentration of recognised authority for the common good and of power for common action; a final social authority capable of commanding the loyalty of the great mass of citizens'. But such power or authority can only rest on consent, and must be limited in practice by many forces, moral, religious, scientific, by numerous social sanctions that both check and complete state action. There are hundreds of forces determining the sovereign will; how exactly they work is perhaps largely an academic matter.

CHAPTER VI

HOW THE STATE CARRIES ON ITS BUSINESS

I. GOVERNMENTS AS THE AGENTS OF THE STATE

FOR its exercise of power according to the law, the state needs ✓
an instrument, and this we term its government. 'The state',
said the United States Supreme Court, 'itself is an ideal person,
intangible, invisible, immutable. Government is an agent,
within the sphere of its agency a perfect representative, but
outside of that it is a lawless usurpation.' As Wilson remarks
in quoting the above passage, 'The state is juristically wholly
organised in its government and can only speak through the
government'. The state has authority inherent in itself but this
is only exercised by the government as its agent, and without
a government there is normally no state—normally, because
there are periods in the history of states when one government
ceases to function and an interval occurs when anarchy
predominates. But such intervals are short, and it is not long
before some new government takes over the task.

The Continuity of the State.—It would not be quite accurate
to say, however, that 'governments come and governments go
but states go on for ever', for states are not eternal. They do
come to an end, usually by forceful annexation, sometimes,
but rarely, by voluntary union with another.[1] But governments can and do change, and that often, without the permanency of the state being thereby disturbed. 'France' has
had many forms of governments between 1789 and today,[2]
each of them claiming to make an entirely new start in political
organisation, but 'France' remained; she remained first of all
as a unit in international law, each successive government
being bound by the diplomatic engagements and foreign
debt of its predecessors; while at home her identity continued

[1] For instance, the merging of Scotland into Great Britain by the Act of
Union of 1707.
[2] The form of government changed in 1790, 1792, 1795, 1799, 1804, 1814,
1815 (twice), 1830, 1848, 1852, 1870, 1940, 1944.

by each maintaining all the laws of its predecessors[1] unless
formally repealed or altered, and rightly claiming to continue
representing the political entity, 'France'—'Monsieur, il restait
la France' (Sir, France was still left) said the President of the
court-martial to Marshal Bazaine, who tried to excuse his
surrender at Sedan in 1870 by pleading that, the emperor
having abdicated, 'il ne restait rien' (nothing was left).

And France was indeed left, and that not only in a purely
spiritual sense. Governments might change, and emperors
abdicate, but no one could alter the whole political and administrative structure of the country. The great mass of the
civil service of the *ancien régime* may have been changed by
the revolution but afterwards the bulk of the new service
passed on to work under Napoleon and later under the restored
monarchy, and so forth until now. It is this administrative
continuity that has preserved the identity of many countries
in the throes of revolutionary change.

In the same way 'Italy' remained 'Italy' from constitutional
to Fascist monarchy and now on to republic; 'England' was
still England under the Commonwealth and Protectorate and
after the Revolution of 1688; the Russia of the Bolsheviks
continued the Russia of the Tsars. But while Germany remained Germany from its formal proclamation as a state in
January 1871 to the fall of Nazism, in spite of its changes
of governmental forms from empire to democratic republic
and from democratic republicanism to national socialism,
she ceased to be a state when she lost her central government,
her international status, and became divided into zones of
foreign control.

Government and State are Practically Identical.—Although
then we must distinguish between state and government,
the fact remains that, at a given time and in a given territory,
the government tends to incarnate the state as its sole agent
and representative, because it wields in its name and on its
behalf that legal coercive authority which is characteristic
of the state; and in daily life it is not so much with the abstract
state as with the government that the ordinary man comes
into contact. As Croce says, 'For those who seek concreteness

---

[1] The Fourth Republic has even recognised the validity of some of the
decrees of the Vichy regime, based on the direct authority of Marshal Petain.

rather than abstraction, the state is nothing but the government, and assumes complete reality only in the government'. It is the type of government in power that gives any state its distinctive political form. When we say that Rome was at first a republic, then an empire; that France from 1814 to 1870 was in turn a monarchy, a republic, an empire and again a republic; that Britain is a constitutional monarchy, we mean that their governments are, or were, of that particular form.

Of What does Government Consist?—We mean by government then all those persons, institutions and agencies by which the will and policy of the state is expressed and carried out. In current speech we sometimes speak of the government when we only mean its controlling element: the ministry in Great Britain and France, the President and his cabinet in the United States, and refer to 'a change of government' if any of these change. But such speech is only an illustration of that inaccuracy of terminology which we have already deplored. A change in those controlling elements is very important but ministers are not the whole government. This includes the whole network of local institutions, elected bodies and appointed officials, the whole civil service in all its ramifications, down to the lowest official charged with the carrying out of policy.

But, however numerous all these may be, the largest of governments is at best very small in relation to the rest of the state. 'That small body of men to whom is confided', as Laski says, 'the legal power of making decisions.'[1] What kinds of decisions? What do we expect governments to do? Innumerable answers have been given to the question, to which we must return in greater detail later. All we can do now is to glance briefly at what may be called the fundamental inescapable purposes of all government, and their connection with various aspects of governmental activities.

The basic fact of all government is that it acts for the whole community. This means, first, that the whole community will come under its control; no individual or group may claim the right to evade the operation of measures designed to apply to all. Here and there, the claim has been put forward, sometimes

---

[1] The question of the relation of the government to a governing class within the community will be discussed later.

with success; the abolition of privilege has been a slow process, whether for social classes or groups such as churches, especially as regards taxation. In many countries, the clergy are exempt from certain duties such as military and jury service, exemption for which they usually pay by being ineligible for public office. In the main, however, the universality of law is generally admitted.

It follows from this that there is no department of organised human activity that can claim to be permanently excluded, in its own right as it were, from the operation of government. The only standard is public utility.

Essential Duties of Government.—In this direction of the whole community, all governments have what may be called primary duties to perform. They must all keep a minimum of public order by a system of police and criminal justice; they must provide machinery for the peaceful settlement of private disputes by civil justice; they must secure to their members the certainty that they will not be interfered with in their orderly everyday life either by their fellows or by agents of the state; and, nowadays, they must build up some kind of system protecting their citizens against the accidents of life such as illness, destitution and unemployment; finally, they must guarantee the security of the community against foreign attack by the organisation of common defence, and conduct its peaceful relations with other communities by diplomacy. They must also ensure that a great many social activities shall be carried on in a uniform way, in order to secure a certain unity of effort and a certainty that essential things not only shall be done but shall be done in one single way. It may be unwise or unnecessary to nationalise the railway system but it would never do for the railway companies to be able to change their rates as they pleased: the public is entitled to know beforehand what it will have to pay—hence the need for laws to regulate fares. And so for many other things: 'There must be', as Merriam puts it, 'reasonable expectation as to what is to be done, and by whom, in the field of social behaviour.'

This is, of course, an extremely vague programme, capable of an unlimited variety of practical application, from the *laissez-faire* governments of eighteenth-century England, to the collectivism of Russia or the totalitarianism of Fascism. But in all cases the primary purpose will be the same. Government is charged by the community with the double task of maintaining what McIver calls 'an established code of living and of adjusting this order to new conditions and emergency needs'. 'When it shall be said', wrote Paine 150 years ago, 'my poor are happy, neither ignorance nor distress is to be found among them; my jails are empty of prisoners, my streets of beggars; the aged are not in want, the taxes are not oppressive,—when those things are said, then may that country boast of its government.'

Government and State Purposes.—The function of government being thus to put into execution the decisions of the state through which it exists, it follows that its forms will vary with these purposes. And it is curious to find such a great thinker as Rousseau putting, as it were, the cart before the horse when he writes: 'I perceived that everything depends on politics, and that the nature of a people will inevitably be what the nature of its government will cause it to be. The question therefore of the best possible government comes down to this: What is the nature of the government capable of making a people as virtuous, as enlightened, as wide, as good in the fullest sense of the word, as is humanly possible?' This is obviously wrong; any government will only reflect the moral state of the people it represents, not the reverse. The utmost that can be said for Rousseau's point of view is that a type of government set up at a time of enlightenment may tend to keep the people enlightened and that one set up at a time of political cynicism or immorality will make it difficult for the people to rise out of that condition. We do not want to exaggerate the truth of the old dictum that people have the kind of government they deserve,[1] because they may have been temporarily foolish or unlucky, and then find it hard to get rid of their tyrant—but the saying remains largely true.

The form or quality of the government is therefore the expression of the particular purposes of the state at the time; it will express the policies of that position of the members

---

[1] Or at least they are likely to have a government corresponding to their degree of political maturity.

of the state who have been able to make their policies effective; and get them recognised in current legislation. What we call 'politics' is in fact largely the conflict, peaceful or otherwise, of various groups and interests in the state for the control of the machinery of government; and at any given time the victors will tend to be those who control the machinery of economic production and distribution.

A change in the political system corresponds therefore as a rule to a change in the economic system, and the will and policy of the state are largely determined by the character of class-relations. The institutions of any particular age and country will tend to be those suitable for the defence of the interests of those who are politically and economically dominant.

2. FORMS OF GOVERNMENT

Evolution of Government Forms.—The form of a government is in fact the product of numerous factors, historical, geographical, social, economic, psychological. Some are comparatively permanent and tend to give a certain continuity to the evolution of institutions; others change and account for variations within that evolution. But in the last resort, no two forms are absolutely identical any more than two human beings, whatever likenesses there may be. And, like a human being, no government remains quite the same: change is at work all the time, imperceptible day by day, but visible enough over a period of years. Few political systems are more stable than the British and American, yet such classics as Bagehot's 'English Constitution' and Bryce's 'American Commonwealth' are now very much out of date.

The direction of the change is again never constant. There may be at certain times a tendency towards a certain type of organisation—constitutional monarchy, republic, dictatorship, collectivism—but it is never sufficiently universal to allow much generalisation; and not even in one single state is the movement uniform. The most that can be said is that over a number of years, the majority of states seem to indicate a move which so far has been along two main lines, distinct though connected; as regards political forms, from irresponsible to limited monarchy[1] and from limited monarchy to republic, in other words towards more popular control; as regards social organisation, from irresponsible *laissez-faire* to various forms of economic control or planning, this also being due to the pressure of popular forces. But few if any countries would show a uniform progression in that direction, action and reaction being the rule. And in that evolution forgotten influences tend to reappear, discarded ideas regain unexpected strength. Nationalism and religion as political forces were thought a few years ago to be definitely on the wane; few would affirm this now. You never can tell.

Essential Factors of Effective Governments.—Anyone trying to analyse the form of a particular state will therefore have to look beyond its formal political machinery. He must take into account its economic structure, whether primarily agricultural, or industrial, or commercial, and in each case distinguish between the countries of large estates employing hired labour and those of farmer-owners; between large-scale and small-scale industry; between manufacture for export or for domestic use; between dealing with home-made goods for local consumption or acting as distributive middlemen for large areas. And in every case the nature of the property system will have to be considered, from primitive family-economy to collectivism. Next the student must examine the social organisation: which types of groups predominate, the influence of bodies such as hereditary castes or Churches, the degree of education and the type of culture. He will want to know whether the people are by nature peaceful and law-abiding, or violent and rebellious; whether the population is fairly homogeneous in nationality and class, or whether it contains sharp divisions into castes and irreconcilable minority groups. And last but not least he will ask 'What is the aim of that state? What do its people want: Property? Power? Freedom? Order? Security? Tell me what you want and I will tell what sort of government you really have.'

We must therefore not be deceived by the outward forms

---

[1] 'It is in my power', said Queen Elizabeth in 1593, 'to call Parliaments and it is in my power to determine the same.' 'The King', answered Chief Justice Coke a few years later, 'hath no prerogative but what the law of the land allows him.'

of a particular state: the old classification of monarchy, aristocracy and democracy have become practically meaningless for they give no clue to the real purposes of the state. All governments have in fact elements of all three: monarchy, in the considerable power of a few people at the top; aristocracy, in the selection of the members in representative bodies,[1] democracy in the (nowadays) widespread distribution of the right to vote. Differences occur in the varying degrees in which those elements are weighted. In one sense all governments are 'oligarchic' in that the few ultimately decide essential policies, and some would say that all tend to be 'plutocratic' because in the last resort it is economic power that matters.

The same is true of other classifications, such as monarchy as against republic. The former may be much nearer the democratic ideal for which the republic is supposed to stand than the republic itself. One must look beneath the surface. No one could seriously pretend that republican France had a really more representative government than monarchical England, or that the new Italian republic will achieve fuller democracy than the Dutch or Scandinavian 'monarchies'. Many of the South American 'republics', and others of the same model, are mere 'oligarchies', i.e. governed by a small clique who pay lip service to 'democracy' and 'run the show' without any reference to liberty or public opinion.

Outward Forms and Inward Reality.—Even when confining ourselves to political forms, therefore, we shall avoid being deceived by mere terms; we shall fasten on essentials and not on outward forms; we shall not ask what the head of the state is called, but how much personal discretionary power he can exercise, if any; how much initiative he possesses in the selection of his ministers; how broad is the basis of the suffrage by which assemblies are elected (even democratic Switzerland still refuses the vote to women); how free are elections and whether assemblies really represent public opinion; how direct is the control of those assemblies over both the selection of ministers and their daily administration; what parts do favouritism, good birth, and fitness for the job respectively play in the

---

[1] 'Parliament is an elective aristocracy. The principle that a child, a lunatic a criminal cannot vote is really aristocratic.' (Seeley.)

selection of officials; how far is law obeyed by all or how effective is bribery in evading the consequences of disobedience; how impartial and prompt is the administration of daily justice; how vast is the extent of government control in the common life; how educated is the electorate, and how capable of taking a broad intelligent view of the issues on which it has to judge;[1] only when such questions are answered can we then assign to that particular government its proper place, and label it accordingly.

Many of the questions raised, however, are not easy to answer, and to a great extent we have to be content with classifications according to outward ascertainable forms. But even then the size and freedom of the electorate and the extent of its influence over the selection and work of the government is more important than differences between monarchy and republic; while again the distinction between states based on 'socialism' and those based on 'private enterprise' is wearing pretty thin.

3. THE GOVERNMENT AND THE CONSTITUTION

Constitutional Varieties.—We are, however, practically driven to take the constitution of a state as expressing the kind of government it possesses. We have already seen that a constitution is the body of rules and principles according to which governments, as agents of the state, exercise the powers entrusted to them, what Professor Friedrich calls 'a technique of effective regularised restraint'. These constitutions vary enormously in all kinds of ways; and, like the forms of government they define, no two of them are identical. Some are very old, some are young; the British being probably the oldest, those of new Asiatic states the youngest to date. Some go into elaborate detail, some confine themselves to general principles and allow many points to settle themselves by everyday practice. For instance, whereas the French constitution of 1875

---

[1] 'A constitution', says the Swiss jurist Borgeaud, is 'essentially a law of political protection, a law of guarantees guaranteeing the nation against the usurpation of the authorities to which it necessarily confides the exercise of the sovereign power, guaranteeing the minority against the omnipotence of the minority.'

assumed most of the practices of British parliamentary procedure, that of 1946 (following in this the German republican
constitution of 1919) laid down in detail the circumstances in
which cabinets must resign and the procedure by which new
cabinets were to be chosen and approved. Again, while most
constitutions are contained in a single document with its sub-
sequent amendments, the British is to be found in a number of
enactments, on the exact list of which no two students would
absolutely agree.[1] Finally, while some constitutions, like the
British, can be amended by ordinary legislative procedures,
most of them, such as that of the United States, need special
processes, often extremely elaborate.

No constitution, however, is completely covered by formal
constitutional laws, whether rigid or elastic. One must add
numerous legal decisions which interpret and supplement
them. Freedom of the press, of public meeting, of association, is
in many countries guaranteed by the refusal of the courts to
allow the government's right to limit it as much as by any
formal enactment. Nor must we forget what we termed the
'conventions' of a constitution, practices which have acquired
the sanctity of law, as for instance the fact that a defeated
cabinet must resign or appeal to the country by dissolution,
that the British Premier must be in the House of Commons,
that if the Lebanese President is a Christian, the Premier must
be a Moslem, or vice versa. Actually the distinction between
law and convention has tended to be exaggerated; a convention
is usually a practice that does not need defining because its
disregard would, sooner or later, involve the government in a
breach of the law, or would create such opposition as to bring
all government to a standstill. A cabinet remaining in power
in defiance of parliament would soon be confronted with an
empty treasury and no legal means to levy any tax; in Britain it
would also soon find itself without any armed forces.

But in any case it is clear that no written constitutions can
cover the whole complex of national politics, because life is

---

[1] Most people would include the Habeas Corpus Act of 1662, the Bill
of Rights of 1689, the Mutiny Act of 1693, the Acts laying down England's
relations with Scotland, Ireland, the Dominions (from 1707 to the present
day) the Act of Settlement of 1714, the Parliament Act of 1911, the Franchise
Acts from 1832 to 1928, and all measures defining the powers of local
authorities. But the list could be lengthened.

always changing, and law is apt to be slow in adjusting itself to new circumstances. We may say that for all practical purposes 'the constitution is that which the government in its several departments and the people in the performance of their duties as citizens recognise and respect as such, and nothing else is'.

What is Meant by 'Constitutional'.—This is perhaps the best answer to the question: 'What do we mean by "constitutional"?' It is not enough to say, 'Whatever is allowed by constitutional law', since much of the practice of government is not included in this.   What is accepted as constitutional both by the Courts of Law and by public opinion is legally constitutional for that particular country at that particular time.

There is, however, more to it than that. The term 'constitutional' is commonly used in political controversy as an epithet applied to proposals or measures involving a breach with the established traditional lines of political evolution. Their strict legality is not called into question; but it is implied that the country has permanently adopted certain principles of action and development which may not be altered without a quasi-revolutionary departure from the country's true political genius and principles.

Here are some instances of what we mean. Conservatives denounced as 'unconstitutional' Home Rule for Ireland, on the ground that any weakening of the Union was an unwarrantable break with the evolution of Britain towards closer unity, not towards less. They similarly condemned reform of the House of Lords as an interference with one of the foundations of the British constitutional system, and more recent nationalisation policies have been attacked on the same lines. Liberals on the other hand objected to the Education Act of 1902 as an infringement of constitutionally established religious liberty,[1] and Labour said of the Trade Union Disputes Act of 1926 that it was unconstitutional as a violation of freedom of association.

In the United States, the 'New Deal' came in for the same criticism. Some of its measures were, in fact, declared legally unconstitutional by the Supreme Court; but the term was

[1] The objection was to alleged preferential treatment given to Anglican elementary schools.

used by its enemies in a much looser way, to designate a departure from the established principles of freedom of contract and absence of state control in economic affairs.

The point is, of course, that such a use of the term involves an altogether unwarrantable stretching of the term 'constitution' and 'constitutional'. A constitution is a set of rules and legally recognised practices; all constitutions have in fact so been altered in the course of history that in most cases their framers would not recognise them now. The innovation of yesterday has become the sacrosanct tradition of today which tomorrow will have to discard as obsolete. Let us be accurate in our speech; a measure we dislike is not therefore contrary to constitutional law.

The Functions of a Constitution.—But although constitutions can only define outward forms, they fulfil a number of essential functions. They guarantee citizens against possible arbitrary acts of the government, and enable them to know what to expect, and especially what not to expect. They provide for peaceful methods of changing the government and thereby the policies of the state. 'A general election', said Sir John Seeley, 'is a kind of peaceful revolution.' They give opportunities for the expression of public opinion. They may be compared to the set of rails along which the state train must proceed, and ensure that it will not ride ever all the countryside. Of course, formal constitutions, like rails, lack elasticity, and they will only deal with outward things, with the letter of the law. The citizens must provide the spirit, or, to take another metaphor, the constitution is the set of words to which the citizens must provide the tune. And it is an interesting fact that different words, sung to the same tune, sound more alike than the same words sung to different tunes. By which we mean that the form of the constitution matters less than the spirit which animates it, and that, for instance, the subject of the British monarchy and the citizen of the Swiss republic will understand each other's political way of life better than a Swiss and a Russian, though both are members of a federal republic. Again, the old Balkan kingdoms had really little in common with the theoretically similar kingdoms of Scandinavia. 'The differences between governments', says Bentley, 'are not differences of principles, but strictly differences of technique for functioning of interests, adopted because of group needs, and which will continue to change in accordance with group needs.'[1]

Four Main Types of Governments.—Having said all this as a warning against taking appearances for realities, we may then, confining ourselves to forms, say that the governments of the world today tend to fall into the following four broad categories:

1. *Parliamentary*, in which the government of the day is dependent on the constant support of elected assemblies: of these most are monarchies (Britain, Belgium, Netherlands, Denmark, Norway, Sweden), a few are republics (France, Italy, and some South American states, Germany under the Weimar Constitution, 1919-33).

2. *Direct*, in which the government of the day, while elected either by the people or by the assemblies, remains in office for a specific period, irrespective of the support of the Parliaments, while being unable to act freely without it. They are now all republics (the United States would be included), but the former German and Austrian imperial systems would probably come under that heading.

3. *Dictatorial*, in which the government, while elected in some popular way, and therefore claiming to represent the nation, remains independent of parliamentary support. Spain, Portugal, Communist republics, Nazi Germany, Fascist Italy are the main examples. It should, however, be noted that some of these would not accept this classification but would claim inclusion in category 2.

4. *Absolute*, in which power is in the hands of an irresponsible monarch usually hereditary; Saudi Arabia is, we believe, the only one extant since the fall of the Japanese empire; the old Russian monarchy was another. It may be some time before we know exactly where to place some of the newest republics.

This classification takes as its basis the relation of the final controlling power to public opinion as expressed in representative bodies. But we could also divide states between those

[1] 'Government', says Merriam, 'is a way of adjusting personality patterns that struggle for expression, and this adaptation of energies, interests, and value systems lies at the heart of the governmental problem under all forms of political and social types.'

with one single authority (unitary) and those with authority divided among local units (federal). Britain, France, Belgium, the Scandinavian states, Italy, would be together against the United States, Switzerland, Russia, Brazil. This, however, gives us no clue to the real nature of the ultimate power. Nor does classification between flexible constitutions (which can easily be altered) and rigid (which cannot).

We are in fact inclined to agree with Cook when he says that there are only two forms of government, democracy and oligarchy. Each of them expresses one of the two answers to the question raised in the last chapter, 'Does a state aim at the freedom of its members, the encouragement of their spontaneous, creative activities, or is it secondary to the building up of power at home and abroad?'

4. THE INSTRUMENTS OF GOVERNMENT: POLITICAL INSTITUTIONS

For the carrying out of their function governments will require certain 'tools' or agencies. These are the institutions of the state.[1] In one sense most of them are somewhat alike in their general form, yet so different in their detail and in the scope of their work, that no two states have ever possessed identical systems. They vary according to history, tradition, customs, temperament; they are moulded by the people in the course of its development, expressing its evolving purpose and character, and in their turn tending to influence this development. 'Individuals can make society', writes Disraeli, 'but only institutions can make a nation.' And how true this is can be seen when watching newly-formed states trying to create the institutions they need, usually obliged at first to copy those of other states, and doing this often in an unintelligent and mechanical way, then slowly adapting them to their own needs. The fact is that, as we shall see later, institutions as described on paper are one thing, and as actually working quite another.

Essential Institutions.—Constitutional lawyers have for many centuries divided these governmental organs into three

[1] 'Institutions are the vehicles of the impersonal relations between individuals in which all societies have their existence, because all primitive societies, even the smallest, are built on a wider basis than the narrow circle of individual personal ties.' (Toynbee.)

categories according to their function, distinguishing between
making law, putting law into practice, and enforcing and
interpreting law—legislative, executive and judicial. When we
study the institutions of a modern state we shall see how far
this traditional triple division corresponds to reality, and only
remark here that 'law' must be taken in a very broad sense as
an expression of common policy. The first task of a government is, as we saw, to carry out the purposes of the particular
state for which it acts, and those purposes will be shown in
numerous acts of which strict laws are only a part. The real
question is, what are the institutions which determine policy,
and how is this carried out?

What are the governmental institutions which we would
include under this heading? Taking Britain as our starting-
point, we have the Monarchy, Parliament, the Ministries with
their different Departments, Boards and Committees, the
Civil Service, both Home and Colonial, the Judicial system and
Police, the Local Authorities, the Armed Forces, the Established
Churches in England and Scotland. The test of what is such
an institution would probably be whether it derives its authority, directly or indirectly, from an Act of Parliament.[1] In
other countries a more or less similar list might be made—
sometimes with a President instead of a King, with one or
three chambers instead of two, in most cases without a colonial
civil service, since the possession of colonies is the exception
rather than the rule, often without an established Church,
occasionally with some additional body which has no counterpart in the British system.[2] In a federal state many of these
organs are duplicated centrally and locally. And the more a
particular state undertakes, the more institutions it will need.

Unofficial Agencies.—We must also remember that the
institutions of the state are not the only tools at the disposal of a government. It may depend on forces, such as
custom, tradition, religious feeling; it can use the press, the
school, the radio; it can appeal to the imagination by ceremonies and symbols; it can shelter itself behind the prestige

[1] Anyone wishing to see a more or less complete list of those would find
it in 'Whitaker's Almanack'.
[2] Such as the Conseil d'Etat in France, the Supreme Court in the United
States.

of a great leader or a successful soldier. 'I can tell you how
to make up the public mind', Hitler is reported to have said
to Hindenburg, stating in simpler terms what Mosher calls
'the manipulation of stimuli to secure general conformity'.
Nor can we neglect the existence of non-political institutions,
i.e. not created by Parliamentary action, on which the government may often rely, but which may develop a power of their
own, sometimes hostile to the government: non-established
Churches, trade unions, parties, trusts, economic bodies,
dangerous allies to weak government, liable to become
formidable foes. As Merriam remarks, 'gold is no less than
government an agency of social control.' Even a political
party may, as it were, take the bit between its teeth and
become more powerful than the government itself. Of
course, where the government is representative of the community it will express the same general tendencies as those
social bodies, 'Political action', Merriam goes on to say,
'is impossible unless the practices of the government are
closely akin to those of the social groups.' These therefore will, no less often than the government, express the policy
and purposes of the community and direct the lives of its
members; they will tend to form what may be called a private
or social by the side of the public or political government,
dealing with many problems that are often too exclusive
or personal for direct legislative or administrative control.

'Good' and 'Bad' Institutions.—How can we tell good institutions from bad? It may be answered first of all that few
are in fact good or bad in themselves. Most are morally
neutral instruments of purposes that may be good or bad;
police, tribunal, administrative services can be used well or
ill. What matters is the intention behind it. But while this is
generally true, it may be said first, that an institution with a
purpose that is in itself evil cannot be good. No one could
describe the Gestapo or the Inquisition as 'good' institutions.
Secondly, even an institution with no inherent evil motive
may become bad if its purposes became twisted and distorted;
originally an eminently useful protection against 'big people'
whom the ordinary courts dare not touch, the Star Chamber
became an engine of tyranny against ordinary folk. And
thirdly, such an institution may be bad if it uses wrong methods

even for right ends: the 'third-degree' discredits any police system, even if used against notorious criminals.

In the main, however, the test of an institution is its efficiency for the purpose for which it was intended. Does it work smoothly and rapidly, with the minimum of waste? Is there a proper relation between the effort involved and the result produced? Is it responsive to the ultimate purpose pursued by the particular community? Another test is elasticity, capability of rapid adjustment to changing circumstances. It must really be both stable and adaptable.

It is obvious that few if any institutions can pass that double test. Almost invariably they sacrifice adaptability to stability; 'they are so protected by checks and balances that they find adjustment extremely difficult and cannot stand the strain of new social forces, of new aptitudes, emotions or ideas, burdens which no set of institutions was originally designed to carry'. Then, Toynbee goes on to say, 'one of three things happens. Either they work through new institutions or through the old which they adapt; or they enter indiscriminately into existing institutions, and either blow them up or somehow make them work in new ways for which they were not prepared, or finally you obtain die-hard anachronism, social enormities, which are the penalties a society has to pay when the process which should have brought an old institution into harmony with new forces is not retarded but altogether frustrated.' There is, of course, yet a fourth possibility, revolution.

Causes of Change.—The impact of new social forces is not, of course, the only cause of changes in the forms of government. A new government may be set up because the fallen system had become associated with national defeat and humiliation. The fall of the two Napoleons is a case in point, so is that of the Romanovs and Hohenzollerns, and of the House of Savoy. Sometimes it is because of the system's utter incapacity to 'deliver the goods', in efficient administration, or to understand the needs of a situation; the Stuarts were finally expelled from Britain because James II would not grasp the popular attitude to Roman Catholicism. Or a particular ruler may incur such unpopularity that both he and his house have to go. But in the main, changes occur because the existing system will not, or cannot, adapt itself to new situations, usually expressed in a demand for reform. And these situations usually involve the emergence of new elements in the state, demanding that share in the government which their new power justifies.

5. FACTORS IN CONSTITUTIONAL CHANGE

Political change seems, in fact, to be mainly due to economic transformations; that is, the shift of economic power to a new class in the population, or the emergence of a new class, makes inevitable a change in the location of political power. And those economic changes themselves usually come from alterations in economic processes, new techniques, new sources of wealth, new possibilities. As a rule, therefore, the new political regime reflects the change in the economic organisation.

New Forms.—The form of new systems may be determined by the past failure of all other systems and the absence of alternatives. Dissatisfaction with a particular royal dynasty leads to a republic if no alternative dynasty be available; otherwise an experiment may be made with some other claimant to the throne. France became a republic in 1870, in spite of a monarchical majority in parliament and in public opinion, because three dynasties had been tried and found wanting—Bourbon, Orleans, Bonaparte—whereas England in 1688, and again in 1714, found royal families both willing and able to take on the task. Many countries are republics for lack of a suitable king.[1]

One must also take into account the influence of world opinion. Certain forms of government are 'in the air' at particular times. In the first part of the nineteenth century the move was towards 'constitutional monarchy' on the English model—a success in Belgium, in Scandinavia, in Italy even; a failure in France, Spain and Portugal. Then came the republican phase, inspired by the success of the third republic in France, followed by the discredit of so many monarchies in the First World War—Germany, Austria, Russia, Spain. And finally came the move towards authoritarian states either

---

[1] Even perhaps the United States, where many wanted to make Washington king.

on the Fascist or the Communist pattern. And tomorrow, what?

Methods of Change.—Now for the question as to how the change takes place. It might be either legal or revolutionary. It is legal if it is done in ways recognised by law; that is, if the law realises the need and possibility of change and provides for it by laying down what lawyers call 'methods of constitutional revision'. But it is more usually done by action which violates or ignores the law, and this is 'revolution'. Revolution need not be violent; the expulsion of the Stuarts from Britain, of the two Napoleons, of the Bourbons, of the Vichy regime in France, were all bloodless, or practically so. So was the substitution of republican for monarchical regime in Germany and Austria after the First World War, in Yugoslavia, in Italy, in Rumania, in Bulgaria, after the Second World War. On the other hand, France, the United States, Russia, all offer examples, along with different lines, of changes accompanied by some form of violence, either foreign war, or internal disturbance, or both.

Revolution.—It is in fact a striking, and perhaps surprising feature of our existing political systems that almost every one of them owes its origin to revolutionary action—that is, to a breach with strict legal continuity. The only European governments which are an exception to this rule are those of Switzerland, and of Denmark. The Dutch royal house owes its position to a successful war of independence three and a half centuries ago; the British to the Revolution of 1688, the Belgian to that of 1830, the Swedish to the election of the French Marshal Bernadotte in 1810, the Norwegian to its separation from Sweden in 1905, while the upheavals which created the present regimes in Portugal, in Spain, in France, the states of central and eastern Europe are still fresh in our memories, the oldest of them being that of Russia only thirty years ago. And outside Europe we would find much the same story, from the establishment of the United States after the revolution of 1776 to that of the South American republics after the forcible overthrow of Spanish rule, down to the Chinese revolution of 1912.[1]

[1] The new independent governments of Burma, India and Pakistan were established by strictly legal and peaceful methods, while those of Indonesia and Communist China were revolutionary in origin.

People's Right to Change.—The right to power of the great majority of present-day governments is therefore based on the right of peoples to change their rulers by violation of constitutional law, if this law does not make it possible to effect the change by legal method. If that right is denied, the heirs of the Stuarts should now rule in England;[1] the Bourbon heir, the Comte de Paris, should be King of France, the Hohenzollerns, Romanovs, and Hapsburgs should still be on their respective thrones, the United States should be a British dominion, and the King of Spain rule not only in Madrid, Antwerp and The Hague but in South America. In fact, the world would have to go back several centuries. Without the admittance of the rights of revolution, history becomes a chaos, and the conservative of today is often only the descendant of the revolutionary of yesterday.

Tests of Legitimacy of Government.—The question is not, therefore, whether a revolutionary regime can become constitutional, but when does it become so? In other words, what makes a system legal since its origins evidently do not? The answer would seem to be that a government, whatever its origins, acquires legitimacy when it fulfils certain conditions.[2]

First of all it must have lasted a certain length of time. How long? There is obviously no single answer. Long enough to have made itself acceptable to the majority of the people, to have lost the fear of being itself overthrown by a fresh revolution and to be able to govern therefore without any of the restraints used by governments who feel their hold on power is precarious. 'A legitimate government', said Talleyrand, 'be it monarchy or republic, hereditary or elective, aristocratic or democratic, is always one whose form, existence, and mode of action have been strengthened and sanctioned over a long period of years, I might even say of centuries. The legitimacy of sovereign power stems from the ancient state of possession, as property for individuals.' Next, during that time it must have proved that it harmonises with certain tendencies in the national history and character. Most people would say, for instance, that neither the Vichy regime in

---

[1] But why stop at 1688? Why not go back to 1485—1399—1066—55?

[2] The argument that follows is borrowed from Ferrero's 'Principles of Power'.

France, nor the Franco regime in Spain, nor even Fascism or Nazism, ever acquired legitimacy in that sense; in spite of its thirty years' duration they might feel like denying it to the Soviet system; but thirty years is a generation, and a generation should be long enough to legitimise any system.

The condition of legitimacy is thus that the governed should recognise in the government the application of certain principles they hold as valid, and that the governments should apply those principles in a manner both rational and honest.

Government Depends on Consent.—Both those principles in fact boil down to one. What makes governments legitimate is their free acceptance by the governed. History shows there is no other criterion. The 'freedom' of acceptance may lack enthusiasm, but it is difficult to admit that, in the long run, any government, however harsh its methods, would remain in power without at least the negative consent of the mass of the citizens. Nor on the other hand will constitutional forms by themselves guarantee democracy or liberty; constitutional guarantees will only work when the people are determined that they shall work.

Many of the questions raised in this chapter will be dealt with at greater length later. The advantages and disadvantages of republican and monarchical forms will be discussed when we come to consider the institutions of democracy. The problem of consent will need fuller treatment. Scarcely anything has been said of the necessary functions of government. We must now pass on, and conclude with two most useful reminders. One was given by the American jurist, Frankfurter, to the effect that government is not easy but 'a most difficult business, an art, and one of the subtlest of the arts. It is neither business, nor technology, nor applied science, but the art of making men live together in peace and with reasonable happiness.' The other comes in the words of President Wilson, 'Government is not a machine, it cannot be conducted upon a mechanical theory. It is a living thing and falls not under the theory of the universe but under the theory of organic life. It is accountable to Darwin, not to Newton.'

CHAPTER VII

FREEDOM AND RIGHTS

I. THE PROBLEM OF FREEDOM

WE have now completed a survey of the essential characteristics of any political organisation or state, irrespective of its particular form, its history and origins, its constituent elements, the basis of its functioning. But states are not all alike; they differ in all kinds of ways. There are republics and monarchies, parliaments of one and two chambers; centralised and decentralised administrations. There are differences of form, but there are also great differences in the number and kind of activities the state may control or undertake. Will it nationalise mines, transport and industry? Will it have a censorship of the press? Will it control, or even prohibit, the formation of groups within its borders, Churches, trade unions, political parties, propaganda organisations? Will it control all forms of education? How much will it tax and how? Will it establish state theatres, hospitals, research stations or not? And such a list could continue indefinitely.

Freedom as the Central Problem of Politics.—But, if we look more closely, we shall find that all these questions, whether of form or function, are all aspects of one problem, which can be stated in several ways perhaps, but nevertheless is really one; how much of the common life shall be organised and directed by or through the state, in the name of the community? How much shall be left to individual citizens to manage as they please, whether by their private efforts or by concerted action in voluntary groups? In other words, how much of a man's life and activities shall be legally controlled and guided, how much shall legally be left to his own initiative?

Political life is in fact a perpetual pull between two conflicting forces, the desire of the government for power and the resistance of the governed. The former we have dealt with

126

when discussing power. We have seen that governments are always seeking for more power—partly because most men instinctively like to exercise it, and, after all, normally only those who do will be interested in the work of governing; partly also because the greater the power, the easier is the task of administration; those responsible for it dislike being hampered by restrictions, being told what they may and may not do, having to give an account of their rule. Governments in a word will normally press for wide powers and only accept with reluctance any limit on these. One limit comes from precise constitutional and legal restraint, the other from the less precise, but no less real barriers of what the public will not stand. For all through history there appears among men, both as individuals and as members of groups, an irregular, spasmodic, confused dislike of and resistance to authority. It is by no means universal in time or space, it is often unreasonable and violent, but the desire for freedom is nevertheless an element in politics as fundamental as the desire for power.[1]

What does it mean to be Free?—Originally to be free was not to be a slave, to have legal guaranteed control over one's person and this is still its essential meaning. To be free is not to be prevented from doing what one wants to do, and not being forced to do what one dislikes doing. Any limitation of this two-fold power is an interference with freedom, however excellent its motives, however necessary its action. It may well be that to interfere with the freedom of some people prevents their interfering with somebody else, and is therefore a guarantee of that latter's freedom; if I were not forbidden to steal and murder, neither my property nor my life would be safe. But all the same it is interference with my liberty of action in those directions. So is the rule that one must keep when driving on one side of the road; it secures order for

---

[1] We are unable to make any satisfactory distinction between the terms 'freedom' and 'liberty'; the only difference is that one is English, the other Latin; and we cannot follow Mr. Carritt, when in his 'Morals and Politics' he defines 'Freedom' as 'unconstraint from human action, especially from socially organised and legal constraint', and 'liberty' as 'a voice in deciding among claims to unconstraint and between ourselves and others'. 'We claim', he says,'the liberty to vote for or against the limitation of Freedom.' This distinction strikes us as artificial.

traffic, and makes for safety, but it is an interference with the desire one might have to drive on the other side because the surface is in a better condition. Freedom thus is essentially an absence of restraint—'what happens to elude the machine'. What exactly will evade restraint and elude the machine we shall discuss later, but it is evident that everything cannot do so. In the most liberal state there will be some constraint; otherwise, as we saw in the previous chapter, conflicts of wills and desires would mean just that anarchy which the state is meant to prevent. On the other hand, the most authoritarian state will leave people free for certain things, choice of occupation, of husbands and wives, of place of residence. Neither freedom nor authority can be absolute and complete.

Freedom a Matter of Adjustment.—Essentially then the problem is one of relation between two necessary and legitimate forces, the individual desire for personal expression and the community's obligation to lay down certain common and controlled lines of social behaviour. 'Freedom unrestrained by responsibility becomes mere license', says Dewey; 'responsibility unchecked by freedom becomes mere arbitrary power. The question then is not whether freedom and responsibility shall be united, but how they can be united and reconciled to the best advantage. This is indeed the central problem of all political philosophy and practice.'

It is thus all a matter of very delicate adjustment, but this delicate adjustment is nevertheless the essential point of difference between states, which, forms of government apart, fall into two broad categories according to their primary stressing of freedom or control. Is freedom the aim, and control only exercised as a necessity? Or is it the reverse? Some states may indeed be difficult to place on one side of the line or the other, but the principle holds generally good.

Variations of Freedom and Authority.—Why are particular societies on one side or the other? In one of the Harvard Essays on 'Authority and the Individual', Dr. Gini gives a helpful list of what he terms 'variations of freedom and authority in time and space'. Which factors make for the predominance of freedom? External security, self-confidence, self-reliance and initiative in the average citizen, social and national homogeneity, a good average level of moral and intellectual qualities, adequate economic resources and a satisfactory equilibrium of population. On the other hand, external danger, apathy and frivolity in the people, social and national disparities, excessive economic inequalities, poverty, unemployment and both excessive and insufficient population will create conditions of instability and insecurity that will make freedom appear dangerous.

We must pass now from freedom in general terms to its concrete realisations. To quote Mrs. Wootton, 'freedom has to be perpetually re-interpreted into freedoms; in daily life it is freedoms that you want, though all freedoms have a common quality—the fact of freedom, the ability to do what you want'.[1]

Concrete Expressions of Freedom.—To be free means first of all having the capacity for action, for spontaneous creative activity, living one's own life as one wants to live it as regards occupation, marriage, location, use of leisure. As Fromm says in his 'Fear from Freedom', 'there is only one meaning in life, the art of living itself', and this art cannot be practised if we are surrounded with commands and restrictions. We must reduce the sphere of the compulsory and the forbidden. Also we want some freedom of action because we want to feel secure, and without some such freedom there is no guarantee of security. 'Political liberty in a citizen', wrote Montesquieu two hundred years ago, 'is that peace of mind which comes from the sense that each one has of his own security—and in order to have that, it is necessary that the government should be such that a citizen has nothing to fear from another citizen. There can be no personality, no sense of adventure without a sense of safety—that is, the establishment of conditions in which man may be free without being a danger to others.'

Freedom of action implies the capacity to change one's life, to make every day practically new, to try to alter our environment, the world we live in. This involves a minimum of sharing in the government and organisation of the country, by the possession of the vote, by capacity to belong to, and to

---

[1] Bowman, in his 'Introduction to Political Science', distinguishes five aspects of freedom: opposition to slavery, or physical liberty; freedom from arbitrary arrest; national freedom or absence of foreign rule; self-government as opposed to tyranny; the opposite to over-government.

5

create, groups for the defence of a particular interest or point
of view, and especially by the capacity to disseminate ideas
and get them assimilated into the social system. In the end,
as Powicke says, 'the salt of freedom is the duty to think for
oneself. If a man cannot use his mind, his civic liberties are
fruitless.'

'By liberty', wrote Ramsay Muir, 'I mean the secure
enjoyment by individuals, and by natural and spontaneous
groups of individuals, such as nation, church, trade union, of
the power to think their own thoughts and to express and
act upon them; using their own gifts in their own way under
the shelter of the law, provided they do not impair the corresponding rights of others.'

2. LIBERTY OF THE MIND: TOLERATION

What is this true intellectual freedom? Some centuries ago
Giordano Bruno defined it in terms we can scarcely better
now. The intellectually free man is 'a wakener of sleeping
minds, a tamer of presumptuous and obstinate ignorance,
who in all respects professes a general love of man, and cares
not for the Italian more than for the Briton, the male more than
the female, the mitre more than the crown, the toga more
than the coat of mail, the cowled more than the uncowled—
but loves him who in intercourse is the more peaceable,
polite, friendly and useful—whom only propagators of folly
and hypocrites detest, whom the honourable and studious love,
whom noble minds applaud.'

'By liberty', says Lord Acton, 'I mean the assurance that
any man shall be protected in doing what he believes his duty
against the influence of authority and majorities, custom and
opinion. Liberty is not a means to a higher political end.
It is not for the sake of good public administration that it is
required, but for security in the pursuit of civil society and
private life. A generous spirit prefers that his country should
be poor and weak and of no account, but free, rather than
powerful, prosperous and enslaved.'

Religious Toleration.—This freedom of the mind involves
of course complete and absolute religious toleration. This is
essential, partly because religion is of the innermost essence

of a man's personality, and it is there, more than anywhere else, that compulsion must be absent; partly also because freedom of religion is the condition of the freedom of all those cultural activities, without which all other forms of freedom become meaningless. 'The spiritual field must not be under political control.'

In theory nearly everybody would agree with this, and religious freedom is in fact generally guaranteed by law, the only exceptions we know of being restrictions on change of religion still existing in certain Moslem countries. But this is not enough. Any legal advantage or preference given to a particular religion or Church, however slight, is a limitation on the freedom of others. Anglicanism in England, Presbyterianism in Scotland, Roman Catholicism in Eire, Spain and Italy and many South American republics, Lutheranism in Scandinavia are all cases in point. Russia may proclaim legal toleration, but no believer in God may hope for any official position, and there was a time not so long ago in France when attendance at church was a bar to advancement in the state. In spite of all legal guarantees of religious freedom, to be a Roman Catholic is still an obstacle to certain positions in the United States, as Mr. Alfred Smith found to his cost in 1928, and it was thought a triumph of toleration for a Jew, Leon Blum, to become Premier of France in 1936.

Freedom of Political Criticism.—Scarcely less essential than religious toleration is the freedom to criticise the state and the existing social, political and economic order. 'The liberty to disparage to the full extent of one's capacity for ridicule and invective the democratic institutions which have permitted the disparagement is the life-blood of society', says Joad,[1] and it is worth quoting the great declaration made by Chief Justice Hughes in the American Supreme Court in January, 1937. 'The greater the importance of safeguarding the community from incitements to the overthrow of our institutions by force and violence, the more imperative are the

---

[1] 'The distinguishing characteristic of the system of beliefs expressed in the phrase "Western Values", is that there is a moral law of universal validity, part of the essence of which is the principle that men should be free within large limits to disobey its commands, so that they may have the opportunity of conforming to them freely and deliberately.' (*Times Literary Supplement*, March 6, 1948.)

constitutional rights of free speech, free press and free assembly, in order to maintain the opportunity for free political discussion, to the end that government may be responsive to the will of the people, and that the changes, if desired, may be obtained by peaceful means. Therein lies the security of the republic, the very foundation of constitutional government.'[1]

Professor Gordon Catlin, in his 'Anglo-Saxon Tradition', gives four reasons for the maintenance of liberty of opinion. First, disbelief in anybody's infallibility and willingness to reason. Second, the fact that comprehension of truth can never rise above accumulative probability and therefore cannot be forced. Third, that toleration favours the climate in which the discovery of new truth thrives. Fourth, that variety in living and thinking are themselves part of a tradition of living, and that this tradition has to be taught and defended. And Norman Angell explains as follows, 'Why freedom matters, even in war-time.'[2] 'The habit of subservience to State authority in matters of opinion tends to destroy in the individual that capacity for private judgement in politics by which alone, in the last analysis, a democracy is able to rule itself. The destruction of the right of private judgement involves finally the destruction of the capacity for public judgement. The habit of irresponsible power on the one side, and docile subservience on the other, must finally make impossible that moral atmosphere in which alone the general instinct for self-government can survive and develop.'

But the last word on the subject rests with Mill, in his 'Essay on Liberty.'[3] 'If all mankind minus one were of one opinion, and only one person were of the contrary opinion, mankind would have no more justification in silencing that one person than he, if he had the power, would be justified in silencing mankind.'

Belief in the Value of Personality.—What is the ultimate basis

[1] C.J. Hughes in the De Jonge case, January 5, 1937.

[2] The extent to which freedom of speech was tolerated in war-time England is well illustrated by an extract given by Allen in his 'Democracy and the Individual', p. 56.

[3] This and Milton's 'Areopagitica' are the two classic defences of the principles of freedom and should be read by all students of politics; if these do not convince them, nothing will. Laski's 'Liberty in the Modern State' is a very valuable restatement of the problem.

of this belief in the preciousness of freedom? It rests surely
on a belief in personality as the ultimate value.

In the last resort, 'the thought and conscience of the
individual are the only thought and conscience there are',
says Laski. 'Perverse, foolish and ignorant as our conscience
may be, it is the only guide we have. It is at least ours, and
Freedom comes from acting on its demands.'[1] It is from the
individual human mind that everything has come. All values
for persons, and the good of the whole, like any other good,
must be a good for persons.

Everything in history is ultimately personal. There are no
'currents of thought', but many persons thinking along the
same lines; there are no 'armies', but regiments of individual
soldiers, each a world to himself; there are no impersonal
social forces, all such forces are 'lodged in the individual,
deriving energy from individuals and operating through
individuals'. Social forces are personal influences, passing from
person to person and producing activities constituting
behaviour.

In a word, 'the choice between liberty and suppression of
liberty is not on the same plane as a choice between things
of different values, one of which may be reasonably preferred
to the other—the first means human dignity and civilisation,
the second the debasing of men until they are either a flock
to be led to pasture, or captured, trained and led to the cage.
Men want freedom because they are, and in so far as they are,
separate persons. The difference of each individual experience
the inescapable variety of human wills, the need for freedom
as the need for air'—these phrases are all of them variations
on Father Tyrrell's profound words, 'Man is driven on to
follow the dominant influence of his life, even if it should
break the heart of the world'.

Freedom Must be Guaranteed.—All these statements are of
course largely assumptions, not proved facts. 'The view that
the human being possesses a quality worth safeguarding for

[1] 'As soon as the individual, his consciousness, his wits, his reason are no
longer granted as the most fundamental of all the laws of the moral order,
then any system one builds up must inevitably lead to an arbitrary arrangement
of society, and of the whole universe, according to the fancies of the philosopher or the priest—and to their passions—and there is no guarantee of
justice.' (Laski.)

its own sake is clearly a matter of faith, or hope, or charity, or all three', says Allen, and we shall see presently in what ways these assumptions are challenged. Granted, however, for the present the validity of the argument and its assumptions, it follows that freedom does not depend on the state, but that the state depends upon free men. If freedom of the individual is desirable, both for the individual and for the society to which he belongs, it must be guaranteed and be placed beyond the reach of the perpetual desire of governments to increase the range of their authority, and deprive their subjects of the power to criticise and interfere. Governments are naturally quick to resent this criticism, and that is why it is essential that they should not possess the power to check it, by censorship or arbitrary arrest. Only courts of law, preferably with juries, should have the power to decide when the bounds of public order have been passed.

Society in fact needs freedom in its members. It needs it, first of all, because any living civilisation needs perpetual renewing by new ideas which alone will prevent stagnation; it needs it again because freedom guarantees peaceful change which is the only alternative either to revolution or to tyranny. It needs it, finally, because constraint is not a healthy condition, and societies can only thrive if their general way of life is freely accepted. It is on these principles that certain societies, the Anglo-Saxons in particular, have always, in the words of Mr. Gladstone, 'set a high value on liberty for its own sake. They desire to give full scope to the principles of self-reliance in the people. . . . They mistrust and dislike the centralisation of power, and they cherish municipal, local, even parochial liberties, as nursery grounds for the general training of public virtue and independent spirit. They regard publicity as the vital air of politics.'

It goes without saying, however, that the society's need for free individuals is equalled by their need for society. Freedom in isolation is meaningless—freedom, to be real, involves the capacity to do or enjoy things in common with others, and no individual can permanently separate his own good from the common good. 'We move in and out of the herd', as has been said, and the healthy free individual is the man who knows when to stress his need for freedom and when to realise to the full the advantages of social life, with all the restrictions this inevitably implies. 'Man thinks alone and acts with others', said the poet Lamartine,[1] and this remains the key to social life.

This means that, for the sake both of the individual and of society, the essential freedoms we have discussed must be clearly guaranteed and protected. Those protected liberties we call rights—'the assurance', to quote Lindsay, 'that freedom along certain lines will be protected from arbitrary interference, both of other citizens and of government officials'.

3. RIGHTS AS GUARANTEES OF FREEDOM

All doctrines of freedom assume the existence of rights which may be defined as those liberties without which man cannot be at his best or give of his best—what is needful to the adequate development and expression of his personality; rights can also be looked at negatively, as those opportunities, the absence of which would deprive him of something essential. A man without rights, absolutely dependent on the daily caprice of a superior authority, is a slave.

Basic Rights.—What those rights are vary, of course, with time and place, but it may be said that civilised communities guarantee, in normal times, freedom from arbitrary arrest (i.e. without due formalities, trial and sentence according to clearly defined laws), freedom to acquire and hold property (within the limits of state taxation), to speak and write for publication, to meet publicly, to form associations for peaceful ends, to make contracts for all purposes not specifically illegal. In addition to this, most adults in most countries have a right to vote, to be elected and to hold official positions. Further, many countries offer guarantees against economic insecurity and exploitation, opportunities for free education, and many other social facilities, as a matter of right not of grace. The kind of rights granted and maintained by each state is in fact one of the ways in which states are recognised and differentiated; that is, rights are what each state considers necessary to enable its members to fulfil their function according to the nature

[1] 'Il faut, pour méditer, s'isoler de la foule.
Et s'y confondre pour agir.'

and purpose of that particular state—always assuming, of course, that they will be used for the common good.[1]

Now it is clear that, in normal times, the exercise of ordinary rights raises no problem for the great mass. These rights represent, after all, what the majority thinks it ought to enjoy. Obviously it would not stand for any wholesale suppression of these rights, from which it would be the first to suffer; and, no less obviously, any extension of rights it desired would have to be granted.

Problem of Minority Rights.—The problem is that of the respect of minority rights. We mean by this a right which certain individuals or groups will use in a way distasteful to, or even hostile to, the majority which controls the state. Dissenting religious groups obviously run counter to the established church; pacifism and anti-Imperialism weakens the world-status of the country; Communism saps the basis of its economic and social system; Fascism undermines any free life.

What then can a man reasonably claim from a majority with which he does not agree? Surely, all that he needs in order to be able to bring round to his point of view those who are now on the other side, and thus have the opportunity of changing the minority to which he now belongs into a majority. Those necessary instruments of peaceful persuasion are books, press, radio, public meeting, propaganda associations. Short of direct incitement to violence or law-breaking, let him say what he likes, and write what he likes, any doubt being resolved by courts of law, not by officials.

Some would distinguish between authorised criticism of incidentals and forbidden attack on fundamentals. But surely such a distinction is futile. Who is to make it? Far better place the only reservation in the manner of the criticism rather than in its content. A Hyde Park orator is allowed to advocate the peaceful abolition of monarchy in England, and the formation of a republican party would be perfectly legal. But

[1] In his 'Theology and Politics' Dr. Nathaniel Micklem joins the 'inalienable human rights of man as man, together with three others as basic factors of human nature, which no battle of words can ever prove or balanced human judgement ever deny'. The others are 'a sense of the sanctity of the home, of the claims of our country upon us and of the duty of loyalty to our conscience and to God'.

let speaker or writer propose arming for the purpose, and plan
a march on Buckingham Palace, the law will interfere, not
to defend monarchy as an institution but to protect the person
of the monarch and uphold the principle of peaceful propaganda. Communists may, in the same way, proclaim the
need for radical changes in our social and economic system,
and urge the exploitation of wealth; they must not suggest
burning down the Bank of England, or use violence to break
up meetings for the defence of capitalism.

It is, of course, true that this wide toleration of dissent is
partially due to the conviction that virtually unlimited freedom
of speech acts as a safety-valve, and has no practical result.
'Let my subjects say what they like, as long as I do what I
like', said Frederick the Great of Prussia. But this is only
partly true. The foundations of the present Labour majority
in Britain were laid in open-air meetings, so were those of
women's suffrage. You never quite know what free speech
may lead to.

Need to Tolerate Dissent.—The last word on the matter
is surely that free societies must defend minority rights
because, by denying them, they deny themselves. There are,
of course, certain conditions to the healthy exercise of those
rights. The price to be paid for the expression of disagreement
is surely the present acceptance of majority decisions pending
the day when the exercise of freedom of speech may have
turned the minority into a majority. A striking instance of this
is the way in which the opponents of the new American
constitution at the Philadelphia convention in 1787 accepted
a system they disliked, and, far from endeavouring to wreck
it in daily practice, did their best to make it a success in spite
of its alleged defects. On the other hand, the majority must
not misuse power; in a word, there must be on both sides
moderation and give and take, an agreement to differ, which
is really a form of unity. 'Our political machinery', once said
Lord Balfour, 'supposes a people so fundamentally at one that
they can afford to bicker.'

When all is said and done, however, the state which
guarantees any rights must face the fact that these rights may
be used against itself. And the problem then arises, how to
secure that rights given by the state will not be taken away by

5 *

it because it disapproves of the use which is made of them. The answer is that this cannot be fully guaranteed. Attempts have been made to do so by enumerating rights in a constitutional document as has been done by the United States and France. But constitutions can be amended; or worse, they can be interpreted so as to lose all significance; or they can be ignored and the victims have no real redress.[1] It is noteworthy that Britain (where individual rights are certainly respected as fully as anywhere else) has no such constitutional guarantees. Any right can be suspended by Act of Parliament or lie at the discretion of judicial interpretation.

Rights Depend on Public Opinion.—It follows that the only guarantee of rights is 'what the people will stand'; they depend ultimately upon the liberalism of the community. An intelligent community understands the social need of freedom; it does not fear healthy criticism; it knows that varieties of opinions are good for growth, that willing co-operation is better than enforced uniformity. In one word, it believes in freedom, and it assumes that in a free atmosphere men will, on the whole, use their freedom in a way which is not, in the long run, detrimental to the real interests of society—criticism being one of these. But beyond this it is difficult to go; nothing will make up for an illiberal public outlook and a judiciary that will yield to every pressure either of the government or of opinion.

4. NATURAL RIGHTS

Are there 'Natural' Rights?—The importance of rights to any real personal life has led to the idea that certain rights are so essential that they should be called 'Natural'. The idea rests on a belief in 'Nature', as the original creating force which gave to every man the powers of finding by his reason the right principles on which to organise his life. This originated in ancient Rome, and came from the discovery that men of all races and countries living under Roman rule seemed to have some common rules of life, some objective standards of right and wrong given to them by the mere fact of their being men with a human nature. This body of principles apparently

---

[1] This is the position of negroes in some parts of the United States.

common to all men the Romans called 'Natural Law' and based on it a considerable part of their legislation. The essential basis of the theory was, in the words of Cicero, 'The existence of a universal and world-wide law, which is one with reason both in nature and human nature, and which accordingly knits together in a common social bond every being that possesses reason, whether God or man. The principle of natural law becomes a recognition of intrinsic worth in human personality, with the necessary implication of equality and universal brotherhood.'

The theologically-minded Middle Ages identified this natural law with the law of God and of the Church. But as long as the source of political obligation was not a practical issue, the doctrine remained, as it were, in abeyance, and was only revived when it became a vital problem in the seventeenth and eighteenth centuries. Then, however, it was stripped of its medieval metaphysical form, and restated in purely philosophical terms in England, France and America. As Locke puts it, 'The state of nature has a law of nature to govern it, and reason, which is that law, teaches all mankind who will but consult it, that being all equal and independent no one ought to harm another in his life, health, liberty or possessions,' or it may be stated in the words of the eighteenth century 'Encyclopédie' from which all later statements drew their inspiration, 'Rights are given by nature to men to dispose of their persons and of their goods as they deem best for their happiness, within the limits of the Natural Law imposed by God to all men and discoverable by the light of their reason, if they consider carefully their nature and their condition. Law and Right are termed "Natural" because they derive exclusively from the constitution of our being before the establishment of societies.'

Natural Law.—The doctrines of natural law, joined with the Anglo-Saxon tradition of self-government, formed as Dr. Stapleton points out,[1] 'a good summary of some very practical ideas about political relationships', and was found thus by the leaders both of American independence and of the French revolutionary movement. It provided them with the universal validity which they claimed for their principles. For either

---

[1] In 'Justice and World Society' which contains in Chapter 2 an excellent survey of the question of natural law.

natural law was only the creation of imagination, or it was independent of time and place. It affirmed four fundamental facts—first, that justice is not merely an ideal of man's desiring, but a part of nature; second, that justice is intelligible, that is, can be apprehended by the human mind, because the law of nature is the law of reason, so that what is arbitrary or irrational cannot be just; thirdly, although majority judgement is not infallible, there is no other just way of deciding what is best for mankind, and this involves the direct consultation of every man; fourthly, the law of nature is universal, and universality is the criterion of justice, for as Montaigne remarks, equity and justice cannot be attached to one particular country.[1] 'What kind of goodness is it', says Pascal, 'that I saw yesterday held in honour, but that tomorrow shall no longer be so, and that is turned into a crime by the crossing of a river?'

Declarations of Rights.—The Americans were seeking a principle by which to justify their struggle for independence and freedom from foreign control; and the French to justify their desire for self-government and freedom from arbitrary rule. Natural law was this justification, and both stated their new political faiths in their historic declarations of the Rights of Man. 'We hold those truths to be self-evident', said the Americans, 'that all men are created equal, that they are endowed by their creator with certain inalienable rights; that among these are life, liberty and the pursuit of happiness. That, to secure these rights, governments are instituted among men, deriving their just powers from the consent of the governed; that whenever any form of government becomes destructive of those ends, it is the right of the people to alter or abolish it.'

Fifteen years later the French National Assembly, evidently echoing Jefferson's words, declared that 'the ignorance, the oblivion or the contempt of the rights of man were the only causes of public misfortunes and of the corruption of governments', and resolved 'to state in a solemn declaration the natural, inalienable and sacred rights of man'. The first of these was

---

[1] Dr. Stapleton, from whom we are quoting, sums up those four points in the terms, reality, intelligibility, representativeness and intelligibility of justice.

equality in rights; next come liberty, property, security and resistance to oppression, together with the fact that sovereignty resides in the people.

What is the significance of those documents? 'The declaration of rights', said Lincoln, 'meant to set up a standard maxim for a free society, familiar to all and revered by all; constantly looked to, constantly laboured for, and, even though never perfectly attained, constantly approximated, and thereby constantly spreading and deepening its influence and augmenting the happiness and value of life to all people everywhere', and in another passage Lincoln refers to it as 'a promise that in due time the weights shall be lifted from the shoulders of men, and that all should be given an equal chance'.[1]

Assumptions of Natural Law.—It is evident that neither natural law nor the natural rightness of rights can be proved either historically or metaphysically. But neither can the axioms of geometry, and just as their negation leads to absurdity in mathematics, so does the denial of any of those abstract propositions lead to social and moral chaos. There is no security or civilised life if rights depend on the whim of the state,[2] and the only alternative to this is a vigorous belief in 'natural' rights, that is, powers without which man cannot be a rational person, having to account for his actions to his conscience. If the doctrine be unprovable, its reverse is even more unthinkable. The truth of this is becoming more and more recognised, as we see the effects of its denial in the excesses of totalitarian systems. We are no longer told, as we were a century or more ago, that 'Natural Rights is nonsense upon stilts' but rather, as by the French philosopher Maritain, that 'Natural Law is the ensemble of things to do and not to do, which follow in necessary fashion from the simple fact that man is man—that we must be good and not evil'.

International Guarantees of Rights.—Far from dismissing the doctrine of rights as metaphysical and historical nonsense,

[1] Lord Acton called the Declaration 'the triumphant proclamation of the doctrine that human obligations are not all assignable to contract, or to interests or to force', and added, 'this single page of print outweighs libraries and is stronger than all the armies of Napoleon'.

[2] Besides, by what 'right' would the state either deny or grant rights? Either because of the consent of the governed, and consent becomes the irrational natural right, or by power, and we are back in the reign of brute force.

many thinkers today are engaged in an attempt to restate it
and place it on a broader basis than the individual state and its
laws. Several plans have appeared, all of them in one form or
another laying down the duty of every state to recognise
certain rights fundamental to man as man.[1] These would
include life, liberty, property, religious practices, speech,
including access to all channels of communication, use of
native language in special schools for national minorities,
admission for all to public instruction, exercise of economic
and professional activities, freedom of assembly and organisation in groups and parties, and, in two drafts at least, free
right to participate in the government by free election, and
right to adequate living and labour conditions.

These rights are thus of two kinds; some apply exclusively
to natural minorities in multi-national states, and will be
better discussed when we deal with nationality problems.
Others apply to all citizens as such, and do not as a rule go
beyond usually existing rights, except in the insistence that
that they must be applied equally to both sexes. What is important and interesting is the assertion that no 'civilised'
state has any alternative save to recognise those rights, that
they do not depend on the circumstances of any particular
community but are fundamental to all.

The United Nations Declaration.—The United Nations
Economic and Social Council[2] is in fact at work on the ques-
tion and appointed a commission for the drafting of an
International Declaration of the Rights of Man. This has now
been done, and the scheme circulated for comment and criticism.
But the crux of the matter is the remark made by the Inter-
national Academy of Diplomacy, to the effect that the
Declaration contains no suggestion or allusion to any steps by

---

[1] See H. G. Wells's declaration in his 'New World Order' (1940); the
proposals of the commission to study the organisation of peace (1943-44),
of Dr. Lauterpacht of Cambridge in his 'International Bill of Human Rights',
and the 'Statement on Essential Human Rights' drafted by an international
committee of the American Law Institute (1944).

[2] It should be noted by the way that the members of the United Nations
are committed by the Charter and other declarations to the recognition of the
existence and reality of rights. The clause about the promotion and encouragement of respect for human rights and fundamental freedom occurs five times
in the Charter and several times in the Mexico City Inter-American Conference
on War and Peace.

which those rights and liberties will be effectively guaranteed.
'Every state must. . . .' How 'must'? Several devices have,
of course, been put forward, if not officially—appeal to the
world court or to some special world tribunal, which would
give citizens the rights to lay a complaint against their own
government? Giving facilities for publicity by radio in each
state, including the offending one, to any denial of rights?
Exclusion from organs of international co-operation such as
the United Nations and its allied bodies? Refusal of normal
economic intercourse and essential raw materials, going as
far as boycott and even war? The Polish delegation suggested
stating that a nation which issues laws contrary to the Declaration of the Rights of Man shall be deemed to be an aggressor.[1]

The problem bristles with difficulties, and we are really
back again where we were when discussing guarantees of
rights in particular states. It all depends on opinion. That alone
can ensure that governments should surrender enough of
their internal sovereignty to allow any external law or tribunal
to interfere between them and their citizens—a thing which
has never happened in recorded history; without the support
of such opinion no international tribunal can feel independent
and secure. It is true that all signatories of the United Nations
Charter pledged themselves to 'submit to any rules that may
be necessary to make their pledges and promises really effective'.
But will they really? There is still much education of public
opinion to be done.

The 'Natural' Equality of Men.—Of the unprovable but
essential principles of natural law, none is more fundamental
than that of the natural equality of men.[2] It is perhaps best
stated in the words of the 'Encyclopédie' : 'natural equality
is that which exists between all men by the very constitution
of their nature. It is founded upon that human nature which
is common to all men who are born, grow, live and die in the
same way. Therefore each must treat all others as equal to
himself. The consequence of this is: first, that all men are
naturally free, secondly, that we are to treat our inferiors

---

[1] It must be regretfully noted that none of the Russia-led Slav states
finally approved the Declaration, and all abstained from the decisive vote.

[2] 'Its most accurate name', says Maritain, 'would be "unity of mankind".'
'Inequalities', he adds 'are fragile and human, so men stress them by insignia
and signs, manifestations of power and fear.'

as by nature our equals; thirdly, no one may claim any particular right above the rights of others unless he has acquired it (i.e. not by birth or wealth).'

What Equality Involves.—Such is the basis of the doctrine. What does it involve? First of all, absence of legal discrimination against any one individual, group, class or race; next, equal claims to a minimum of education, housing, food, and guarantees against economic insecurity; in other words, recognition of the fact that there can be no difference inherent in nature between the claims of men to happiness, and especially, that no one, person or group, may be sacrificed to another. 'There cannot be supposed by any such subordination among us', said Locke, 'that may authorise us to destroy one another as if we were made for one another's uses, as the inferior ranks of creatures are for ours.'

Nobody pretends, of course, that men are actually born equal in brains, health, looks, wealth. What the doctrine of natural equality means is that none of those inequalities can be recognised by law as creating inequalities in rights. The law must treat all alike, keep all doors open to all, admit of no official predominance due to anything else but capacity shown by objective proofs which all may try to offer. It also means that law should work at reducing those inequalities, rather than perpetuating them, by providing those social and economic opportunities that equalise chances. Natural equality may be to some extent an ideal rather than an immediate reality, but the ideal must be taken as both desirable and realisable, as a guide for immediate practice. Granted that, as Croce says, 'there is something mechanical and mathematical about the concept of equality'; granted with him that social life is nothing more than 'an imperceptible and interrupted progression of unequal fortunes, with each man surrounded by inferiors and superiors and equals'. What then? How can law recognise these inequalities without perpetuating them? How can it calculate their value except by entering into concepts far more mechanical and mathematical still? 'Treat all alike' may be rough and ready; it may occasionally involve injustices but 'treat them all differently' is far worse, for you have no objective standards by which to evaluate the differences.

Freedom and Equality.—It is sometimes argued that equality and liberty are incompatible concepts, because liberty involves leaving each man free with such natural advantages as make him different from his fellows. But it is, on the contrary, natural and legal inequality that hampers freedom, by depriving men of opportunities they need for that adequate self-expression and self-development which goes with freedom. Freedom, as we have seen, means security, and security demands the disappearance of those inequalities that place the weak at the mercy of the strong.[1] All this, of course, is unprovable. Neither equality, nor, indeed, the belief in the value of every man can be proved, either by logic or by expediency. But then, 'There you are, Sir', says Walter Lippmann 'and there is your neighbour. You are better born than he, richer, stronger, handsomer, better, wiser, kinder, more likeable; you have given more to your fellow men and taken less. By every test of intelligence, virtue and usefulness you are demonstrably a better man than he, and yet—absurd as it sounds—these differences do not matter, for the last part of him is untouchable, and incomparable, and unique, and universal—either you feel this or you do not.'

No Rights Outside Society.—Before we leave this question of rights let us not forget that rights, and all the concepts that go with them, are meaningless outside organised society. Apart from communal life they are hopeless abstractions. And since rights imply common life, they imply duties— for our rights are the duties of others towards us and their rights are our duties towards them. It follows that rights must be compatible with a common good expressed in 'a complex of rights and duties linking men to each other', as Hobhouse puts it, 'Rights are what we may expect from others, and others from us, and all genuine rights are conditions of social welfare. Thus the rights anyone may claim are partly those which are essential to every man in order to be a rational human person, and partly those which are necessary for the fulfilment of the function that society

[1] Middleton Murry rightly remarks in his book 'Adam and Eve' that the tragedy of the nineteenth century has been the frustration of the hopes set upon political equality as the guarantee of genuine freedom.

expects from him. They are conditioned by, correlative to, his social responsibilities.'[1]

5. OBSTACLES TO FREEDOM

The Freedom of Others.—We have been arguing so far as if freedom were something absolute and universally desired, but there is obviously another side to the question. Freedom is not absolute; it has to face a number of external and internal obstacles and limitations. They are, of course, first and foremost the limits that each man's freedom sets to that of his neighbours, and that their freedom sets to his. Their freedom includes their security, and we would agree with Professor Laski's definition that 'limits to freedom are set by the imminence of danger to the social peace'. There can be, of course, no final objective test as to what constitutes this danger; it is not the same in time of war as in ordinary times; it must vary with the level of culture, with the coherence and stability of each society; all we can say is that governments easily tend to exaggerate the danger, and that public opinion must keep a constant watch on any tendency to restrict freedom of expression.

Restraints and Happiness.—Next comes the fact that freedom itself is no guarantee of happiness, and that restraints on freedom can actually add to happiness. They save the community, or at least some of its members, from perpetually going back to first principles, or from making over and over again experiments that have proved disastrous. They point out that certain apparent highways are really blind alleys. Marriage laws, and in general all restraints on lines of conduct commonly defined as immoral, are of that kind. They represent past experience, failure and success. Restraints may also make for security by automatically checking us along certain lines that can only make for conflict. State action may help freedom by liberating the individual from the grip of custom or tradition, or from subservience to family or other groups. After all, slaves had to be liberated, and their freedom

---

[1] The denial of the reality of rights comes largely from those who deny the reality or desirability of freedom—and we shall come to this later on in this chapter.

guaranteed by law. 'The state', says Hocking, 'can promote the rational meaning of social life by setting its elements free from every situation which is purely accidental or mechanical.' But, of course, it does this by restraining the freedom of those who would want to maintain this accidental or traditional order.

It is also true, as T. H. Green says, that 'much modern legislation interferes with freedom of contract, in order to maintain the conditions without which a free exercise of the human faculties is impossible'. Laws limiting the hours of labour are restraints on workers just as much as on employers —restraints imposed on them for their own good, originally against their bitter opposition, but saving them from the temptation of injuring their health by excessive labour. The same holds good of legislation forbidding child labour and establishing compulsory education; they were fiercely resisted by the parents who did not want to lose the money the child might earn, and were condemned by well-meaning sincere people as interferences with freedom. So they were, but these interferences secured a fuller life for the children, and ultimately for the parents themselves. After all, no man is allowed to sell himself into slavery, and this is a beneficent limitation of his freedom. And the same is true of numerous other measures, such as those enforcing hygiene. It is curious, in fact, how an automatically accepted freedom in one age may become an automatically accepted restraint in another. Compare for instance our present restrictions on currency and trade with the assertion of a seventeenth-century pamphlet that 'it is the birthright of every man to be alike free to transport that of any commodity into what parts beyond the seas seemeth most advantageous to him'.[1] As Whitehead judiciously remarks, 'the conventions and regulations of groups other than one's own always appear hampering. To the outsider the rule is a restriction and nothing more; to the native it has become the obviously right way to behave and implies no conscious restrictions to his initiative. Order made possible by sensible laws and conventions opens up a number of possibilities which would not have existed otherwise.'

Human Intolerance.—Turning now to the external obstacles to freedom, the first would seem to be the natural

---

[1] 'The Golden Fleece Defended', 1647.

intolerance of man. He may be ever claiming freedom for himself, but he finds it very hard to recognise his neighbour's claims. We want to make others conform to our beliefs and ways of life, and have an instinctive distrust of the non-conformist, whether in religion, politics, dress, or food. His nonconformity seems to imply a blame; what is good enough for us should be good enough for him. And so through-out history majorities of every kind have endeavoured to make minorities conform, to make their own standards the only and universal ones. As a rule, minorities accept this, because they are helpless, or because the struggle isn't worth while; occasionally they rebel, and either obtain toleration for their way of life or thought, or fail, and sullenly wait for another chance.

In fact it may be said that only very lately have majorities willingly tolerated minorities. When they have done so, it has been usually because the minorities were just too powerful to be forced. The voluntary abandonment of the power to coerce is a rare phenomenon, and is only to be found either in communities which have come to the conclusion that co-ercion was not worth the trouble, or in those which have achieved a considerable degree of political intelligence and self-control.[1]

And here it may be noticed that there is nothing like an oppressed minority for being tyrannical if the tables are turned. One might instance in religion the fanaticism of the New England sects who had migrated in order to avoid persecution; in politics the bitter handling of her national minorities by newly liberated Poland, or the ruthlessness shown by the Russian Communists, themselves the victims of so many years of savage repression. So naturally intolerant is man that he is incapable of granting to others the very free-dom which he craves.

> 'Nature hath put this tincture in our blood,
> That each would be a tyrant if he could,'

wrote Defoe, and his lines are as sadly true now as when he penned them.

---

[1] 'Liberty is the non-use of power—the supreme form of generosity—the rights of the minority given by the majority—sharing its existence with its enemy.' (Ortega y Gasset, 'The Revolt of the Masses', p. 83.)

Freedom is thus precarious; it lies largely at the mercy of the commonsense or the indifference of the majority. So, if we happen to be in a free minority, let us treasure our freedom and never take it for granted. 'Its price', as has been said, 'is eternal vigilance.' And if we are on the side of numbers let us be no less vigilant in keeping alive in us the spirit of moderation, remembering that today's position may well be reversed tomorrow.

Privilege.—Next, but closely allied to this natural intolerance, comes the dislike of holders of privilege, a form of freedom in one sense, to share this with others. Every extension of the suffrage, for instance, has been a struggle, orderly or violent, with those who were unwilling to see their rights extended to those who were still their inferiors. People do not voluntarily give up either power or prestige, and tend to justify their retention by the most specious and fallacious kinds of argument. 'It seems to be a law of nature', wrote the Reverend Townsend some 125 years ago, 'that the poor should be to a certain degree improvident, that there may always be some to fulfil the most servile, the most sordid, and the most ignoble offices in the community. The stock of human happiness is thereby much increased, whilst the more delicate are not only relieved from drudgery, and freed from those occasional employments which would make them miserable, but are left at liberty, without interruption, to pursue those callings which are suited to their various dispositions, and most useful to the state. As for the lowest of the poor, by custom they are reconciled to the meanest occupations, to the most laborious works, to the most hazardous pursuits; whilst the hope of their reward makes them cheerful in the midst of all their dangers and toils. . . . When hunger is either felt or feared, the desire of obtaining bread will quietly dispose the mind to undergo the greatest hardships, and will sweeten the severest labours. The peasant with a sickle in his hand is happier than the prince upon his throne.'

Freedom is Difficult.—There follows closely on these, a third obstacle in the reluctance of authorities to extend the sphere of freedom because it is so much easier to govern without it. Listen to Robert Owen's conversation in 1817 with the Austrian secretary of the congress of sovereigns then in session:

'I stated that now, through the progress of science, the means existed to saturate society at all times with wealth sufficient to supply and amply the wants of all through life. What was my surprise to hear the reply of the learned secretary: "yes", he said. "we know that very well; but we do not want the mass to become wealthy and independent of us. How could we govern them if they were?" '

6. THE FEAR OF FREEDOM

All these obstacles, however, are external obstacles. They can be met, by organisation, by education, by propaganda— by the methods, in fact, in which freedom has largely been realised so far, however perfectly. Far more deadly, as recent history shows, are the foes of freedom within man himself. 'The most significant phenomenon of our era', said Professor Barthelemy nearly twenty years ago, 'is that whole peoples become or seem to become enthusiastic for slavery.'[1]

The fact is that, however loudly man may clamour for freedom, one part of him is afraid of it; so that only one-half believes in it.

The Fear of Freedom.—Why do people fear freedom?[2] Mainly perhaps because it implies responsibilities and most people fear responsibility. The idea that men want to make their own lives is largely an illusion; some do, of course, but many want to be told what to do, from the cradle to the grave;[3] while some, though desiring freedom in their strictly private affairs, feel no need of it in public life; they do not object to being tyrannised, as long as they have their share of tyrannising others—'A man is often a millionth part of a tyrant and the rest of him a slave'. The wonders of 'discipline' are sung both by those who want to enforce it, and by those who welcome it as an escape from themselves.

The Great Inquisitor, in Dostoievsky's novel 'The Brothers Karamazov', prided himself on having made men happy by removing their freedom. Liberty is intolerable, he argued,

---

[1] French Academy Proceedings, October, 1933.

[2] See Fromm's 'Fear of Freedom', a penetrating analysis of the problem.

[3] ' The danger to democracy comes not from the people who want to govern, but from those who want to be governed.' (Petre, 'Life of Loisy'.)

both for man and for society. Man wants to be fed, not to be free; and he prefers peace, and even death, to the freedom of discerning between good and evil, for nothing is more painful than freedom of choice. Man, in fact, is not strong enough to bear the burden of liberty.

Does Man Want Freedom?—Half a century ago, Bryce wrote that 'When a people allow an old established government to be overthrown, it is because they resent its oppressions or despise its incompetence. But that does not mean to say they wish to govern themselves. As a rule, that which the mass of the people desires is not to govern itself, but to be well-governed,' and we may conclude with Dewey that the danger to freedom, 'is not the existence of foreign totalitarian states. It is the existence within our own personal attitudes, and within our own institutions, of conditions which have given a victory to external authority, discipline, uniformity and dependence on a leader in foreign countries. The battle field is here.' Is it necessary to spend any time in proving this point further? What else is the modern history of Germany but its illustration? And the tragic episode of the Vichy regime in France shows how a normally freedom-loving people can forget its history and tradition—not indeed for the first time, as the discreditable Second Empire shows. As to us Anglo-Saxons, let him that thinketh he standeth take heed lest he fall![1]

Freedom and the 'General Will'.—More serious because more fully reasoned and resting on a deeper philosophical basis, is the challenge to individual freedom in the 'general will' of the community, represented by the state. We saw in the chapter on sovereignty how the foundation of the theory is that the state stands for the more purely 'rational' and 'moral' side of the individual. It is therefore only his 'lower' self that will be inclined to resist; his 'higher' self will always want to conform. The state therefore has the right to coerce him against his 'lower' will, knowing it really has 'the support' of his 'higher' will, even if this is for the time being dormant. Further, the state, being perfect reason, understands what is good for the individual better than he does himself.

The function of the state is, therefore, according to that

[1] See Upton Sinclair's novel, 'It Couldn't Happen Here' about an imaginary Fascist revolution in the United States.

view, to guarantee freedom for 'good' things and to deny
it for 'bad'. It is evident that this involves an entirely different
view of the nature of freedom. It is no longer general absence
of restraint, but it is limited to action for good. 'The true
development of man consists', says Green, 'in so living that
the objects in which self-satisfaction is habitually sought
contribute to the realisation of a true idea of what is best for
man.' Freedom, in other words, consists in an identification
of the self and will with some entity to whom, in fact, we
abdicate our personal freedom. It is exactly the conception of
freedom that was expressed by a young Communist student in
Belgrade a few months ago: 'Liberty is the abandonment of
one's liberty for the benefit of our party; so that we may have
more liberty to act on behalf of Communism'.[1]

Confusion of the Doctrine.—This theory, it seems to us,
confuses a number of entirely different things. The sacrifice
of one's freedom to a cause, whether of country, party, or
person, has been one of the great moral forces of history.[2]
This sacrifice is one of the most fundamental of human rights,
and can be a cause of the greatest happiness and inner harmony.
And states have always claimed the right to demand such
sacrifice in times of common emergency, such as war or
economic crisis, and there are few, even of the most ardent
defenders of individual freedom, who would dispute such a
right. But it is surely playing with words and with ideas to
call this sacrifice of freedom true freedom. It involves an
abdication of personal decision, personal choice, even conscience at times, for it consists in trusting another's decision
as to what is good or bad for me, as to what is my 'higher'
and my 'lower' self; and to call this 'freedom' is a contradiction in terms. 'The idealistic view of freedom through
experience' writes Laski, 'contradicts all the major facts of
experience. I cannot be more free by subordinating my
judgement of right.'

The doctrine of the general will is based, in fact, upon the
assumption that there is someone—the state—who knows

---

[1] Quoted by Madam Tabouis in a lecture at Beirut, January, 1948.

[2] 'A man may, and frequently ought to sacrifice his life but not his
personality. The person within him he ought to realise, and sacrifice is
the condition of realising personality.' (Berdyaev, 'Origins of Russian
Communism', p. 216.)

better than we do what is really good for us. This was true of us in our childhood, and we therefore had to obey—but we were not free. To be free is one thing, and to obey someone who knows better is another. When the pilot steers the ship he is master and the crew obey; it is for their good but it does not make them free. Following a guide on an unknown mountain is necessary for my safety and enjoyment, but it does not make me free. It may be excellent to be restrained from foolish or wrong actions, though we learn from our mistakes; but restraint is not freedom, and must be defended on the ground that it is expedient, not that it is a producer of liberty.

Restraint is not Freedom.—It is all the more necessary to face this issue that the state is the claimant to our obedience. The believer who puts his implicit trust in his Church does at least believe in her dependence on a divine supernatural guidance, but what is this state whom we are to follow? In the most democratic country imaginable the voice of the state is at best the voice of the majority. We shall later on defend majority rule as the most workable form of government, but would also say that whoever can believe the majority is always morally right can believe anything.

The truth is that the doctrine of the general will, while trying to reconcile the need for freedom with the need for government, really sacrifices the former to the latter. As Hobhouse puts it, 'The Hegelian conception of the State was designed to turn the edge of the principle of freedom by identifying freedom with the law of equality, by substituting the conception of discipline—of personality, by merging the individual in the State—of humanity, by erecting the state as the supreme and final form of human association.'

There is yet another element of confusion in the doctrine of the general will embodying the personal freedom of the citizens. How can this will be formed and determined, if it is to be 'general', and not a mere addition of individual wills, without a full and unfettered discussion in which all take part? On its own showing, as it were, the state that represents the general will needs the active co-operation of the mass of free citizens. A general will based on coercion and restraint is a contradiction in terms.

More realistic in his facing of facts, in contrast with the young Communist who identified his freedom with that of his party, was the young Nazi, who actually said that what he felt during a stay in France was need of freedom—and he explained that there was no true freedom in France because nothing that happened there had any importance; since anything could happen, no action had any significance; no doubt one was more free, but such a freedom which had no value or purpose resolved itself into vain, fruitless agitation. In his country there was less tolerance, but everyone was conscious of working for something and making his contribution to a new order.[1]

It is impossible, in other words, to have it both ways. It is possible to believe that a community is happier and more effective if closely controlled by a powerful state, whose will the citizens will accept as their own and obey accordingly. It is also possible to believe that a healthy community will leave the greatest degree of initiative possible to its members and restrict to the minimum the coercive and restraining action of its state. But it is impossible to pretend that the two are the same.

Is Freedom an Illusion?—Some, however, deny that freedom can really exist. In the world of today, they ask, what freedom has man left? 'The right to express our thoughts', as Fromm says, 'only means anything if we are able to have thoughts of our own.' We are living in an age of mass-minds, standardised by factory-made education, by commercialised radio and press. And the pressure of manufactured ready-made thinking is increasingly difficult to escape. 'There is, in fact, no such thing as real individual behaviour', says another voice. 'It is true that there may be in man a small element of personal uniqueness but most of him is based on imitation and culture patterns. Our psychology is socially conditioned; we have really no minds of our own for which to claim freedom.' And this view is that of the Communist to whom, says the Russian Christian philosopher Berdyaev, 'freedom of conscience is impossible, because it assumes that there is a spiritual principle in the individual which is not dependent on the community.'

[1] Caillois, 'The Two Faces of Freedom', in *La France Libre*.

And then comes the economist with a twofold challenge. 'Your mode of life', he cries, 'is determined by the economic system under which you live, and as this is itself the dominant factor in your individual character-structure, it follows that your character is fixed by your economic system. Besides', he goes on, 'what "freedom" is there in economic insecurity? Of what use is a "free tongue in an empty stomach"? "*primum vivere, deinde philosophari*"—live first and then discourse. What freedom of speech is there for the sweated worker? Who dares offend his boss by expressing subversive opinions? Is not liberty just as much as religion the opium of the people? Your so-called rights are a pure illusion.'

Freedom and Security.—What answers will be made to those criticisms? As a matter of fact, it is perfectly true that economic insecurity is a great hindrance to a free life. But, in the first place, some individuals have transcended this limitation; and secondly, it can be, and to some extent is being, removed. The extension of social services and insurances is definitely destroying in many countries the bugbear of insecurity and giving a more solid basis to freedom. On the other hand, it may be remarked that the much greater economic security which Russia claims to have established has certainly not brought greater personal freedom—and even if one identifies freedom with security it does not appear that Russia is as yet the paradise of the proletariat.

But all the other obstacles we have been discussing belong to the mind. Intolerance, love of power, fear of responsibility and desire to be led are moral diseases, for which, were there no cure, the outlook for freedom would be poor indeed. But the fact that, though common, they are not universal shows that the cure exists—in education of all kinds, in all that develops independence of mind and spirit. We should also note that the various 'pressures' referred to are, after all, human elements, that is, the pressure of mind against mind. Some men have the freedom to oppress others; all men cannot be slaves to each other. The defender of freedom claims the right of all men to be free, or at least to be given the opportunity of achieving freedom. For it is true, that while in one sense, man is born free, that is, with a right to freedom and the capacity for it, this freedom must be acquired. It is an achievement; and it is only at the cost of the most painful efforts that man can affirm his true personality, by freeing it from the innumerable outward pressures that try and force him to conform, and by subduing in himself the instincts that would make him shun freedom. 'In fact, the aim of liberty', says Ruggiero, 'is to assist the individual to discipline himself and achieve his own moral progress.'

Is Man Fit to be Free?—The greatest problem of freedom is, therefore, man himself. 'Political Liberalism', says Canon Lloyd, 'is based on the assumption that men can and will rule themselves, that men are rational, that they know their own interests, will respect the rights of others, and will make good use of the freedom they have won.' Liberalism assumes that men are real persons. But the problem of today is precisely the depersonalisation of the individual. In his striking book 'The Revolt of the Masses', the Spanish philosopher Ortega y Gasset distinguishes between 'persons who make demands on themselves', and the mass, 'for whom to live is to be at every moment what they already are', who wants to 'feel just like everybody', sets no particular value on itself, and thinks that 'to be different is to be indecent'.

'The characteristic of the hour is that the commonplace mind, knowing itself to be commonplace, has the assurance to proclaim the rights of the commonplace mind and impose them wherever it will.' The trouble with the mass-man is that, 'he regards himself as perfect'; he is inhibited from comparing himself with other beings, and cannot go out of himself.[1]

How can the mass-man use freedom properly? Obviously he cannot without becoming a person. The mass will either ignore its rights, remain apathetic and indifferent, absentee voters, evaders of taxation, shirkers of responsibility, or it will use its freedom to impose its commonplace way of life. Only its intellectual and spiritual regeneration can save the rest of the world from the fate that has already befallen

---

[1] 'The conflict between the individual and the mass has always been the conflict between maturity and infantilism, and on a social level it is a struggle against the effort of people who are everlastingly infantile to prevent intellectual maturity anywhere in society. The meaning of individualism, of the attainment of individuality in society, is the same as the struggle for personal maturity out of a childish world.' (Martin, 'The Conflict of the Individual and the Mass', p. 109.)

Russia and Germany and is threatening our own free countries in the increasing standardisation and vulgarisation of life.

Freedom Cannot be 'Proved'.—But, finally, whatever road we take, and whatever line of argument we follow, we always come back to the conclusion that freedom rests on assumptions, and that those assumptions are ultimately of a spiritual nature—that is, that liberty exists in the mind and soul of man, or not at all. 'There are nations', writes de Tocqueville, 'which have tirelessly pursued freedom through every kind of peril and hardship. They loved it, not for its material benefits; they regarded freedom itself as a gift so precious and so necessary, that no other could console them for the loss of that which consoles them for the loss of everything else. I attempt no analysis of that great emotion for those who cannot feel it. It enters of its own accord into the generous hearts God has prepared to receive it; it fills them, it inspires them; but to the meaner minds which have never felt it, it is past finding out.'

> 'It is the land that free men till,
> That sober-skirted Freedom chose,
> The land where girt with friend or foes,
> A man may speak the thing he will.'

And either you like Tennyson and Tocqueville's ideal or you do not; there is no arguing about it.

CHAPTER VIII

THE FREE DEMOCRATIC STATE

FREEDOM, we have seen, seems to be the only possible basis for a healthy Society. And the State in which this free Society will realise its existence organised is usually termed a 'Democratic' State, so that 'Democracy' can be defined as 'the political and social framework of a society based on principles of freedom', or as 'the body for a would-be free spirit'.

I. BASES OF DEMOCRATIC THOUGHT

What Do We Mean by 'Democracy'?—The terms 'democracy' and 'democratic' have been used so often and so differently that they are like coins on which all inscriptions and designs have become effaced, with the result that they can be made to apply to anything one wishes to defend or to attack according to one's preferences. A republic is more 'democratic' than a hereditary monarchy, though a president may be more powerful than a king. It is 'democratic' to have the broadest suffrage possible, yet Switzerland, universally acknowledged as one of the most democratic states in the world, has no women's suffrage as yet, while France, another democracy, only introduced it very recently. The educational systems of these last two countries and of the United States are 'democratic' because the enormous majority of the children attend one single type of community-supported schools. It is supposed to be 'democratic' to travel third class rather than first, but democratic France is one of the few countries to have retained two classes in her bus, train and municipal railway systems. It is 'democratic' to take your place in food queues and 'undemocratic' to patronise the black market. It is 'undemocratic' to be ashamed of humble origins and poor relations. Tsarist Russia, of all countries, was called 'democratic' by some because of the habit of addressing all people, even the highest, by their Christian names joined on to that of their father or by some such 'equalitarian' appellation as 'little Father'. And others call 'undemocratic' any sharp inequalities of income, and describe as 'democratic' any system of taxation that tries to reduce them. Scandinavian kings are called democratic because they dislike pomp and ceremony, and the French President Faure's liking for military escorts was called the reverse. 'Democracy is simplicity' said the headline of a paper of a newly independent republic, complaining of the way some ten miles of main road had been cleared of all traffic for two hours at one of the busiest times of the day to enable the President to drive back without impediment or delay from a luncheon party.

It may indeed be true that, as someone has said, 'democracy has a context in every sphere of life', but there is no doubt as to the confusion produced by the indiscriminate use of the word. Out of the terminological chaos, there would, however, seem to emerge some three kinds of uses of the term. One obviously identifies democracy with some kind of social equality—no snobbery, no sharp class differences. This may be described as democracy in social organisation, or social democracy. To some the essence of the term lies in economic policies that attempt the levelling of inequalites of wealth. To others the term is essentially descriptive of a certain type of political organisation, of which many descriptions have been given but which may be loosely described as one in which power is entrusted by the governed to the governors, and in which authority, coming from the people directly or indirectly, submits itself at every stage to popular control.

Democracy in Government.—To put it in more technical language, a system of government is democratic if it is based, more or less, on the doctrine of popular sovereignty. Many definitions have been given of this doctrine and its applications: 'government of the people, by the people, for the people', said Lincoln.[1] 'Our democratic system', said an English newspaper some forty years ago[2] 'rests on the assumption that "the wise cannot be trusted to speak for the foolish, nor the rich for the poor, nor the learned for the ignorant", or,

---

[1] A letter in the *Listener*, on June 22, 1946, pointed out that this famous passage, quoted as Lincoln's own composition, is actually an adaptation from the preface to Wycliffe's Bible, which reads 'This Bible is translated and shall make possible government of people by people for people'.

[2] The old *Westminster Gazette*, about 1908.

as in a familiar saying, that "only the wearer knows where the shoe pinches" '.

This type of democratic state has been dominant during the last century or two in the west—Great Britain, France, Switzerland, the United States. 'What the average Englishman means by democracy is a political system under which there is universal suffrage, regular elections honestly conducted, a number of political parties, freedom of speech and writing, toleration of minorities and a competent independent judiciary. To us democracy is the antithesis of dictatorship.' [1]

Another type of state, also claiming to be democratic according to its own interpretation of the term, has appeared of late years in the Communist system of Soviet Russia. To the Russians the western system with its economic and social inequalities, is not democracy, but plutocracy, and the toleration which is to us the life-blood of democracy, is to them, hypocrisy, for it does not really operate in the one vital sphere, the abolition of economic privilege. 'The best criterion of the democracy of a government is its policy', wrote Alexei Sokoliev in the Moscow *Novaya Vremya*.[2] 'Whom does it serve, for whose benefit does it exist—for the benefit of the people or of their most bitter enemies, the traitors and betrayers of the people's interests?' And he goes on to defend the 'democratic' regimes in the liberated East European countries—Rumania, Bulgaria, Hungary and Yugoslavia. 'To the Russians', said Lord Lindsay, 'police regulations, the Moscow trials, the dictatorship of the proletariat are all democracy. Democracy to them is power in the hand of a government on behalf of the poor; therefore it must not be limited by any written constitution or law or respect of individual rights.' To them our democracy is limited in so far as it is limited by any of these things. Opposition to the will of the people is undemocratic and must be suppressed in the name of democracy. So is toleration of individual wealth.

Here are indeed deep and fundamental differences, and it is obviously confusing to use the same term for both.[3] But

---

[1] *The Friend*, January 18, 1946.   [2] Summarised in *Soviet News*.

[3] On the same occasion Lord Lindsay pointed out that the common use of the term democracy 'in common declarations was the only common moral basis possible between Russia and the west after 1941'; but no attempt seems to have been made to see if there was any agreement as to the meaning of the term.

since both sides insist on using it, we cannot do otherwise, using for want of better adjectives the terms 'Political' and 'Economic'.

Democracy and Rights.—Our political democracy is really the mere application of the doctrine of individual rights. Man must be able to feel, as Hocking puts it, that he is rightly placed, is counting as a human being, is changing things in the direction in which they need to be changed, and will stay changed so that in one's own way one is altering the universe for good.

Why do people believe in democracy? For the same reasons that they believe in freedom, namely a belief in the rights of the ordinary man. Nobody has ever defended democracy on the grounds of efficiency, but only on the grounds that, as for freedom, its denial involves the denial of certain personal values more important than efficiency. 'A democratic society', says Wolff, 'is a society of free, equal, active and intelligent citizens, each man choosing his own way of life for himself and willing that others should choose theirs.'

The Four Implications of Democracy. What are the implications of such an assumption? First, that uniformity of belief and action is neither necessary nor desirable. Agreement to disagree, even on vital issues, is essential. It believes that truth will come by the clash of opinion with opinion, that every citizen may have something of value to contribute and must not be hindered in bringing it forward.[1] 'Democracy', writes Sir Stafford Cripps, 'is a system of government in which every adult citizen is equally free to express his views and desires upon all subjects in whatever way he wishes, and to influence the majority of his fellow-citizens to decide according to those views, and to influence those desires.'

The second implication is the rejection of any 'absolute' in political theory or practice. It is an admission of relativity in politics. The state has no final truth to proclaim or establish, infallibility may be a religious concept, it has no place in

[1] See Friedrich, 'Democracy and Dissent', *Political Quarterly*, October, 1939. We would not go so far as he does, however, when he urges that not even 'common agreement on the point that political decisions have to be based on consent rather than force' is necessary.

politics.[1] There is no belief in the 'state in itself' as apart from its members, or in mysterious mystical entities. The only reality is the individual citizen.

The third implication is that political rights must be the same for all, irrespective of birth, or wealth, or even education. 'Democracy', says Shaw, 'means the organisation of society for the benefit and at the expense of everybody indiscriminately and not for the benefit of a privileged class'; its aim is 'to prevent the operation of policies excluding some people from the benefits of the State; without it, some men become the tool of others.'[2] Democracy is therefore rooted in equality, not as something already attained but as an aim to be kept always in view.

Fourthly, and lastly, democracy is inseparable from a belief in methods of peaceful persuasion, in the ultimate reasonableness of man, and his response to rational argument.

2. DEMOCRACY IN HISTORY

The Ancient World.—How far back must we go to find the origins of democratic theory? To the earliest affirmations of the natural equality of all men, to be found implicit or explicit in all the great world religions and in the philosophical systems which have come to us from antiquity. But it was many centuries before these affirmations were tried as a basis for political organisation. The Greek city-states were indeed democratic in the participation of all citizens, not only in the election of officials but in the daily routine of administration and justice; they pushed their belief in equality to the extreme of filling many posts by drawing lots, on the assumption that one man was on the whole as good as another. But they only applied their principles to a small number of citizens, excluding 'foreigners' (i.e. fellow Greeks from other communities), and slaves; and no Greek philosopher ever accepted democracy as desirable; it was at best only less objectionable than tyranny. Nor was there any real democracy in Rome, even under the 'Republic'; the participation of citizens in government was only formal; effective power was in the hands of an

[1] Cf. Lacroix, 'Y a t'il deux démocraties?' *Esprit*, March 13, 1946.
[2] Article 'Democracy' in the 'Encyclopaedia of Social Sciences'.

aristocracy of wealth and education. Slavery was maintained
and only in the respect for law as binding on officials as much
as on private citizens did Rome lay down any principle of importance in democratic evolution.

The Medieval World.—Nor did the coming of Christianity make much immediate difference. Its equality was
spiritual, not legal or economic. But the Middle Ages
developed the notion of contract, freeing the people from
their duty of obedience if the ruler broke his side of the
supposed bargain and insisting on the theory that government is for the sake of the governed; they also discovered
the idea of representation, which solved the problem of
democratic government in large communities, and stressed
the concept of authority as a trust. But the idea of religious
dissent, vital to any form of political freedom, was alien to
the medieval mind.

The Reformation.—Democracy as the affirmation of man's
right to dissent from the state was born of the Reformation,
even though few of the reformers believed in applying the
principles to those who disagreed with them. Some principle had to be found by which to justify resistance, passive or
active, to the state's prohibition of the new worship and enforcement of the old, while in Protestant countries Catholicism
also was driven to such a defence of disobedience. The notion
of contract was again brought forward on both sides; the
rights of kings were severely limited and even tyrannicide
had its apologists.

Protestantism not only defended the right of the individual
conscience to differ from the state religion, it also proclaimed,
although very spasmodically, the principle that strict uniformity was not only impossible but unnecessary and even
undesirable. Roger Williams, in Rhode Island, established
toleration on the ground that there was always 'more truth
and light to break forth from God's word' and that therefore
uniformity of religious practice was bad in itself; progress
would come from encouraging diversity, 'No one individual
or group can express the whole idea of God'. Protestantism
was in fact rooted in discussion, and discussion implies freedom
for all parties concerned.

The practical translation of all this was first of all the

independence of the Church from the state, either legal by formal separation, or practical by virtual autonomy within a régime of establishment. And it meant in most cases the autonomy of the individual congregation, often through the impossibility of centralised control in countries where the new faith had to maintain itself against persecution. 'Our democracy', said Lord Lindsay, 'is inspired by the seventeenth-century idea of self-governing congregation'; there lies the origin of that Anglo-Saxon reliance on voluntary association which Tocqueville rightly considered the distinguishing feature of American democracy.

The Protestant Basis of Modern Democracy.—It is, in fact, among the English Protestants of the seventeenth century that we find the earliest clear proclamation of democratic theory. 'Who would live where he hath not the freedom of his mind and the exercise of his conscience?' wrote Walwyn. 'In civil affairs', said Henry Robinson, 'we see by experience that every man most commonly understands best his own business'; and Saxby stated the basis of any democratic state in the words that 'every man born in England cannot, ought not, either by the law of God or of nature, to be exempted from the choice of those who are to make laws for him to live under, and for him, for aught I know, to lose his life under'; while a little later (1649) John Warr declared that 'the great men of the world, being invested with the power thereof, cannot be imagined to eclipse themselves or their own pomp unless by the violent interposition of the people's spirits who are most sensible of their own burdens and most forward in seeking relief'.

By its insistence on the 'priesthood of all believers' and on the equal rights of all Church members, Protestantism emancipated the common man. It was in fact a widespread complaint that the new sects allowed the public speaking and religious leadership of all kinds of ordinary people 'such as common preachers, cobblers, tinkers, pedlars, weavers, sowgelders, and chimney-sweepers, confectioner, smith, boxmaker, soap-boiler, glover, meat-man, chicken-man, buttonmaker, tailor, sadler, porter, shoemaker, mechanick', and aristocratic leaders of the popular party were so disgusted that we find Lord Essex in 1644 declaring his 'determination to devote his life to repressing the audacity of the common people'.[1]

Democracy in England.—The political struggle of the English civil wars was of course not limited to the problem of religious freedom. The issue was also concerned with the royal right to interfere with private property by taxation not sanctioned by Parliament, and we find that liberty of conscience is inextricably mixed up with liberty from arbitrary interference with ownership: 'all free subjects are born inheritable as to their land and so also to the free exercise of their industry. Tyranny may be justly esteemed the greatest calamity because it is in opposition to the chiefest felicity which lies in liberty and in the free disposition of that which God and our own industry hath made ours', said a pamphlet of 1642, and the 'Common Soldier's Apology' of 1647 declared that 'the meanest subject should freely enjoy his right liberty and property in all things. Upon this ground of hope we have gone through all difficulties and dangers.' We already see the identification of English liberalism with *laissez-faire* in the economic sphere.[2]

Whether in the field of religion, of economics or of political theory, the point at issue was the relation of the king to the common law and the respective rights of people and monarch. The Bill of Rights settled it in 1689[3] by proclaiming the doctrine of contract, the subordination of the king to the law, and the right of the people to change a sovereign they no longer trusted. John Locke's 'Treatise on Civil Government' (1691) gave these decisions a philosophical justification, declaring a man's inalienable right to 'whatever he hath mixed his labour with', and, probably unconsciously, laid down the principle of equality by declaring that 'there cannot be supposed any such subordination among us that may authorise us to destroy one another as if we were made for one another's uses, as the inferior ranks of creatures are for ours'.

[1] These and the preceding quotations are taken from Petrogorsky's 'Democratic Ideas in Seventeenth Century England'.

[2] See the quotation from a 1647 pamphlet on the right to trade given in a preceding chapter.

[3] The first written constitution based on the subordination of the government to law is not, however, the Bill of Rights, but that of Connecticut in 1639.

Democracy in Switzerland.—This democratic philosophy is the political application of the philosophy of religious freedom and individualism derived from the teachings of John Calvin in Geneva, and his Genevan city state was democratic in so far as all its members shared in the management of its affairs, under supervision of the assembly of ordained ministers. In this sense, democratic theory is of Franco-Swiss origin, and it is interesting to note that the earliest known communities that were definitely political democracies were those set up by Swiss farmers in some of the oldest of the areas or 'cantons' that formed the nucleus of the Swiss Federation. Schwyz, Uri, Appenzell, Unterwalden are to this day the only 'direct' democracies in existence, in which citizens settle all their affairs in popular assemblies as in the days of ancient Greece.

This, however, was on a small scale, affecting at most a few thousand people. It was not until several centuries later that a whole nation issued a clear statement of the rights both of the individual and of a collectivity. But fourteen years before America declared her independence, the doctrine of popular sovereignty had been restated on a secular basis, and again by a man from Geneva, Rousseau.

3. THE WILL OF THE PEOPLE

The French Revolution.—Rousseau's theory is expressed in two treatises, the 'Discourse on the Causes of Inequality among Men' (1749) and the 'Social Contract' (1762). The influence of the latter has tended to overshadow the other, which is, in some ways, a fuller proclamation of individual rights, but it is the 'Social Contract' that counts in history. 'If it be closely read', says Belloc, in his 'French Revolution', 'it will be discovered to say all that can be said of the moral basis of democracy.' And it is worth remembering Carlyle's grim words: 'a man called Rousseau wrote a book called the "Contrat Social". The noblemen of his day laughed at the work. But the second edition was bound in their skins.'

Democracy and Constitutionalism.—Later democratic theory was concerned less with the re-affirmation of principles than with the attempt to find an institutional expression for the three dominant ideas bequeathed by the eighteenth century: first, the English belief that liberty is best found in parliamentary government; second, the American insistence on the right of a people to dismiss its governors; third, the French revolutionary attack on privilege as the child of autocracy. Each of the three great western powers concentrated both in its practice and in its thinking on its own main line of interest. In England, parliamentary reform, individual rights both to free expression and to whatever benefits are to be derived from membership of the state, found defenders in the utilitarians, Bentham and Mill, with their distrust of authority and their belief in law as the protector of the citizen. The Americans, on the other hand, starting with the same heritage of belief in individual freedom in politics and religion, developed not only a profound belief in equality and free initiative, but also a system of government in which popular control by frequent elections endeavoured to make popular sovereignty an everyday reality.

British and Americans in fact would possibly present to the rest of the world a common view of what they meant by democracy, admirably summarised by Pierre Maillaud in his book, 'The English Way'.

"The individual is not merely the subject of the state but an object in himself.

"The State must not be stronger than the Society it represents, not turn it into a regulated machine. Whether by law or public opinion, the rule of the majority must be tempered by the protection of the rights and convictions of the minority.

"Every man is entitled to hold and profess his own beliefs, irrespective of the policy of the executive.

"The object of the State is to serve, not to coerce, the community; therefore no discrimination can be made between citizens: therefore there is equality of rights."[1]

Revolutionary Democracy.—In France and in the rest of Europe, however, democracy developed along somewhat

---

[1] Americans would, of course, add the absence of all rights and privileges derived from birth, such as those of monarchy and House of Lords; to which an Englishman might reply that the part these play in his life is greatly exaggerated, and is much less important than the part played by wealth in America.

different lines. It was first primarily concerned with forms of government, particularly with republic as against monarchy. It took France three revolutions (1830, 1848, 1871–75) before her institutions found a definite expression in the Third Republic. And in this struggle for adult suffrage and freely elected assemblies she lost sight of that other aspect of democracy, so important to the Anglo-Saxons, the rights of the individual against the state.[1]

In France also, the early democratic republicans, having to struggle against European coalitions, tended to identify their cause with that of independence from foreign interference or control. In the same way, other peoples, striving to be free from rulers who were both tyrannical and foreign, associated the two causes of democracy and nationalism; the latter was in fact the application to the national group of the doctrine of individual rights.

This aspect of European democracy can best be understood by the study of such episodes as the Greek War of Independence, and especially the events of the year 1848. The republican-nationalist struggles in Poland and in Hungary, the association of constitutional reform in Prussia and Austria with national sentiment, all these contrasted with the peaceful evolution of Britain towards fuller democracy but within the historical framework of the King in Parliament. This illustrates the saying of Sir Ernest Barker that 'In England, democracy has been a doctrine of order, on the continent a doctrine of Revolution'.[2]

Democracy and the Industrial Revolution.—Meanwhile a new type of democratic theory had been developing, born of the problems created by the Industrial Revolution. The extension of the suffrage and other political rights soon showed the worker that these were of little value in the midst of increasing economic inequality. The application of democratic principles to those problems was inevitable and was

[1] We venture to refer readers to our very full treatment of the subject, together with its vast bibliography, in our 'French Political Thought in the Nineteenth Century'(Benn, London; Yale University Press, 1931). Michelet is probably the most typical representative of this republican democratic theory.

[2] See also the later democratic struggle in Portugal, in Spain, in Tsarist Russia.

first made by Frenchmen, St. Simon and Fourrier in particular. With them appeared 'Socialism', with its demands that the political machine should be used to remove the economic inequalities of the industrial world, by legislation to improve working conditions and guarantee security, by ruthless taxation of wealth for the providing of social services, and by freedom for workers to combine in their unions for the defence of their individual and collective rights.

The later development of economic democratic theory into the Marxist philosophy of the dictatorship of the proletariat will be dealt with in a later chapter. We shall content ourselves now with quoting the following passage as a clear statement of the problem: 'There can be no true freedom without a remoulding of the economic structure. In the liberal State, every man leads a double life—one as a citizen, one as a producer. As a citizen, he has rights, which he cannot really enjoy because they are only exercised in and through the State, over which he has little or no real control; as a social being he is a slave. Before and after the declaration of the Rights of Man in actual practical life, he is still either an owner of property or a wage-earner, in the one case secure, in the other insecure.'[1]

The bases of democratic philosophy are therefore varied but clear. At the foundation lies a spiritual concept, that all men are equally children of God and thereby equal in their needs and their rights. Each must count for one, and for no more than one; each has something to give and must therefore be given his chance to contribute it. It follows from this that government exists for persons, and not the other way round; the state is only there to give individuals their fullest opportunity of living a good life, they, not the state, being the judge of what 'goodness' is for them. And finally authority cannot come from above or from outside; its only source is the people themselves; its only justification its derivation from popular authority.

The 'Dogmas' of Democracy.—In an article published in 1948 in a Beirut paper,[2] the French thinker Julien Benda sums up in particularly felicitous language the essentials of the democratic philosophy of the French Revolution. Its

---

[1] Lacroix, *Esprit*, March, 1946.   [2] *L'Orient*, Jan. 27, 1948.

essential dogma is the individual and his sacred rights, for whom society was created, the state being unable to infringe upon these rights, save for a superior and temporary emergency or because of their unworthiness. This dogma is directly opposed to that according to which the foundation of society is society itself, not the persons who compose it.

A second dogma is that of the sovereignty of the nation, rulers being only its delegates, whose powers may be recalled at any time. It follows that all power can only be exercised under control and supervision.

A third dogma is that relations between states must be constructed on the same basis of equality of rights, thus ruling out all conquest, annexations and wars of aggression. Finally, it is laid down that a man can achieve on earth conditions of adequate happiness, rejecting the doctrine proclaimed in the French Parliament in 1850 that 'man is here below to suffer'.

These doctrines are all based on the rational element in man, not on his physical make-up such as race. Men are bound together by common ideals, not by common blood; they form nations because they wish to do so. A nation is a group of people who want to live and work together; that is the only test.[1]

Democracy a Doctrine of Human Optimism.—Democracy is therefore an optimistic creed in so far as it believes in the ordinary man's political common sense. We mean by this his capacity not to make policies and carry them out, but to choose between alternative policies and the principles on which they are based, not to govern but to choose his governors, his right to know in a general way what kind of state he wants, and to try and persuade his fellow-citizens to work with him towards its realisation. Now obviously in the last resort this belief cannot be proved, any more than its ideals can be perfectly and completely achieved. How can you 'prove' democracy? You may defend some of its institutions as efficient, or less inefficient than others; you cannot defend them as ideal, any more than you can proclaim the infallibility of majorities. 'But when you think you have crushed out of existence the principles on which democracy is based, you find they have

---

[1] M. Benda has written a history of France under the title 'A History of the French People and their determination to be a Nation' (Histoire des Français dans leur volonté d'être une nation).

eluded you, and that there still is a democratic reality which has to be translated into concrete terms. There are popular aspirations towards greater welfare and a desire for more justice in human relationships; wills making for peace and progress. This is the reality, of which government by universal suffrage is only the rough and ready expression.'[1]

4. WHAT MAKES A STATE 'DEMOCRATIC'?

Confining ourselves now to political democracy, what are the distinguishing features of a democratic state, by which it can be distinguished from non-democratic?

Opportunities for the 'Common Man'.—The essence of democracy consists, it seems to us, in the kind of life it opens up for the ordinary citizen. Taking one such from his earliest years, he will be offered the fullest educational possibilities, both for his own sake as an individual, and for the sake of the community that needs well-educated citizens. And under education we include not merely basic schooling but preparation for whatever career he seems best fitted by taste and capacity. Whether this education should be one uniform system or whether variety is desirable, whether it should be state-controlled or largely independent is a matter on which opinions may differ; the one essential thing is availability for all on equal terms, irrespective of wealth or social position.

This training completed, the young citizen must be enabled to enter the profession of his choice without being debarred by absence of means. A man should be able to live on his pay in any branch of the public service, civil or military. Professions such as the law, where progress is very slow, should be compatible with part-time occupations giving the young barrister a living until his income from fees be sufficient to give all his time to the bar.

In all his professional activities he will expect society to protect him against anything that may make him the instrument of another and not a free human being. He will want to be defended against economic exploitation of all kinds, and will demand that all activities be directed from the point of

---

[1] 'Letters' of Henri Franck, a young French writer of the First World War.

view of a common good rather than personal advantage, without implying that these two aims are necessarily antagonistic. Believing that democracy implies solidarity, he will demand the pooling by common insurance of those hazards of life for which he is not responsible, especially illness and unemployment.

Equality of Rights.—Turning from his private existence and activities to his life as a citizen, the member of a democratic society has political rights equal to those of any of his fellows. He votes and is eligible for office on a level with them all. The old adage, 'one man, one vote', is the only basis for a democracy. But apart from voting the citizen will have been free to contribute to the making of public opinion in speech or writing, in public meeting and press, by forming parties, associations, groups, without any hindrance or regulation. He enjoys complete freedom to praise or blame the institutions and leading men of his country; he can criticise policy, suggest other lines of action; he has no fear of the police, unless he has broken some positive law. He is free in all these things because the political life of his community is based on a complete freedom of discussion out of which emerges the public opinion which is the ultimate source of authority.[1]

Our democratic citizen cannot of course pretend to universal knowledge, or to an understanding of the technicalities of all the problems involved in common life. He only claims two things—first, his capacity of understanding broad issues, the essential principles on which policies and programmes rest, and to choose between them. Second, his right to offer his opinion when study and experience have enabled him to form an independent judgement. 'People', as Ward remarks, 'should be consulted on matters of desire, not of facts, by a clear revelation of possibilities.'

---

[1] 'There is certainly no lack of the means of discussion nowadays. Who but an actuary could reckon the number of media through which any subject is discussed? When we think of the *voces populi* to-day, we have to take into account not only the political parties and meetings, but the parish debating society, the local constitutional club and reform club, discussion groups in the Forces and among civilians, the bar parlour, the women's institutes, leagues, guilds and fellowships' (and we would add the trade unions, the co-operatives, the school and college debating societies, the suburban trains). (Allen, 'Democracy and the Individual', p. 61.)

Assumptions and Conditions of Democracy.—This building of society on a basis of free discussion (the liberal democrat is a creature of dialogue) involves the three-fold assumptions that there are differences, that they do not go too far, and are never settled by violent methods.

Democracy recognises and welcomes differences. It has no belief in uniformity. On the contrary, one of its characteristics is to provide the machinery for their free expression. Its political organisation rests on various devices which admit the existence of contrasting policies and of politicians ready and eager to replace these in power. It knows that there are as many opinions as there are men (*quot homines, tot sententiae*) and does not believe in their suppression or control: free expression is a safety-valve, repression means explosion.

But these differences must not go so far as to make impossible any common life between those who differ. Irreconcilable minorities, parties or classes are a perpetual danger. Any democratic system requires a broad agreement as to general principles and methods. You may disbelieve in democracy as much as you like, but either you must keep out of politics or you must accept its general way of life and not plot its overthrow. And this way of life includes the right of all to share in its advantages and the belief that persuasion is the only satisfactory way to effect any change. If discussion be the life blood of democracy there must at least be some agreement as to the rules of debate. 'Whatever the form of government', says Guérin in 'le Problème français', 'a régime is democratic when the will to social co-operation of its members is stronger and more spontaneous than its anarchical impulses.'

Discussion and Change.—Discussion involves change, and a democratic society is bound to be a changing one. In fact all societies are perpetually changing, but democratic societies recognise and welcome the fact. They cannot be static; they must evolve with the development of new points of view, new techniques, new possibilities for human life. But the change will be conscious because it will be directed as far as possible by conscious wills and as little as possible by irrational forces. It will be the result of decisions, to which each citizen will have contributed according to his capacity.

'Living', says Whitehead, 'is a continuous process, during which practical decisions involving action are always being made, and the evolution of society depends on the type of consideration which influences those decisions.'

Majority Rule.—In the last resort those decisions will have to be those of the majority, for democracy is in daily practice the acceptance by the minority of majority rule. Already Aristotle had laid it down some 2300 years ago that 'to democrats justice is that to which the majority agree and to oligarchs that of which the wealthier class approves'. Any democratic system, of whatever form, depends on the ultimate authority of majority opinion, for the alternative would be the supremacy of some minority and this would be neither democratic, nor effective. As we saw when discussing minority rights, the passive acquiescence, if not the active co-operation of the minority is the only method of orderly free government.[1]

The necessity of majority rule is, of course, no admission either of its moral right to dominate or of its infallibility. According to Burke, the majority has no right to alter the framework of society even if it be its pleasure. But if the majority has no such right, then who has? We also find Ibsen, in the 'Enemy of the People', declaring that 'the majority is never right; it has might, unhappily, but right it has not; the minority is always right'. But there is surely no more a Divine Right of the minority than of the majority. The rule of the latter is an expedient, nothing more, but its acceptance solves many practical problems and avoids many a conflict. Of this, however, more later.[2]

The Price of Democracy.—Our supposed citizen must, of course, face the fact that a democratic society is obviously one that makes heavy demands on its members. It requires self-control, discipline, devotion to a common cause, capacity

[1] 'I had rather be ruled by the folly of the many than by the corruption of the few.'—Stephen McKenna in *Sonia*.

[2] 'A majority held in restraint by constitutional checks and limitations, and always changing easily with deliberate changes of public opinion and sentiments is the only true sovereign of a free people. Whoever rejects it does of necessity fly to anarchism or despotism. Unanimity is impossible. The rule of a minority as a permanent arrangement is wholly inadmissible ; so that rejecting the majority principle, anarchy or despotism in some form is all that is left.' (Abraham Lincoln.)

to subordinate to it private interests and desires.[1] It relies on the spirit of give and take.[2] It is 'civilised' because it means precisely being 'civil' to each other, that is, having a concern for other people. It also demands time to share in common activities, to study the issues involved. No wonder that it has been described as 'that form of society furthest removed from nature' but as Ward remarks, 'epidemics and cyclones are natural, and the defences against them are artificial'.

What, after all, is the essential aim and purpose of democracy? 'To make it possible,' as Lindsay says, 'for mankind to live in vast and complex communities while preserving, as far as it is possible, the right of the individual to act as he believes best in accordance with his own conscience, the equal weighing of individual claims to happiness by social institutions, the right and the opportunities of making one's contribution to the common life by one's work, one's reason, one's whole personality'. Democracy is participation, it means doing things in common with others, and taking your share of the responsibilities involved. 'The democratic problem', he concludes, 'is the control of the organisation of power by the common man.'

The Spirit of Democracy.—If these be the marks of a democratic society, it is evident that there is not and never has been, a really democratic society. Democracy is a goal, desirable or undesirable according to one's preferences, and societies have approximated, and are approximating to it in various degrees and in various ways. Driven out by one door, inequality, privilege, injustice, oppression, are apt to come back by another because of the imperfections of human nature. No political system will do away with the evils inherent in the tangles and short-comings of modern society. One just has to go ahead and try, and we may conclude this section by quoting a famous

[1] 'Restrictions, standards, courtesy, indirect methods, justice, reason, sum-up civilisation, making possible a common life, taking others into consideration—in a word, the will to live in common.' (Ortega Y Gasset, 'The Revolt of the Masses,' p. 82.)

[2] 'What about the C.I.O.?' said Mr. White, 'It may be that as a manufacturer I would prefer not to have the C.I.O. and sit-down strikes; it would be simpler and easier; but now here they are, a force, a reality; they must be met and dealt with. How? By bringing our problems into the open and keeping them out in the open; by compromising and getting along somehow as free citizens of the same country.' (Adamic, 'My America,' p. 493.)

passage from the great philosopher Bergson's speech on his reception as a member of the French Academy. 'What is the Democratic Movement?' he asks. And he answers: 'a persistent single-minded aspiration, the natural sequence to the biggest effort ever made to adjust the government of men to the level of reasoning. By proclaiming the equality of rights and the independence of the individual person, the Revolution had erected the Democratic regime into an ideal but had not realised it; for neither in a day nor in a century could sentiment and tradition, which had hitherto been as it were the cement that kept together human societies, be superseded or at least overlaid by that purely rational principle of unification, without which there is no true democracy, and which is a fellowship of freely consented obedience to a superior intelligence and moral quality. How to recruit, how to build up as a governing class, as counsels of government, that new aristocracy, always to be renewed, of talent, efficiency and especially of personal character? There lies the whole problem of democracy; we haven't solved it yet.'

That is unfortunately true enough, but the spirit of democracy does occasionally manifest itself. 'In the harbour of Dunkirk', wrote the *New York Times*, 'the rags and blemishes that have hidden the soul of democracy fell away. It was not mere courage or discipline, nor careful planning . . . it was the common man of the free countries rising in all his glory out of the mill, office, factory, workshop, mine, farm or ship . . . a democratic improvisation of the free creative spirit of people taking charge of events.' Democracy does not always dwell on those heights. It is, as Professor Laski remarks,[1] 'Untidy, slow to act, often confused; it quarrels within itself. But it has deep reserves of energy upon which it can call. If it bends often enough, it very rarely breaks. If it is slow to mobilise its powers, when they are mobilised, it goes on to the end with an impressive determination.' And the Franco-American writer, de Sales, concludes a study of the problem with the optimistic words that, 'Great Britain gives a basis to the hope that new democratic solutions to world problems are possible nationally and internationally.'

[1] In his review of Brogan's 'Free State' in the *Manchester Guardian*.

CHAPTER IX

DEMOCRACY AT WORK

HAVING established democratic principles as the basis for any free society, we now turn to the instruments by which those principles will be realised in practice. Any state, as we saw, has a government—institutions by which the principles on which it rests will be expressed. What institutions will be those of a Democratic free society?

We must begin by admitting with Zimmern that, 'while we live in an age of Democracy, Democracy has not yet discovered its appropriate institutions, nor yet found its form of government; it is still carrying forms from preceding régimes', especially from that of a limited monarchy with a broadly recruited oligarchy or governing class. We shall return to this at the end of the chapter, but it should be borne in mind all the time.

I. REPRESENTATIVE ASSEMBLIES

Direct Democracy.—In a democracy the source and centre of all authority is the people. Not only is everything done in its name, but every law must be traceable back to it, every official must show that his power is exercised as a mandate or trust from it. The ideal would be of course that the people should itself manage its own affairs, decide itself all matters of importance, and choose directly those who carried on in its name the daily routine of government. This was indeed the practice in ancient Athens, where many minor offices were filled by drawing lots, surely the most extreme form of equality of citizen rights. In an assembly meeting practically every day, and in which anyone could speak, the ordinary citizen did really get his share in the business of the state. Athens was not fully democratic, because the citizen class was limited, but citizens really governed the city.

The same condition and practice prevailed wherever democracy of any kind appeared in small communities such . as the medieval city state. Not indeed that all medieval city states were democracies; many restricted political rights to a very small group of wealthy men, usually merchants. But we do know many instances of communities where the citizen class was large enough to form a broadly democratic basis and yet small enough for the town assembly to exercise direct control. The same is true of many small agricultural groups that preserved their autonomy within large states, and sometimes acquired complete independence. In England much local government was carried on for centuries by parish assemblies small enough to need no election of delegates; in America the township meeting remained for long years the centre of public life. In Switzerland, we have seen that several of the smaller cantons have maintained to this day their old tradition of direct government; the popular assemblies, or Landsgemeinde, of Appenzell for instance, still held in the open air at regular intervals, are the survival of this old practice.

Representative Democracy.—Direct democracy is, however, obviously impracticable in large communities, and representation has become almost universal. We have seen how it originated in the Middle Ages as a device used by certain monastic orders and was applied to bodies called by the kings for consultation on questions of broad interest, especially taxation. Under various names: Parliament in England, Estates General in France, Cortes in Spain, Diet in Germany, such bodies appeared towards the end of the thirteenth and the beginning of the fourteenth centuries and were soon playing an important part in national affairs. For instance in 1360 the French Estates rejected and annulled a treaty with England, signed by the French king John in exchange for his liberation (he had been captured at the battle of Poitiers in 1356) and allowed the war to continue and their king to die in prison because the proposed terms seemed humiliating. And by that time the English Parliament had acquired rights of taxation and consultation that made it an indispensable part of the government machine.

These assemblies were of course in no sense democratic. They only represented certain elements in the population, the aristocracy, landed gentry, the rich business men, the higher clergy. But these elements were probably fairly expressive of what may be called the politically conscious elements of the community; there is no reason to think that a larger electorate would have acted differently in any important issue.

Parliament.—With the end of the middle ages monarchy grew more powerful and assemblies were reduced to mere formal duties or indeed altogether ignored. There was no meeting of the French Estate between 1614 and 1789, and the Diets and Cortes did not fare much better. But the English Parliament not only survived but grew in powers, until by the end of the seventeenth century England was the only major country in which a representative body had obtained practically supreme political control. It was not until 1832, however, that the first change was made in the system of representation fixed in the Middle Ages.

During the nineteenth century a number of new processes were at work. In Britain, by the extension of the suffrage to an ever-increasing proportion of the population (Acts of 1832, 1867, 1884, 1918 and 1928) Parliament became more and more representative and powerful, especially in its popular assembly or House of Commons. In other countries the creation of a parliament and its 'democratisation' by a broadening of the basis of the suffrage became the aim of all champions of democracy. In the main, monarchies survived only in so far as they made concessions to the general demand for parliamentary systems.

Modern Popular Assemblies.—Representative institutions, both central as parliaments and local as elected councils, boards, committees, became the distinguishing feature of a democratic state and its indispensable instrument of government. They provided the solution of the problem of reconciling effective authority with the wide treasure of political freedom. It was incompatible with autocracy on the one hand, and with the vagaries of mob-rule on the other. It enabled the authorities to know what was generally desired, and particularly what was not wanted. It guaranteed in other terms a general harmony of purpose between government and governed.[1]

A modern parliament[2] comprises in general two chambers, each elected on a different basis.[3] In a democracy one is elected by adult suffrage, the details and methods of which we shall discuss presently, and this for fixed periods, usually from two (U.S.A.) to five years (Great Britain), four being the usual practice, as in France, Switzerland, the Weimar Republic, etc. It elects its chairman and fixes its own procedure; in most countries it judges of the validity of the elections to itself; in some countries, Britain for instance, this is left to the Law Courts.

It is in that chamber that parliament really claims to represent the people. But this implies the existence of a class of citizens who have the right to choose the community's representatives, and immediately a number of questions arise. What proportion does that citizen class form of the total adult population? How exactly are the desires of this active citizen class reflected in the existing government composition and policy? How close a check does it keep on the activities of that government? How far are the rights of the minority respected?

2. THE ELECTORATE AND THE 'POPULAR' CHAMBER

The Electorate.—Taking first of all the extent of the citizen body, let us remember that there was never any real democratic representation before the establishment of broad adult

---

[1] 'If there be any excellence in the constitution of England, it is that it leaves the inhabitants of every locality to manage their own affairs. It is, in fact, an infinity of republics under one head, which head is not intended to exercise any influence or control over the executive in the different parts of the provinces, but is established to poise and regulate the whole by preventing the jarring which would otherwise be inevitably occasioned by the separate independencies. It is, in fact, the fly-wheel of society interfering with none of the intricacies of its machinery but regulating the movements of the whole.' (Richard Oastler, a Tory Radical of a hundred years ago.)

[2] We shall use this term of all representative assemblies in general.

[3] Medieval parliaments often had more than two. There were three estates in France, and originally four in England. Then the clergy broke away to sit in convocation, leaving only the Bishops in the House of Lords, sitting there first as landed aristocrats, then as spiritual leaders, while the Knights of the Shire and the Burgesses joined forces as Commons, i.e. the communities of the realm, rural and urban. There is nothing sacred or inevitable about bi-cameralism.

suffrage in the second half of the nineteenth century. We have already seen how very small was the citizen body in ancient Athens, and in the medieval city states and in the medieval consultative assemblies, and how slow was the movement for the extension of the franchise. On the other hand there are few, if any, countries today in which the universalisation of the citizen class has not become a fact. A few countries still exclude women, but of these Switzerland is the only one which otherwise would qualify for recognition as a democracy. For good or evil, adult suffrage has come to stay. Not only so, but the equal weighing of all votes is also practically universal. This was not always so; in Prussia voters were divided into four categories, according to wealth, each category having the same number of representatives in parliament, thus securing a heavy over representation of property. In England those who had voting qualification by residence or property in more than one constituency could vote several times, and a university degree also gave an extra vote, but these anomalies have disappeared. One vote, one person, is now a virtually unanimous practice.

Adult Suffrage.—This equality of voting has, of course, been criticised, but is the result of slow evolution or practical experience. To assert off-hand that every person of the age of twenty-one or more has an equal right to a share in the direction of public policy is at first sight absurd. General education, specialised knowledge, a higher level of intelligence and wider experience obviously make some people far better qualified than others. It is also evident that certain people, by their economic interests, have a greater concern than others in the management of public affairs. And yet universal equal suffrage seems to have come to stay. Why?

It is largely the result of experience. To limit the suffrage to those with 'a share in the country' means in practice the running of the country for their benefit, especially in the incidence of taxes, so that these fall mainly on the unrepresented classes. No class likes to tax itself; it always tries to shift the burden on to other shoulders. Democratic suffrage has, of course, tended to put it on the wealthy classes, perhaps to excess, but the overtaxing of the rich is a lighter evil than the overtaxing of the poor, and it seems a choice between the

two. As regards other aspects of fitness for voting, it seems
that no objective method has yet been devised. Who can
measure political intelligence? There may be something to
be said for literacy tests, but many who are technically able
to read never in fact open a book, and rarely a newspaper
outside the sports page, while there are illiterates with plenty
of common sense.

Apart from all this it seems a matter of justice that all those
concerned should have their say. Few problems are more
technical than those of foreign relations, but if all men and
women are to be asked to risk their lives in case of war, they
all have the right to be consulted on policies that may lead to
war. Again, a restricted electorate is not likely to concern itself
with the welfare of the masses, especially when this means
expenditure; only the access of these masses to political rights
has given them the benefits that political rights bring with
them, namely the conduct of public affairs in harmony
with their needs. As Laski says, 'Exclusion from power means
exclusion from the benefits of power', and we may take it as
an axiom of modern politics that the suffrage is both a fundamental right that cannot be denied to anyone, and a contribution that everyone is entitled or expected to make to the life
of the community. The same applies to eligibility; in most
cases whoever may vote may be elected. There seems to be
no sound principle by which the choice of a free electorate
should be limited; if mistakes are made, it must bear the
responsibility and consequences.

Types of 'Constituencies'.—If, however, there is practical
uniformity in the rule as to 'who is to vote', there is no such
uniformity as to 'how people are to vote'. For historical
reasons modern representation has been based on geography.
Members of Parliament represent a particular district, and
are elected by the qualified voters of that area. The elector is
looked upon exclusively as an inhabitant of a certain house,
in a certain street, in a certain village or town. In some countries, the United States for instance, this geographical basis
is reinforced by the rule that the representative must be a
resident of the district he represents.

This is explained in the fact that in the early parliaments it
was indeed the local unit as a group that sent members. It was

the particular town, the country district that was being represented, not the individual inhabitants; the city with its wealth and its wide interests because it was going to be asked, as a city, to make a contribution to royal expenses, being left free to distribute the burden among its citizens as it pleased; the country district as an area of land also worth so much for taxation, and as a unit in the royal system of justice and administration.

It is obvious, however, that geographical residence need not be the only basis. Representatives could stand for professional and religious groups, for instance. It is, however, simpler to keep to the other system, because it gives one a simple basis on which to calculate the proportion of members to electors, and the whole organisation of electoral campaign and election is thereby much easier. It also emphasises the fact that the citizen is acting in his strictly personal capacity. None of these arguments is, however, final, because with modern technique, any basis of representation can be effectively organised if it is desired. If, for instance, a professional is preferable to a geographical basis it can certainly be established. But is it? Professional representation will tend to stress social and class divisions, and to look too exclusively on the citizen as a producer. But he is also a consumer, a member of a family, a churchman and many other things, which are probably better expressed through his home than through his trade union. The suggestion of using function as a basis for a second Chamber may, however, have something to recommend it.

Methods of Election.—Direct election is now the almost universal rule. But indirect or second degree election, has been used and has certain advantages in a very young democracy. It consists in the elector choosing not the representatives, but another group of citizens who alone will make the final choice. The old French Estates were selected in that manner, and, according to the original scheme, so was to be the President of the United States: the American electors do not elect the President, but deputies who will vote for the particular candidate they recommend.

The advantage of the indirect system is that it enables the elector to vote in a much smaller constituency for people whom he knows and trusts, that the 'intermediate' representative is in close touch with the electors and is likely to be better educated and able to make a more enlightened final choice. And indeed the argument is unanswerable where the electorate is illiterate, ignorant of broad issues, and practically able only to choose between two or three men whom it knows. But experience shows that the system breaks down once the selection is made for a party programme rather than for a certain individual. If the elector is voting Red, Blue or White it matters little whether he chooses directly or indirectly: by whatever method his party selection will triumph. The organisation of American parties completely defeated the scheme of the electoral college, which might as well now be dispensed with.

Having secured our electorate, we have to decide exactly how its votes will be expressed. Methods are numerous and cannot be all enumerated and discussed. Small constituencies each choosing one representative? Large ones choosing several? Counting the votes and proclaiming elected the one or those who have the most votes, or a relative majority? Declaring that no one will be elected who does not obtain half the votes plus one, what is termed an absolute majority?[1] Or the system of proportional representation, by which seats are distributed to each party or group in exact mathematical proportion to the number of votes obtained? This last method (or methods, for there are many) is very popular on the continent of Europe. It tends to be accompanied by the equally mathematical distribution of seats in the government to each party in the same exact proportion. The main results are first the encouragement of small parties who have no chance of being numerous enough to form a government but hope for a few seats and perhaps one day one cabinet post; secondly the stereotyping of party divisions and lastly but chiefly, the distortion of the true nature of politics and political representation.

Politics are not mathematics, and the will of the people is not ascertained by arithmetic. Instead of concentrating public opinion on a few broad issues, proportional representation encourages local and sectional interests, and breaks up big coherent forces into small units incapable of adequate

[1] The former has always been the British custom, in most other countries the latter method prevails.

action. It makes impossible the broad large majorities on which effective government is based, and turns every government into a precarious combination of group representatives, liable at any time to be withdrawn by their patrons. It has been an effective agent of ministerial instability, surely a great curse of democratic politics.[1]

Is the Vote Worth Having?—A century ago such a question would have sounded absurd, almost blasphemous! Men made revolutions and sacrificed their lives for the vote. To the disfranchised it appeared as the door for liberation from all their chains. 'Adult suffrage', said Victor Hugo, the poet politician, one day in the French parliament, 'went to seek for man abandoned and despairing, and told him to hope; for the passionate man, and told him to think; for the poor, the rejected, and crowned him as a citizen. What a marvellous increase of dignity for the individual, and therefore of morality! What a satisfaction and therefore what a pacification! See this working man entering the polling booth, he goes in with the sad demeanour of an oppressed proletarian, he goes out with the look of a sovereign.' And coming very much nearer home, many of us remember the violent agitation for women's suffrage in the early years of this century. 'Elections today', wrote Charles Péguy, the French Radical thinker, to a conservative friend,[2] 'strike you as ridiculous, lies, trickery. You have a right to your opinion, but men without number have lived as heroes and saints, men have suffered, men have died, in order that even the most utter fool should have the right to indulge in that ridiculous business, however lying and tricked it may be. You may think that elections are futile, but there was a time, my dear friend, a heroic time, when the sick and the dying got themselves carried to go and drop their voting paper into the ballot box. "To drop a voting-paper into a ballot-box"—such an expression strikes you as highly ridiculous, but it was won by a whole century of heroism. "These elections are futile", you say, but the heroism, the saintliness through which results are obtained which seem futile by temporal standards, these are the greatest, the holiest things in the world.'

[1] See Finer, 'The Case against Proportional Representation' (Fabian Society. 1924).

[2] In 'Notre Jeunesse.'

But now in nearly every country the apathy of voters is one of the commonplaces of politics. There are proposals for making voting compulsory, either fining the unexcused absentee or depriving him of his vote at the next election. Voting, they say, is a privilege that should not be despised. Personally we think that to drag to the poll a voter who is not interested is the sure way to degrade political life and to get ignorant or stupid decisions. After all, a man has a right not to use a right, and is not obliged to be interested in political issues; he may be short-sighted and foolish, and cannot complain if things don't go according to his wishes, but voting or not voting is his own business—that is of the essence of democratic freedom.

Suffrage and Public Opinion.—The fact is that the business of voting for parliament is only part of a democratic system. Elections are made for the purpose of ascertaining what the people want, and to make sure that the policies pursued by the government are in harmony with their desires. 'Elections', as Lowell remarks, 'are saying yes or no to issues, but there are other ways of expressing one's opinion.' Attendance at a meeting of protest against a particular measure may be as effective as voting against a particular candidate. So may supporting or opposing a policy through a trade union resolution or letter to the press. The essential thing is that the government may know what the people think. 'Voting', in fact, as Professor Catlin remarks, 'is a rare and solemn function, but it is taking place every day and every hour'; by all we say and do we are perpetually passing judgement on issues and men, and building up the popular judgement which ultimately decides.

If, however, the vote is not the only instrument by which the voter can express his opinion, it is a most important one, for it is the chief instrument by which through his choice of a representative, the elector expresses his opinion. And in showing what he thinks of the way in which affairs have been managed in the years since the last election, he either desires to have a change or to keep on with things as they are. The experience of elections shows that the elector's instinct is to say no rather than yes, to blame rather than to praise. His tendency will therefore be to try new men and a new programme.[1] Changes

[1] In Britain since 1868, when adult suffrage really became effective, only in 1885, 1900, 1910, 1918, 1935 and 1950 was the government in power

of government after elections are thus more indicative of what the people do not want than of what they positively desire, and at best the electorate's contribution to representation is a consciousness and expression of wants, negative and positive; it lacks the knowledge of what is really possible.

Adult suffrage is now the only basis of any electoral system, but its limitations are evident, and it is futile to ignore them: inadequate knowledge, lazy emotionalism, short-sightedness, quickly arouse prejudice. Left to its devices, the public opinion which the electorate embodies would be both dangerously effective and at the same time ineffectual for any constructive action or considered policy.

3. SECOND CHAMBERS

Second Chambers.—The popular chambers whose method of election we have been studying do not, as a rule, form by themselves the whole representative system. In most parliaments there is another, 'second' or 'upper' chamber. These second chambers take many forms. Britain still has a purely hereditary 'House of Lords'; that of France, in both Third and Fourth Republics, is elected by representatives of local bodies, themselves selected by universal suffrage. In some countries, it is selected by the members of the popular house; in some it is elected by the same electorate as the other chamber but with different kinds of constituencies. In monarchical Italy it was nominated by the crown, and is still in Canada and Jordan.

In federal constitutions the second chamber usually represents the individual states on a basis of equality while the other represents the people on a strictly numerical basis. It may be said that the success of a second chamber is closely related to the logic of the principle on which it is selected.

The respective powers of the two chambers differs greatly. Some second chambers enjoyed absolutely identical powers with the first, except in certain matters of finance. This was the case with the French Senate, and with the House of Lords

maintained. The elections of 1874, 1880, 1886, 1892, 1895, 1905, 1923, 1924, 1925, 1929 and 1945 all resulted in a practical vote of censure on the previous administration.

until 1911. But with the growing pressure of democratic feeling they have now nearly all lost any right of absolute veto; all they can do is to hold up a measure for a limited period of time, or demand its reconsideration;[1] in some cases they may get it submitted to a popular referendum. They have also lost any power of forcing a change of cabinet.

The fact that the powers of a second chamber are now universally limited simplifies the problem of conflict between the two houses. Various devices exist to meet this, however—sometimes a joint session, sometimes a new election of the lower house, sometimes the possibility of increasing the numbers of the upper. Many second chambers have certain functions of their own. The American Senate must ratify all treaties and all appointments to certain important posts and this by a two-thirds majority. In practically every country the second chamber tries cases of treason and serious derelictions of public duty by ministers and high officials, on the accusation by the other chamber, a practice termed 'impeachment'. The House of Lords in Britain is also the final court of appeal from any Court in the British Commonwealth, except from certain Dominion courts.

Second chambers are defended on the ground that popular representation can be over-hasty and needs checking by a less impulsive, more experienced body.[2] Few people nowadays would agree with Sieyès, the French revolutionary thinker, that 'if second chambers agree with the first, they are superflous, if they disagree they must be suppressed as standing in he way of popular will'. It is usually agreed that a well-contructed second chamber, with carefully limited powers, has a useful part to play in criticism and suggested amendment, based on the broader experience of its members and the greater stability of their position.

Granting the utility of a delaying authority, controversy centres round its composition and it must be said that a really satisfactory formula is hard to find. A body of men impartial, experienced and wise would be composed of angels. We

[1] Two years in Britain; three months in France. The American and Canadian Senates are the only important second chambers whose consent is still necessary to any legislation.

[2] For a defence of single chamber government, see Laski's 'Grammar of Politics'.

would incline to a chamber with two elements, permanent members, up to the age of seventy or seventy-five, men who had held certain high offices in the state (colonial governors, ambassadors, retired chiefs of the civil and military services, former prime ministers no longer in the other house)—say fifty of these; then some 200 elected by the county councils for six years, one-third retiring every other year. This suggestion is mainly based on our opinion that the French Senate, shorn of absolute veto power, was as good a second chamber as is likely to be found.

4. THE FUNCTIONS OF PARLIAMENT

The Budget.—It is now time to discuss the proper functions of parliament. Its first duty is to vote the annual budget, without which the state could levy no taxes and have no money to spend. This happens at the beginning of the financial year. This done, it would in theory be possible for parliament to disperse for the next twelve months. Actually parliaments sit usually for two sessions, which cover together rarely less than half the year, usually more. They do so because they insist on doing so, and any government that did not summon them in regular sessions would be violating the written constitution, or, if it did not, would be promptly refused all support when at last it had to call the house for the next grant of financial supplies.

General Control.—What is there besides the budget? First of all, to see how the government governs—by asking questions about the routine of administration, protesting against what may seem to be any abuse of power by officials, expecting the ministers to explain the policies of their departments, ratifying foreign treaties and, in some cases as we saw, certain important appointments. It keeps the government fully informed of what the country is thinking, of what it wants and especially of what it will not stand.

The Cabinet System.—In most countries the next main duty of a parliament is to create and support the directing authority of the government, the cabinet or committee of chief ministers. Since parliament directly represents the will of the electorate, or at least of its majority, it is necessary that the government should represent the will of parliament, or, again, of its majority. The government, as the phrase goes, must 'enjoy the confidence' of parliament. In this system, commonly called the cabinet system, 'the Government carries on the general administration of the country, with the help of parliament, which help is expressed in a permanent and general control of governmental acts, destined to guarantee that the directing ideas which inspire the government's policy correspond with the opinions predominating in parliament, and that control is made effective by the political responsibility of the government before parliament. Its essential condition is a majority in the nation and in parliament.[1]

The 'Presidential' System.—This absolute correspondence between the government and the parliamentary party majority does not exist in what is commonly called the 'Presidential' system of democratic government. The United States is its dominant type, but it is also found in Switzerland and in some South American states. Its essential feature is the election both of the President, as chief executive officer for a period of four years, and of the House of Representatives for two; thus whereas during the first half of his tenure the President is assured of parliamentary support, since the party that put him in power will also have secured a parliamentary majority, he may after two years be faced with an adverse majority that may block his initiatives at every step. The situation is further complicated by the fact that the Senate, renewed by one-third every two years, may be out of harmony with either the President, or with the Representatives' majority, or with both. There is not, therefore, that close co-operation between government and parliament which is secured by the cabinet system.

In both cabinet and presidential systems, however, parliament is ultimately supreme, and has its way in every department of state activity, and this supremacy of parliaments shows the fallacy of what used to be an axiom of political science, the theory of the separation of powers.

Classification of Governmental Powers.—The institutions by which power is exercised are usually classified into three categories, corresponding to the kind of functions for which

---

[1] L. Duguit, 'Revue Politique et Parlementaire', 1900.

they are responsible, and so we speak of the legislative, executive and judicial branches of government, with their corresponding agencies. Under the first come all elected bodies charged with law-making, with laying down rules according to which the state is to be run; under the second, all officials, from the head of the state to the lowest member of those authorities whose work it is to see that decisions are duly carried out; under the third, all those charged with the administration of justice, deciding whether rules have been observed and with dealing with people who have failed to observe them.

This classification has been accompanied by a principle, a dogma we may call it, that those three branches of power must always be rigidly separated, that is, never exercised by the same bodies or individuals. Each, it was said, has its own distinct sphere to which it must keep, and within which it must be absolutely independent; it must never encroach on other branches or be encroached upon; this is an essential condition for the maintenance of democratic freedom.[1]

The theory has been responsible for almost as much unreality and confusion as the doctrine of sovereignty. It is usually ascribed to the French thinker, Montesquieu, in his 'Esprit des Lois' (1755),[2] and was said to be due to an inadequate understanding of the practical working of the British constitution at the time. Actually Montesquieu did not speak of the separation but of the distribution of powers, and was mainly concerned with the danger of all power being monopolised by one individual or group. 'Powers must be shared', he said, 'and the best way by which tyranny will be prevented and freedom secured will be by each of the three powers seeing to it that the other two discharge their functions properly, by each checking the two others, which can only be

---

[1] It was thus defined by the United States Supreme Court : 'It is believed to be one of the chief merits of the American system of written constitutional law that all powers entrusted to the government are divided into three grand departments, the executive, the legislative and the judicial, that the functions appropriate to each of these branches shall be vested in a separate body of public servants and that the perfection of the system requires that the lines which separate and divide those departments shall be broadly and clearly defined.'

[2] Best translated as 'the inner meaning of laws'. The term 'spirit' is an imperfect rendering.

done by a certain amount of overlapping, not by rigid separation, each being to some extent concerned in the work of
the others, while remaining primarily responsible for its own
business.'

The Unity of Authority.—Leaving now what Montesquieu
meant or did not mean, the essential fact is that while some
kind of divisional classification is convenient, power is really
one, and classification of any kind will always be somewhat
artificial and precarious. If a state is really united, authority
comes from one source, however it may be shared, and
a return to that source is always possible in case of difficulty.
Nothing in fact can be more remote from the old theory of the
separation of powers than this constant, perpetual control and
checking of the executive by representative assemblies.
It is really a sharing of executive by the so-called legislative
authority.

Nor is the latter the only law-making power in the state.
There is first of all the fact that most legislation actually
initiates from the executive: i.e. parliaments rarely legislate
except when asked to do so, though proposed measures are
fully discussed and amended by them.[1] Next we must remember that a great deal of legislation not only originates from but
is solely the concern of the executive; ministerial decrees,
orders-in-council, are virtually laws which have no connection
with the strictly legislative authority.

So parliamentary government is essentially the sharing of
power, both executive and legislative, by its two chief organs,
the representative assemblies and the cabinet. To quote
Duguit again, 'In the Parliamentary system political power
belongs to two organs working in continuous co-operation
and checking each other by the reciprocal action they exercise
one on the other: one is an elected, collective organ, parliament;
the other an unitary organ, the government, embodied by a
head of the state.'

Parliament legislates with the help of the government,
which help is expressed in the government's initiation of

[1] This practical monopoly of legislation by the executive is due largely
to the pressure of business; parliament is too busy with governmental proposals to spare time for proposals by private members. It also comes from the
fact that legislation as an expression of policy is the responsibility of the
executive.

bills, participation in their discussion, and ultimate promulgation, with a more or less extended right of veto.

Parliament and Legislation.—Having said all this, the fact does remain that legislation is a most important function of legislative bodies in democracy. It is important, because it is by legislation that changes are carried out in the political structure, and change, that is, adjustment to new conditions, is of the essence of democracy. This is seen by comparing the number of laws voted by the British parliament in any one recent year with the number voted a hundred years ago. In normal times, every cabinet of whatever party expects to carry through at least one major measure in each session, and the fact already mentioned, that there is little time for any measures to be discussed outside the governmental programme, is the genuine grievance of the ordinary private member who might have very valuable proposals to make. The ordinary member is not, in real fact, a legislator, for his law-making function is limited to formal approval of his party's proposals if in office, and disapproval of the government's when in opposition;[1] his real work is to act as a watchdog on behalf of the general public. 'All that Parliament is good for is the ventilation of grievances', wrote Bernard Shaw some years ago.[2] This is an exaggeration; the value of parliaments as organs of discussion and consultation is at least as great. But the remark is a useful reminder of the essential 'representative' character of modern parliaments, which, when functioning freely, remain the essential protection against dictatorship and totalitarianism.

The Referendum and Initiative.—The supremacy of parliament, which is the basis of both cabinet and presidential systems, is really weakened by a device, mainly used in Switzerland but also adopted by the Fourth Republic in France,

[1] Of recent years the only important private members' proposals made into law have been The Daylight Saving Bill, based on proposals made by Mr. William Willett some years earlier and Sir Alan Herbert's Divorce Law Reform.

[2] And more recently in 'Everyman's Political What's What': 'Parliament must survive as a congress of plaintive, plangent Anybodies, with unlimited licence to complain, criticise, denounce, demand, suggest, supply and discuss firsthand information, to move resolutions, and to take a vote on them—in short, to keep the government abreast of public sentiment.'

7

the referendum and initiative. This means the direct popular voting by acceptance or rejection on certain measures; these must compulsorily include all constitutional revisions, and any 50,000 citizens can request one on any law before the parliament; it is also compulsory for any proposed international agreement of a permanent nature. (The entrance of Switzerland into the League of Nations, for instance, was submitted to a referendum.) The second measure, the initiative, is the right of any 50,000 citizens to request parliament to draft and vote on any law which they desire; that law is afterwards submitted to a referendum. (Both measures are used both in the national federal constitution and in many local or cantonal constitutions.) It can obviously only be used when the matter at issue can be settled by a 'yes' or a 'no', and does not allow for any 'halfway' vote, such as agreeing to a measure but only on condition of certain changes in detail. In Switzerland the general effect has been definitely conservative, the majority of proposals being defeated. In France it has so far only been used twice for the adoption of a new constitution; the first consultation rejected the proposed draft, the second accepted an altered scheme which became the present French constitution. The system may sound more democratic than representation, but if it is frequently substituted for parliamentary decisions it obviously diminishes the prestige and power of national representative assemblies.

Responsibilities of Members of Parliament.—Questions, and debate on proposals, whether financial or general, do not exhaust the activities of a member of parliament. We alluded to some of his time going to committees; these are of many sorts. Some are appointed for the preliminary discussion of particular measures; some are permanent, usually corresponding to each main department of state, and examine everything that belongs to their particular subject. In most parliaments a great deal of work is done in those committees, which are further examples of the impossibility of separating executive from legislative functions, for they have, as it were, their right of entry and enquiry into every single aspect of state activity, and are real agents of government.

But a representative's responsibilities are not limited to parliament itself. His duty is also to explain the government's policy to the electors in his constituency, so as to keep them in touch with what goes on and thus ensure their continuous support (or opposition as the case may be). He must also keep the government fully informed of what goes on in the constituencies, of the reactions of public opinion to events and policies; he is essentially an 'agent de liaison' between the people as the source of authority and the government as their agent. Parliament appears, therefore, at every stage of political life as the indispensable representation and translation of the popular will.

The supremacy of parliament is, it must never be forgotten, limited in time. After a few years the house or chamber is dissolved; and few terms are more aptly descriptive: for a while there is just no assembly, it has vanished into thin air, it is indeed dissolved like a cloud or mist before the sun. And members have to keep in mind the certain fact of this dissolution, just as members of certain monastic orders keep their coffin by their bedside, to remember they one day must die. The shadow of an election is in fact a serious handicap to the activities of a parliament in the last few months of its life; it works with an eye on the electorate, watching every reaction and calculating its chances of keeping the favours of that very fickle body. And in addition to this fatal end, parliament, in most cabinet systems, is liable to have its life prematurely cut short by a cabinet decision to dissolve—an eventuality which we shall discuss presently.

How Parliament Works.—The working day of a parliamentary chamber, while obviously differing in details in various countries, will have certain common features. Sessions are usually held in late afternoon and evening, members needing their mornings both for their private affairs and for attendance at committees. The session is usually opened with 'question time', when members may ask the ministers for information on any point connected with their department; we have already seen how essential is this aspect of a parliament's work. Questions over, the debating of some proposed measure is either begun or continued, and it may be that a vote will be taken either on some suggested change or on the proposal as a whole. This vote may be largely a formality if the cabinet's majority is assured: it may be of vital importance if the majority is small and precarious, since a defeat for the cabinet would involve its fall.

It may be thought that if a cabinet is assured of a solid majority a debate is artificial and almost unnecessary; but this would be wrong. The proposals put forward are always tentative in detail. Though fixed in their main lines, the debate may reveal weak points, possible improvements, sometimes actually unworkable features. The experience of both government supporters and opposition members often supplies valuable criticism—or answers to criticisms. Few measures emerge from debate without important changes, and debate is always a reality, however much foregone the final result.

In both cabinet and presidential systems, parliament, we have said, is ultimately supreme. It follows that their success depends on parliament's efficiency. This will depend to some extent on the methods of its election—freedom of the electors, the level of their education and intelligence, satisfactory presentation and discussion of issues—resulting in a well-selected and representative body of members. Once selected, these members must, in their work, fulfil certain conditions. Measures must be adequately debated, in good order, with sincerity of purpose and genuineness of discussion. The freedom of members in debate must be protected from all interference and fear. The programme of parliamentary activity must be carefully planned and announced beforehand. Rules of procedure must be clear and observed. But above all reason must predominate. That is, while the majority must have an unmistakable final word—otherwise nothing would ever get done—the minority must feel secure and protected, and confident that the majority power will be used with moderation. In a word, as Dr. Finer puts it 'the system of government by parliamentary discussion and decision must be accepted as proper and incontrovertible', and the condition to all this is that the majority and minority, government and opposition, should always remember that their respective positions may soon be reversed, and act on the injunction to do as you would be done by. 'But it remains true' as Dr. Finer says, 'that the whole of Parliamentarism is an edifice of conventions erected on a very fragile basis of civilisation.'

CHAPTER X

DEMOCRACY AT WORK

PART II. HOW THE WILL OF THE PEOPLE IS ORGANISED: PARTIES

WE said in the previous chapter that 'left to its own devices the public opinion which the electorate embodies would be both dangerously effective and at the same time ineffectual for any constructive action or considered policy'. But before going any further we should ask ourselves the question: 'What exactly *is* the Public Opinion of which one hears so much?'

I. PUBLIC OPINION

What is Meant by Public Opinion.—The term is usually applied to what people think and want for their common life. It is manifested in every single department of collective human activity; here we are of course only concerned with its manifestation in the political sphere.

Public opinion in politics is not just what people think, nor even that part of their thinking which they express in public; it is what they want to be made effective in practice. There are many things that people like and dislike, but what matters in politics is what they like enough to demand, what they dislike enough to resist. It must be precise enough to be translatable in actual measures and policies, to be or not to be adopted by a government depending on popular support.

Even within that limited sphere, what exactly is public opinion? It is usually the adoption by the greater part of the population of a point of view, of a policy, ideal or prejudice, put forward by some interested person or group, using the various methods of dissemination or propaganda at their disposal—press, book, public meeting, radio, advertising and especially communication from person to person. As a carefully thought out opinion or policy, it remains usually the opinion of a minority; it is only rarely that the majority form a considered judgement on any except the simplest of issues. Few people really think on public affairs; most people accept, negatively at least, one of several competing minority standpoints, which then become majority opinion, unanimity not being of this world.

The degree of the enlightenment of public opinion will be relative both to the general level of education and intelligence and to the honesty and understanding of the opinion-forming groups and leaders. It is, of course, easier to appeal to its prejudices than to its reason; in England fanaticism barred for many years the admission of Roman Catholics to political rights; in the United States it still prevents equality of treatment for negroes in the south; in many countries it blocked the granting of the suffrage to women. On the other hand it is capable of responding to idealistic appeals on great occasions, of accepting rigid and unpleasant disciplines, 'blood, sweat and tears', of recognising great leadership when it is offered it.

But when all is said and done public opinion is not easy to define. 'It is one of those terms', says E. M. Carroll, 'which eludes precise definition. In its common use, it refers to the composite reactions of the general public, but as a rule the only tangible evidence of those tendencies is to be found in the opinion of the more influential leaders.'

How are those 'composite reactions' of the general public to be made clear expressions of what it wants? How is that mass of desires and opinions to become definite enough for governments to act upon it? The answer is 'the party'.

2. PARTIES ARE ESSENTIAL TO ANY REPRESENTATIVE SYSTEM

Whenever we study democratic government we find parties, that is we find that while there are in one sense, as the Latin proverb says, 'as many separate opinions as there are men', these apparently innumerable opinions are in fact grouped along a certain number of definite lines, which correspond roughly to the programme of organised propaganda bodies which we call parties. 'Party divisions, whether on the whole operating for good or evil, are things inseparable from free government.' So wrote Burke and he defined party as 'a body of men united for promoting by their joint endeavours the national interests on some particular principle'. A more modern and complete definition would be 'a group of citizens more or less organised, who act as a political unit and who, by the use of their voting power, aim to control the government and carry out their general policies'.

Variety of Parties.—There is nothing secret about parties. Walk about the street of any large town in a democratic country and you will see at intervals such inscriptions as Liberal, Conservative and Labour party offices in Britain, Republican and Democratic party headquarters in the United States, and in France similar notices concerning the Popular Republican Movement, the United Socialist party, the Communist party, the Republican Democratic Union, and so on. On the walls will be large placards announcing a great Labour rally, or a Liberal demonstration, a Conservative garden fête, and other countries will offer you a similar variety of party organisation and party labels. Again, pick up a newspaper and as often as not you will find it is the mouthpiece of a certain party.

This is very different from the day when party was identified with rebellious factions, when statesmen violently repudiated party labels, when reputable papers advocated non-party government; and even more different from the time when parties were secret organisations, membership of which was punishable with prison or even with death.[1] So universally acknowledged have they become that they are actually officially recognised in some constitutions: in this country, the leader of the opposition is paid a salary; in the German Republic, the law required the posts in the cabinet to be divided among the parties supporting the government in exact proportion to the membership of the party in the Reichstag.

The Necessity of Parties.—Parties are in fact both necessary and inevitable, from the moment when public opinion is consulted as to the policy to be followed. An electorate left to itself is an incoherent mass ; it is essential that in one way or other it should be presented with alternatives between which it may choose. Parties are these alternatives. They offer the

---

[1] The days have reappeared in certain countries, but the penalties affect membership of some particular parties, not of parties in general.

electorate two or more programmes, associated with particular
political leaders who pledge themselves to carry them out if
given power. These programmes themselves represent a
selection made by each party out of the numerous possible
issues of the moment. The problems to be faced are many,
few can be tackled at any one time. The party settles which of
them, in its opinion, can be taken up with reasonable chance
of success if the electorate will agree to the solution offered.
Behind each party programme lies a heap of rejected policies.
As Finer rightly remarks, 'without parties an electorate would
be either impotent or destructive by embarking on impossible
policies that would only wreck the political machine.' [1]

The first role of parties is therefore to define and clarify
the issue for the electorate. They cut roads, as it were, through
the jungle of conflicting individual opinions, each road
offering either a separate destination, or separate ways of
reaching an agreed goal. But without these roads the electorate
would wander aimlessly and ineffectually; and, to abandon the
metaphor it can truly be said that the will of the electorate is
meaningless except as expressed in party programmes.

Parties or Persons?—Someone may ask why are not the
electors asked to choose between leaders rather than between
programmes? There are two answers to this: first, this does
often happen, especially in countries where there are many
parties, with little real difference between some of their
theses. In such cases personality may well weigh more than
programmes. There are parties, in fact, which have been little
else than the personal followers of some distinguished man.
The so called Republican Socialist Group in France was
practically an association of those who followed M. Briand
when he left the official Socialist party.[2] And for many years
in Britain the party struggle was really one between Gladstone
and Disraeli.

Even when the political scene is not dominated by such
giants, parties cannot do without the leaders who, when the
party is in power, will hold the key positions in the govern-

---

[1] The whole treatment of parties by Dr. Finer, in his 'Theory and Practice
of Modern Government' is to be recommended.

[2] When he successfully broke the railway strike of 1911 by mobilising
the railwaymen.

ment. In the party as in the state, ultimate decisions are the work of a few, sometimes prominent in the public eye, sometimes quietly busy behind the scenes. In all spheres of human activity personalities count for much. But after all, even great leaders must do something; they must offer definite plans of action based on certain principles. The elector's choice will still be therefore between alternative lines of conduct, though the personality of the men involved may have much to do with his decision. Neither person nor programme nor principle can be ever totally eliminated, but, unless there happens to be one or more very dominant personalities, which is rare, principles and programmes will matter more. And this is as it should be. Conflict between personalities can easily introduce into politics a violence and a bitterness which more impersonal policies will avoid; they are in fact the open road to dictatorship. And one of the advantages of strict party organisation is precisely that it tends to depersonalise political controversy, and to keep the struggle within the field of principle and collective interests.

Parties and Programmes.—But in insisting on principles rather than on persons there is a danger of laying too much stress on formal programmes. A party is both much more or much less than its official tenets. It is certainly a body of people who want something done, but it is also a body of people who look at politics from a certain angle, who feel in rather the same way. A party represents a political and social temperament which maintains its identity through changing political circumstances, and its programme may be almost an accident. The Italian philosopher, Croce, calls party principles 'pseudo-theories, which only hide the fact of the party as a political will, historically determined and individualised'. At best, theories, he goes on to say, 'express in a form which is apparently logical but is intrinsically fanciful the sentiments and practical tendencies of the party'. Programmes are also largely theoretical; concreteness and reality do not lie in them but in the actual wills of persons joined in these unstable organic and living associations which are called parties.

It is these temperamental differences between parties that often determine a man's politics. It is scarcely an exaggeration to say with Sir William Gilbert that 'every boy and every gal that's born into this world alive, Is either a little Liberal or else a little Conservative', only that one should now add 'or a little Socialist'. Party affiliation may be in fact as much a matter of family tradition, of environment as membership of one of the great world religions. Many people belong to a party much as they belong to a church; they accept what it generally stands for in the world without necessarily endorsing all that it does or says; they are one thing because they are definitely not the other, and one has to be something. 'A party', as Mocher says, 'represents not a homogeneous block of identical opinions, but a range of opinions lying within rather vaguely determined limits'. It has its left wing and its right wing, and all left wings have much in common and so have all right wings, for these are expressions of temperament rather than intellectual conviction, while people who are just on two sides of a boundary line may be much nearer to each other than to those of the same group at the other extreme.

3. THE FUNCTION OF PARTIES

If parties are necessary in any form of democracy, they are indispensable in the cabinet or parliamentary type of government. As elections will have been fought on party lines, parliament will, in practice, express in its composition the strength of the parties in the electorate, and in its turn the government will be the expression of the party strength in parliament. This expression will not be absolutely mathematically exact, unless proportional representation is rigidly adhered to both in elections and in the distribution of seats in the cabinet, but it will be exact enough to secure the acceptance by the electorate of what parliament will do and reject, and guarantee a harmony of purposes and policy between parliament and government. The cabinet or ministry depends for power on maintaining a majority in parliament; the day this majority disappears, it must resign. Now if there were no parties, if members of parliament were completely disorganised and formed only a mass of men voting one way today and another way tomorrow, the government could not tell how long it could stay in power. It would have no stability, no power to plan any coherent policy. With governments depending on parliamentary majorities, there must be parties and, whether few or many, these parties will inevitably form two camps or sides, the ministerial supporters and the opposition. As soon as the opposition obtains a majority it outvotes the government party and takes its place, and the former ministerial party becomes the opposition.

Thus if the first role of the party is to sort the issues for the electorate, its second is to supply the majorities without which governments cannot remain in power. Its third function is to provide alternative teams to run the Government. It prevents the same people being in power too long and looking on office as a matter of right. It is a guarantee that if the electorate wants a change this can be effected without trouble. And changes in government may be desirable without any radical change of programme. Power tends to corrupt, to make men feel important. How wholesome to know that you can be replaced tomorrow, that you hold your job on good behaviour only![1]

Two Parties are General.—It is evident that this system will work best when there are only two parties. The government will be homogeneous, with a clearly defined policy, and so will the opposition. But in fact two-party systems are rare, and have been usually confined to the two Anglo-Saxon democracies. In Britain a third party has developed in the last fifty years but seems to have succeeded in virtually ousting one of its rivals, the Liberal party, so that the two-party system has in fact been restored.

But this is the exception. Multiple-party systems have been the normal rule ever since parliamentary institutions developed outside Britain and the United States. The reason is, that while occasional issues may appear on which only two attitudes are possible, parties usually stand for programmes, of which there may be a considerable variety. It is also true that a number of problems which still divide public opinion in many countries were settled many years ago in England and America. No opposition to monarchy has ever appeared in Britain, nor

---

[1] This, we believe, is the answer to those who complain like Mr. Belloc in his 'Servile State' that party divisions are artificial and are only fights for office. Even if there were no dividing principle, even if the alternation of power were a virtually 'arranged' procedure, the very alternation itself would be valuable.

to republicanism in the United States. In neither of them are religion, or freedom of association, or liberty of speech and expression political issues. Neither contains a national minority nor important elements advocating revolutionary changes in the social structure. Both have achieved complete adult suffrage. The relation of central to local authority was never a serious problem. And in the issues that remain, either there is a clear cut division, or the differences are more in the speed of progress than in actual direction.

It was therefore an American, Thomas Jefferson, who divided electors between 'those who fear and distrust the people and those who identify themselves with the people', and an Englishman, John Stuart Mill, who said that 'a party of order and stability and a party of progress or reform are both necessarily elements of a healthy state of political life'. But citizens of any other country might shake their heads and say that politics were not as simple as all that.

Party Traditions.—And it should be noted that the reduction of American and British parties to two was only possible by the fact that they admitted very wide divergence of opinion within their borders. We have already remarked that each party contains on its fringes members who were really much nearer to the members of the other party than to their own at the other extreme. Many Conservatives are nearer to moderate Labour than to the die-hards; many moderate Labour men are nearer to the Conservatives than to their own members on the edge of Communism. But the parties remain united before the world because of long historical traditions and attachment, because of similarity in a few essential principles, because of discipline, of the fear that breaking away would only create new political groups, destroy cohesion and bring about the uncertainties and confusion of multiple-party politics.

Things have worked out otherwise in the political parties of continental Europe and of certain other non-European countries. Many vital issues are still undetermined, such as forms of government, relations of Church and state, and they enlarge the area of party conflicts. Parties are also much more recent, have no old traditions to maintain and cherish, and are still sometimes looked upon as abnormalities, hostile to national unity (a proof only that the essential function of party is not yet understood). There is often also a complete ignorance of the essential rules of party politics—moderation in victory, reasonableness in attack, and the discipline which keeps the party together by unity on vital issues and agreement to disagree on the less important.

Parties and Religious Denominations.—In his 'History of European Liberalism' the Italian writer Ruggiero offers an interesting explanation of this last fact: 'In order to understand the positive value of political parties, there is required the experience of religious sects, where the very multiplication balances them and produces an equilibrium, and a new congregation can attempt to prove the soundness of its doctrine by the purity of its life and the skill of its propaganda. Now parties are nothing but religious sects, where the attachment of a common welfare compensates and counteracts their original particularism. A party is a particular way of looking at the whole, an individual conception of the whole government, precisely as the religious sect is a special way of worshipping the one God.' But he goes on to say this can only happen in Protestant countries. In Catholic countries the mass of the population will never be able to grasp this fully. Truth to them is one; there is no diversity in unity; you are either a Catholic or a heretic.

Multiple Parties and Cabinet Instability.—Whatever the reason for the existence of multiple parties, their existence has established in their countries a tradition of cabinets built upon combinations of coalitions and groups, often in a very unstable equilibrium. Parliamentary France had on the average three cabinets a year during the Third Republic, and whereas it is very rare for a British cabinet to last less than one year, it is almost as rare for a French one to last as much.[1] Another

[1] The following comparison between France and Britain between 1871 and 1928 is eloquent. France had thirty-eight premiers of whom twenty-three were premiers for one year or less. Between 1868 and 1929 Britain had eleven premiers (Gladstone, Disraeli, Salisbury, Rosebery, Balfour, Campbell-Bannerman, Asquith, Lloyd George, Bonar Law, Baldwin, MacDonald), of whom only two held office for less than one year.

During those fifty-seven years the French had twenty-eight ministers for War, thirty-two for Navy, thirty-four for Justice, thirty-five for Commerce. Only in the Foreign Office with fourteen incumbents was there any continuity comparable with that of Britain's eleven Foreign Secretaries in the same period (Clarendon, Derby, Salisbury, Granville, Rosebery, Lansdowne, Grey, Balfour, Curzon, MacDonald, Austen Chamberlain).

consequence of these coalitions is that policies are a compromise based on what can be made acceptable to all concerned. Instead of a party winning an election on a definite programme, and settling down to a practically assured tenure of several years, during which it can realise that programme, you get an insecure coalition, with only a vague plan of action, carrying scrappy and piecemeal legislation, not knowing sometimes literally from one day to another how much longer it will be able to carry on.

4. THE ORGANISATION OF PARTIES

Party Permanency.—It follows from all this that permanency and organisation are essential to a satisfactory party system. Organisation, for without it parties will remain vague, shapeless, mere tendencies to similar views but not units capable of doing their real work, which is controlling the government; permanency, because obviously parties that lived only for a short while would never have any definite influence. It is here again that the multiple-group system is at such a disadvantage. Whereas the old parties of Britain and America have many years of continuity behind them, while at the same time adapting to changing circumstances, groups are made one day and unmade the next, often around some passing issue or temporary problem; they rarely have time to develop lasting traditions or loyalties. And the shortness of their life is reflected in the precariousness of their control; instead of dominating government, they often become an instrument in the hand of a clever politician. The history of the Third Republic in France shows that only those two political associations that developed real party organisation and permanence—Radicals and Socialists—were able to exert any lasting positive influence.[1] Practically the whole of the effective legislation of the last fifty years has been the work of the collaboration of those two parties.

Party a State within a State.—An organised party is almost like a small state within the big one. It has its active membership and its passive adherents, its local branches or constituencies, with their agencies for propaganda, fund collecting and

[1] This would also be true of the Communists in the Fourth Republic.

recruiting, its election to the party assemblies or parliaments, responsible for its choice of leaders and officials, and the adoption of the party policy. 'By degrees which to the ordinary citizen were imperceptible', says Finer, 'these nation-wide fellowships have come into being and organise themselves with a gigantic and complex apparatus. They possess buildings and newspapers, printing presses and advertising experts, songs and slogans, heroes and martyrs, money and speakers, officials and prophets, feast days and fast days; like all religions they disrupt families and produce heretics, and among their agencies of discipline and subordination are the novitiate and penance.'

By the side of this central organisation, the local party branch plays a most important part in the life of a democracy. It provides the ordinary citizen with a chance to express his views freely and easily, gives him both knowledge of public affairs and practice in speaking and debating, enables him to influence the policy which will be adopted at the party conference. It is there that he will emerge from obscurity, become known locally and then later in a larger sphere. A well-run party branch is a school of democracy and public life. It also provides headquarters with information as to what is being thought and said, and is a kind of open window on local public opinion. To change the metaphor, the party branch is a local unit of the army, provides the recruits, and is also a centre of intelligence as to what is going on within the party and in the country in general.

An Army that Prevents Civil War.—The military metaphor is not out of place. A party is in fact a fighting organisation and must be equipped and organised as such. It is the army which is out to conquer power and, as Finer says, 'Victory is the first law of Politics'. Its phraseology is one of war: battles, defeats, victories, strategy, tactics, generalship, treason even. There is a constant talk about the need for single-minded action, for unity before the enemy, about the danger of wasted energy. Each attacks the other, often in the most violent terms, and a stranger to party politics, on reading the party press, or being present at party meetings, would easily think that the country was on the eve of a civil war.

And yet civil war is precisely what the party system prevents.

It is essentially the peaceful settlement of disputes that might otherwise lead to violence. It is the alternative to revolution, 'Putsch' or 'Coup d'état'. The stronger the party organisation the more likely it is to face domestic problems with success. It is in the countries with weak parties that constitutional government goes under easily, as in Italy in 1922, in Germany in 1933, and there is little doubt that the strength of British and American party systems is their best safeguard against overthrow by dictatorships of right or left.

5. PARTIES IN HISTORY

Parties arise out of great issues dividing public opinion, provided that this opinion is sufficiently free and able not only to express itself but to exert a direct influence on affairs. Because of this, they could scarcely arise under absolute monarchies, or, if they did they could only obtain their ends by revolution. Such were also the factions that divided the medieval city states, usually held together by common devotion or opposition to particular individuals rather than by common positive principles. But when representative assemblies wrested sovereignty from the kings, they provided a peaceful battlefield for rival groups who fought their battles in elections and in parliament. Ballots replaced bullets in political strife and heads were counted instead of being broken —one of the great victories of commonsense in politics.

English Parties in the Seventeenth Century.—In their modern form parties first appeared in England, the country where representative assemblies first became really powerful or important, and they reflected from the very beginning the variety and confusion of issues along which they were to be divided. Their basis appeared first of all as a mixture of religion and politics, control of government being sought primarily to establish toleration for all Protestants and prevent the development of Roman Catholicism. But as the royal power was identified with the freedom of Catholics, resistance to royal power was inseparable from the religious campaign. The first clear alignment of the English parties can be seen in the division around the Grand Remonstrance in November 1641, a document which condemned in detail both the political and religious policies of King Charles the First. How evenly forces were divided is shown by the fact that it was only carried by a majority of eleven votes; how important was the vote is shown by Cromwell's statement that if it had gone the other way, he would have sold his property and emigrated to America.

The defeated Royalist minority, however, did not accept the verdict and civil war began. With its end and with the restoration of the monarchy under Charles the Second, party divisions seemed to fall into abeyance; but some twenty years later they reappeared when the religious issue again became dominant over the probable succession to the throne of a Catholic prince, brother of Charles the Second. Those who wanted to exclude him in the name of Protestantism, and who asserted the right of the nation through parliament to alter the succession, became more or less organised under the name of Whigs, while the Tories upheld the Divine Right of the King to pursue whatever religious policy he pleased, and denied the supremacy of parliament.

After the Whig victory of 1688, Divine Right died out as a theory of government and the religious problem dropped out of politics. But the parties remained divided, first over the issue of the relative position of king and parliament and, when that was finally settled in favour of the latter, over the broader problem of popular sovereignty.

Parties and Economic Divisions.—This politico-religious division, however, hid another cleavage, as deep, perhaps deeper, arising out of changing economic conditions. As long as the land and agriculture dominated the scene, together with the Church, their control represented a fixed state of things with little change of policy and no room for serious divisions of opinion. As Finer says, 'Government under such conditions is not created or divided by the changing balance of opinion. The opinion of the subject orders has little to do with the policy of the state. The ruling classes ruled together in perpetuity because they depended on tradition, not on opinion. Their rule implied sheer fixity, based on a claim to inviolate right.'

Then came the economic and social changes associated with the increase of trade and commerce and the growth of cities.

The new forces began to organise themselves against the old, and the old to do the same in self-defence. The economically and socially conservative forces naturally became politically conservative also, and the Tory party defended not only monarchical and religious tradition but also agriculture and the interest of the land while the Whigs stood for industry and the interests of the merchant class. Political issues concentrated in the nineteenth century on the extension of the suffrage and on what we call 'social reform', by which time the Whigs had become Liberals and the Tories the Conservatives. But the economic lines of division, while adapting themselves to new circumstances, did not fundamentally change, the Liberals representing the manufacturing and commercial interests that demanded free import of raw material and foodstuffs against the Conservative defence of the farmer, and to some extent of the small independent shop-keeper uninterested in export policies.

Neither of the two original parties was concerned, however, with any drastic alteration in the existing social and property system. Both were dominated by the upper middle class and could well be termed 'bourgeois' parties. And the same was true of the two American parties, and of the less organised but nevertheless quite recognisable parties in European continental countries.

Parties in Other Countries.—In the United States the line of division was originally the degree of autonomy to be left to the individual states of the Union, complicated by the conflicts between agricultural and industrial interests. This conflict was first fought around tariffs and later around slavery and the right of secession. After the civil war both slavery and secession ceased to be practical issues, and economic differences became so attenuated that it became difficult at times to find fundamental points of differences. For many years the party conflict was the shuffle of office and its spoils, though later the issues became more personal and were fought around the personalities of Wilson and F. D. Roosevelt.

The French parties made a brief appearance in the revolutionary era, there being three main tendencies, reforming Royalists, reforming or moderate Republicans and extreme terrorist Republicans. Napoleon destroyed both the issues and the parties, but they reappeared after the restoration of the monarchy in 1814. For many years three main alignments could be seen—Conservative Monarchists, Reforming or Liberal Monarchists, and Republicans. Later on the first of these collapsed and party conflict was driven underground by the repressive measures of Napoleon the Third. With the Third Republic Royalism died out after 1870 and the Republican ranks became divided into a considerable number of groups, whose programmes varied mainly on the relation of Church and state and the questions of social reform. In certain countries another line of party division has been national, parties being the spokesmen of national groups. In many countries there exist parties pledged to the defence of Catholic interests, especially in the sphere of education and social legislation, usually in opposition to parties defending disestablishment of Churches, the state control of schools and easy divorce.

The Socialist Party.—But by the end of the nineteenth century dominant issues were being created by the appearance of Socialism.[1] There are innumerable definitions of this movement, but here we need only regard it as the entrance into politics of the workers as a class, challenging the monopoly of power and policy hitherto enjoyed by the bourgeoisie. They forced the older parties to a drastic reconsideration of their programmes, gained the full adhesion of some of their members, obtained from others a measure of support for some of their proposals, and finally drove others into open or camouflaged opposition to the new force. Its appearance proved once more the fact that the two party alignment is, as Dr. Finer calls it, 'The political form of the great alternative which everywhere presents itself in human activity'.

The problem of the social control of property began to colour all political discussion. In England the Liberal party ceased, as we saw, to be one of the two dominant parties and only maintained a precarious existence; in France the same fate befell the Radicals. In the United States on the other hand Socialism has so far failed to make any deep impression in party politics. It is too early to say exactly what effect the new challenge of Communism will have.

[1] See Chapters XIII and XIV.

Socialism did not transform existing political parties into class parties, but revealed their hitherto hidden class characteristics; together with the newly developed economic interpretation of history. It showed the extent to which, both now and in the past, 'their economic principles turned upon those views of economic constitution with which, at any given time, the nation was deeply concerned', and how 'parties were predominantly organisations which sought to determine the economic constitution of the state, and were only intelligible in the light of that understanding', as Laski puts it. But emphasis must be put on the words 'dominant' and 'predominantly', for economic issues, important as they are, are not the only ones. Parties remain complex products of political and religious factors as well, and all elements can be compounded in a considerable variety of ways, largely determined by historical and psychological circumstances.[1]

Party and Class.—But however important the economic element in party alignment, one must not confuse party and class. 'Class' to begin with is a most difficult term to define exactly. It can be used socially, of people with similar habits of life, people who normally live together and intermarry, and it can be used economically, of people with the same kind of income derived from the same kind of work[2] and therefore with similar interests to defend. A class again has no clear limits, nor any definite programme of action, while party has these, and is in many ways as precise and exact as a class is the reverse.

The difference between party and class is shown by the fact that in a modern state all parties appeal for the support of

[1] An interesting article in the *Revue Socialiste*, entitled 'The Three Dimensions of the Political Heavens', distinguishes in each of the three domains, religious, political and economic, two main attitudes that may be called the dogmatic and the liberal. The author thus obtains eight possible combinations. A—capitalist, authoritarian, dogmatic; B—capitalist, authoritarian, liberal; C—democratic, capitalist, dogmatic; D—democratic, capitalist, liberal; E—authoritarian, socialist, dogmatic; F—authoritarian, socialist, liberal; G—democratic, socialist, dogmatic; H—democratic, socialist, liberal. Of these, A and B represent traditional conservative Catholicism, C and G the Catholic centre and Liberal groups, D the English Liberals, E Russian Communism, H real Socialism.

[2] A clergyman with £300 a year, a laboratory assistant with £25 a month and a skilled mechanic with £6 a week earn exactly the same money but belong to different economic, no less than to different social classes.

the workers, both industrial and agricultural. A real workers' party would have a monopoly of power, for the vast majority of the electors in all countries belong to the working class. The Conservative party owes its position to its successful bid for workers' votes made by Disraeli in his programme for Tory democracy, endorsed by his successors in the Conservative leadership, and for many years the Liberal party lived on the working class votes gained by its appeal to the nonconformists and by its Lloyd George radicalism. The loss of most of this support to the Labour party explains its present weakness. The French Conservative parties depended largely upon the five million small farmer owners. It is hard to see in fact, how any political party, in any country, could subsist without proletarian support. On the other hand the more radical and even revolutionary parties have always numbered adherents from the propertied classes who have often supplied them with some of their most effective leaders. Neither Marx, nor Lenin, nor Jaurès, nor Blum, nor Attlee, nor Postgate, nor Litvinov, are of proletarian origin.

Class struggle would mean in fact the end of party struggle. Instead of rival sets of programmes appealing for support, with the victors of today the possible defeated of tomorrow, you would get solid masses fighting for concrete interests, with the certainty of ultimate proletarian victory owing to superior numbers; after which party divisions would appear in the victorious proletariat, as they certainly would in Russia if freedom of discussion was allowed. It is, of course, open to anyone to advocate class struggle, on the ground that it is real while party controversies are often artificial. But that is another matter. Those who want to reduce to its absolute minimum the element of civil war in politics will continue to defend the party system as their best guarantee; they will welcome the existence of 'Conservative working men's clubs' and the presence in Socialist ranks of numerous men of wealth and aristocratic origin. It may be, however, that the trend of world politics is going to force all of us into defence or attack of a political order where economic class will be the primary consideration.

6. WEAKNESSES AND STRENGTH OF THE PARTY SYSTEM

There are, of course, certain defects inherent in the party system, nothing human being perfect. It does sometimes tend to an over-simplification of complex issues in order to make easier the appeal to an untrained public opinion. It tends to discourage independence of thought and action and to give the non-party man little chance of entering politics; and within the party the independent member is frowned upon by the leaders who like the man who will blindly accept the party lead and programme, speak and vote as he is told.

It is also true that occasions may arise when a party is sorely tempted to profit from some crisis, to exploit to its own advantage a difficult situation. It is hard not to mis-represent rivals, not to benefit from their mistakes and not to watch for any opportunity either of turning or of keeping them out of office. All this is true, but electors are not asked to decide complex issues but to choose between two or more groups of men; these will judge issues as they come, according to certain principles between which any reasonable intelligent person can choose. After all, the number of possible attitudes to political questions is limited. Even if the two sayings of Mill and Jefferson quoted earlier are felt to be over-simple, there are few people who cannot accept the general policy of one of the dominant parties.

Parties and Local Politics.—This also answers a frequent criticism made of the party system, namely its introduction into local politics. Party divisions, it is argued, were built up around national issues, which have no counterpart in the affairs of municipality and county. These are either technical, and local representatives should be chosen on grounds of technical capacity, or they are purely local, and candidates should be chosen on their knowledge of local affairs.

It is probably true that the problems of village councils may have little in common with that of the state. But a county or large town with hundreds of thousands of residents is no smaller than a small state. Further, issues have usually to be decided according to principles or attitudes which are much the same wherever one goes. The arguments for muni-cipal control of public undertakings such as gas, electricity, or transport are much the same as those for their nationalisation. Those who advocate extensive national social services will be the same as those who want their city to be generous in the way of schools, poor relief, hospitals, etc. Actually independent members do get occasionally elected to local councils, where they often do excellent work, but experience shows that they usually tend to side with one party; their election is often due to the non-appearance of candidates of that party, and they often ultimately migrate into a party fold.[1]

As regards other criticisms the answer is, first, that to use to one's own advantage the mistakes of one's rivals, to put the worst construction on his actions, even to misrepresent him is not special to parties; it occurs whenever men compete for power, whatever the system. Nor is excessive independence of judgement welcomed outside the party system. The really independent man is rarely to be found in the management of public affairs. Again the criticism that party means appealing to the masses, sometimes not on their highest levels, is also true of all governments, none of whom, whatever their form, dares disregard public support. A people that misuses and corrupts a party system is not likely to make a great success of any other form of self-government, for which it is probably unfit.

Parties and Administrative Efficiency.—The party system has on the other hand certain very definite advantages. If it is useful to the electorate as a clarifier of issues, it is no less useful to the executive as a check on officials and a great instrument in preventing corruption and slackness. With other parties always on the alert to detect weaknesses in its management of public affairs, a party is kept 'up to scratch'. Scandals are less likely to occur if their detection is a practical certainty. One must admit on the other hand, that party patronage for executive posts outside the initiation of policy leads to the intrusion of party differences where they should not exist.[2]

---

[1] We remember supporting with enthusiasm the candidature of an independent candidate for the city council of a northern industrial town in England some twenty-five years ago. In less than one year he had joined the party most opposed to the views of his supporters.

[2] The elimination of party from civil service appointments by anonymous competitive examinations in Britain and France stands in good contrast to the American system of spoils by which many administrative and even judicial posts change hands with the varying fortunes of a party.

More fundamental than all this is the still fairly widespread tendency to establish a contrast or contradiction between party politics and national affairs,[1] to accuse men of putting the party before country, of taking a party view of the issues of the day. 'What we want', those critics say, 'is not government by a section, but by all able men of goodwill, and capable of sinking their party differences for the common good.' And they speak of 'business governments', or of the 'l'union sacrée' or of the 'national cabinets'.

Party Interest and National Interest.—Many of those who speak in this way are perfectly sincere but fail to understand the meaning and purpose of party. The success of the 'Coalition Governments' in time of war is due to the fact that in war-time there is only one dominant issue, before which all others count for nothing, national survival; co-operation between parties is easy because to all practical purposes there are no longer parties.

Let us go back to our starting point. Parties arise from the variety of opinions concerning the nature of national problems and their solutions. Party is the alternative to unanimity; it only exists because men disagree. When, therefore, there is no disagreement about essentials, as in the case of war, then party disappears. And even then it sometimes happens that the manner of conducting the war, and particularly of ending it, creates divisions, sometimes corresponding to normal party divisions, but often cutting across them.

The same national union might conceivably appear in the face of a national emergency of another kind—some natural disaster such as earthquake or flood. But once the emergency was over and normal problems reappeared, so would party divisions, and this is as it should be, for they correspond to different solutions to those problems. All are equally concerned for the national welfare, but all do not see the same way to secure it. If the doctors around the patient disagree about diagnosis and therefore about treatment, the only chance for the sick person is for him to choose the doctor who inspires

---

[1] 'Although I am a Conservative and would like the support of the Conservative party, I do not agree with the introduction of party politics into local government, and should, if elected, strongly oppose Socialism in all its forms. (Election manifesto, quoted in the *New Statesman*.)

him with the greatest amount of confidence and let him go
ahead. If the doctors tried to 'co-operate' then the various
treatments used would either neutralise each other, or more
probably kill the patient.

'Party' and 'Country'.—It must be repeated and remembered
that party is not in contradiction with country—it is an interpretation of the country's needs and of the programme of
action for which it calls. Inter-party co-operation in normal
times is to ask people to apply measures in which they do not
believe to a situation which they think calls for something
quite different. Insincerity would lie in such a shelving of our
beliefs, not in acting on them. When Mr. Attlee and his
colleagues call for nationalisation of the industries while Mr.
Churchill and his friends urge free enterprise, neither is being
more sincere and patriotic than the other; both are concerned
with the welfare of the country and see its realisation in the
adoption of the policy they recommend. But to ask them to
'place country before party', to 'forget their sectional differences and co-operate in a common programme of national
economic reconstruction' is asking them to be untrue to themselves, to put their real convictions into cold storage, and for
the sake of office, to take responsibility for policies which
they think ineffective and dangerous.

The attack on party politics sometimes comes, however,
not from ignorance or misunderstanding but from downright
political dishonesty. It is common for people to denounce as
'partisan' or 'sectional' whatever they dislike, and to claim
the adjective 'national' or 'non-party' for whatever they like.[1]
Experiments in non-party politics usually turn out to the advantage of the one party which happens to be either less scrupulous than the others, or which for some reason holds the key
positions. The national union of post-First World War France
consisted in neutralising certain political groups which might
have been dangerous opponents to the majority; the so-called
'non-party ticket' became in fact a party ticket camouflaged
under the name of 'national block'. And we all know what
national government has meant in Czechoslovakia. The cry
for a national government, in fact, often comes from a party

[1] 'The choice between the electorate next time will be between the national
government and the Socialist Caucus.' (M.P., *Isle of Wight Country Press*,
quoted in the *New Statesman*.)

that expects to be beaten at a forthcoming election, and should not be taken too seriously.

The Party and Political Life.—Party has thus come to play an essential part in our democratic politics—'the power behind the throne, the centre of political gravity', as Finer calls it. It has become one of those spontaneous groups and fellowships which demand our loyalties and often offer a larger life and fuller activity than can be found in purely individual action. Like the church or the trade union, it is integrated in the collective life, and cannot be separated from it or held up in opposition to it. The party, as we saw in the quotation from Ruggiero, plays in political life the role that the separate denominations play in religious. They are parts of a larger whole which they severally try to interpret.

'The phenomenon of party government is remarkable', concludes Finer. 'Does it not need an extraordinary restraint upon human passions to permit part of the ordinary machine of government, an organised opposition, to undermine the government of the day, to enter upon weeks and years of demagogy and militant tactics to excite the people and return with the power to reverse decision? It sounds as if in other days, it would have been judged, like treason, disruption, revolution or battering at the foundation of the state. It would have been met with executions, proscription, the suppression of the freedom of opinion and open violence. Not all countries have been able to maintain these rules of electoral self-control.'

The party system in politics is not unlike those games in which the team counts for more than the individual player, whose success is bound up with that of his side. It is an important lesson in the necessity of co-operation. Men learn that they must line up with others in order to be effective, that he who plays an entirely lone hand and disregards team work is not likely to achieve much. Finally, party, like the whole of democracy of which it is an essential element, is basically rooted in the belief in the rationality of men, in appeal to argument and discussion, rather than either to emotion or to violence. No wonder that Asquith, the greatest English parliamentarian of modern times, said once that he believed in party because it was 'the most wholesome way of conducting politics'.

CHAPTER XI

DEMOCRACY AT WORK

I. THE DECIDING OF POLICY: THE CABINET

In a Democratic country the body primarily responsible for policy is a committee of men (often now of women too) who are in general control of the whole machinery of the State. This committee is sometimes called the 'Cabinet', sometimes 'Council of Ministers', and its members are invariably termed Ministers of State. It usually numbers anything from half a dozen to twenty or more, each minister being in charge of one (sometimes more than one) of the main departments of State activity, to which we shall come later. It is usually presided over and always formed and directed by one of them, termed Prime Minister, or President of the Council of Ministers.

The Ministers?—Who are the ministers? As a rule anyone whom the head of the state appoints. Membership of parliament is not usually constitutionally necessary. In Britain, however, the fact that no one may speak in either House of Parliament unless he belongs to that House makes it impossible for a non-parliamentarian to hold office for long, since one of his essential functions is to explain and defend in parliament the work of his department, but in France ministers may speak in both Houses even though they are ministers of neither. In practice, however, the only normal road to office is a parliamentary career, and ministers are therefore men (and sometimes women) who have made a sufficient mark in some line of work to be selected as parliamentary candidates, who have successfully run the gauntlet of elections, and have had some years of experience of public affairs as an ordinary member. They come to office therefore with what should be normally a broad knowledge of the way in which politics are managed in their own country, of what the electorate wants, of what the government is likely to try and do, and of the probable reaction of public opinion to particular measures. They may indeed have no special technical knowledge of the particular department they have to administer, but this technical knowledge will be supplied by their permanent staff; what is wanted of them is to be able to relate the general lines of their departmental work to those of the cabinet policy as a whole, to make their department work smoothly and efficiently by getting the best out of their assistants, and be themselves co-operative members of a team charged with responsibilities that may suddenly be of vital importance to the national destinies.

The cabinet thus constituted will, according to the party system of the country, be made up either entirely of members of the same political faith (single-party government) or of members of somewhat differing affiliations, yet able to agree on a programme of immediate common action (multiple-party system). In either case the cabinet is formed by the person who seems, to the head of the state, best able to form a team in conformity with the existing parliamentary majority. Under the single party system there is usually no real choice, the leader of the majority party being the only possible prime minister.[1] In the multiple system there is often some margin of choice, and the head of the state then exercises for a brief moment an influence on affairs that may be decisive. In the United States the President is, as it were, his own prime minister, selecting freely his colleagues save for the provisos of ratification by the Senate and non-membership of Congress.

The Premier.—The premiership of a smoothly working parliamentary democracy is one of the most important centres of real power in the modern world.[2] Although he is

---

[1] In some countries such as France, the head of the state may sometimes preside over the cabinet meetings. The President of the United States is chairman of his cabinet.

[2] The only time since 1868 when the Crown has had any choice in the matter was in 1923 when King George V could have made Lord Curzon Premier instead of Mr. Baldwin but passed him over because he thought the Premier now had to be a member of the House of Commons. Queen Victoria tried in vain in 1880, 1885, and 1892 to keep Mr. Gladstone out of the Premiership.

technically only one of the ministers, and paid as such, the premier is their recognised head, the real initiator of their common policy, the linch-pin of the cabinet. If he resigns the whole cabinet automatically resigns with him, and he has been known to take that step without even consulting it. He has been rightly described as 'the working Head of the State, endued with such a plenitude of power as no other constitutional ruler in the world possesses'.

The prime minister is in fact four persons rolled into one. He is the head of the cabinet, that is of the government of his country, and as such is easily the most powerful of its citizens. He is also the leader of the parliament—the one whose interventions in the debates have the greatest weight, who states and interprets government policy, who is responsible for obtaining its sanction by parliament. Thirdly, he is the person through whom the head of the state normally communicates with the cabinet, with parliament, and ultimately, the country. He is in daily touch with king or president, keeps him informed and on rare occasions may have to speak in his name. Fourthly, he is the head of his party and responsible for the maintaining of harmony between the party and the majority that returned it to power. (It is to be noted that in certain countries he is a fifth person, the distributor of state patronage; in some countries on the other hand such as Britain and France patronage amounts to very little.)

The Premier as Party Head.—It is, of course, the fourth of these positions that gives him access to the others. It is because he is party leader that he becomes prime minister when his party obtains power after an election. A party's choice of leader is often therefore the selection of a prime minister, though the party may then have little prospect of power. In a two party system it is inevitably so—in no case in modern times has the premiership gone to one who was not party leader at the time of the vacancy. In a multiple party system to be elevated to the leadership of the party is not a guarantee of being selected for the premiership, for there are several rivals in other parties but it does mean that the choice of a premier is normally limited to the heads of parties and groups. Thus predominance in a party is in all systems the necessary road to predominance in the state.

Cabinet's First Responsibility.—The cabinet, once constituted, is responsible for the government of the country in all its aspects. Its powers are too extensive to be classified under the conventional headings. Its work will include determining the basic principles on which public affairs shall be run, both at home and abroad, deciding how the public money shall be spent, selecting the chief civilian and military, and in some countries ecclesiastical, officials and the matters on which legislation shall be drafted and proposed for consideration to the parliament. It will also include legislation by decree or order in council, as laid down in constitutional law and tradition and by its appointment of judges it will influence the administration of justice, and although it depends in all these things on the consent of parliament, it possesses in most countries a most effective weapon, in the right of obtaining at any time from the head of the state a decree dissolving parliament.

Dissolution of Parliament.—Experience has shown that the right of dissolution is vital to the smooth working of a parliamentary system. If properly used it is the solution to any possible political deadlock. If cabinet and parliament disagree, the electorate will decide between them. The appeal to the people as the constant source of political authority is the logical manner of settling any serious dispute between rival agencies of the state, and it has been remarked that sovereignty, in a parliamentary democracy, resides in a newly elected House of Commons (or Chamber of Deputies).

But in order to be effective, dissolution need not be resorted to. The mere threat to use it is often its main advantage as is shown by what happens when it is not there. The prime minister, who can at any moment threaten a possibly restive parliament with dismissal back to its constituencies, is in a commanding position. It will never be with a light heart that deputies will take action against the government with the knowledge that this will entail the expenses and risks of a new election. But the prime minister who lacks this power is certain of defeat in case of conflict with his Parliament. He has no alternative to resignation.

The Third Republic in France is the classical example of this defect. By its constitution the Chamber could be dissolved by the President with the consent of the Senate. This right was used once, in 1876, not as a way out of a crisis but as an attempt to get rid of a newly elected Chamber too radical for the tastes of President MacMahon whose policy was the restoration of monarchy. Dissolution in this case was therefore a method of evading the verdict of the people who answered by confirming the Republicans in power; MacMahon resigned shortly after and a Royalist restoration passed out of the domain of practical politics. But unfortunately dissolution had become so closely associated in public opinion with unconstitutionalism and a bid for personal power that no later President ever dared use it, however serious the crisis. This removed the safety valve that the constitution had meant to place on parliamentary absolutism; being safe from dissolution the Chamber could count on four unbroken years of tenure, and during that time could overthrow cabinets with impunity, no appeal to the electorate being possible. This made infinitely worse the tendency towards cabinet instability already created by the multiple-party system; in fact it may be said that the power of dissolution can perhaps be dispensed with in a two-party system, where parliamentary majorities are normally stable, but is really indispensable in the multiple-party system where the threat of dissolution is the one thing that can hold in check the mania of groups to play about with ministerial combinations, in the hope of holding office. Time and time again the President of the Republic, even though limited by the need for senatorial sanction, could have steered through a cabinet crisis if he had not been deprived, by its unfortunate use many years ago, of a device which the framers of the constitution of 1875 knew to be necessary to its smooth working. The error has been rectified in the constitution of the Fourth Republic, which allows dissolutions, under certain conditions, not less than twelve months after an election. It is, of course, too early to say how this will actually work in practice.

Ministerial Responsibility.—The members of a cabinet have a double responsibility in their work: individual for the working of their department and collective for general policy. What exactly is implied in that latter term? It means that the policy is that of the cabinet as a whole, differences of opinion being kept private and the minority accepting the majority decision and making it its own in its speeches, votes, and attitudes, or resigning if it is conscientiously unable to do this. If, therefore, parliament refuses to accept this policy, the whole cabinet must resign, even if that policy seems to involve one single department only. From being a departmental matter it had become the concern of the whole cabinet, who must stand and fall by it. A mistake made by one minister need not, however, involve the whole cabinet, if the error really be personal. There are cases, however, when a weak cabinet is unable to survive the loss of one member, even on a personal and technical point.

In addition to this collective responsibility is the individual minister's responsibility for the administration of his department. Should this be questioned in parliament and an adverse vote appear likely, it is for the prime minister to decide whether to 'throw his minister to the wolves' or to give him the support of the cabinet, and take the risk of defeat and collective resignation.

The 'responsibility' here discussed is of course purely political, not legal. In theory a hostile parliament may impeach a minister for conduct dangerous to national security and welfare, but such a procedure has now fallen into complete abeyance. 'Responsibility' means that the ministers, individually and collectively, must satisfy parliament and give up their posts the moment they fail to do so; loss of office is the sole penalty, but since the whole political machine is built on man's desire for office, its loss is, for the time being, political death. As long, however, as parliament is satisfied the ministers have a clear field; only in a few countries, with a rigid written constitution, are they liable to find any legal obstacle to their proposed actions and in that case they can still set in action the machinery for the revision of the constitution.

The Power of the Cabinet.—Presenting a united front to the world, led by a man of commanding personality, and helped by an independent and efficient civil service, able to draw for advice on the greatest experts available, a cabinet with a solid majority in parliament is extremely powerful. It is a real governing body in the fullest sense of the term, from whose decisions there is practically no appeal, since it need not fear an adverse vote in parliament and, representing a majority of the electorate, need not fear revolt of public opinion against its proposals. But the 'solid majority' is an essential condition, since everything the cabinet does must be either positively agreed upon, or at least passively accepted by parliament. A cabinet without a solid majority is in a very difficult position, because, although powerful, it is insecure. It can only rely on a nucleus of dependable supporters, yet it must somehow keep the support of the doubtful element of its precarious majority. It is therefore hesitant, unable to take long views, anxious not to offend and therefore keen on avoiding action on controversial issues. Its work will be largely limited to daily administrative routine; its decisions and appointments will be essentially safe so as to avoid giving unnecessary offence; instead of really governing its chief purpose will be to remain in office. And this insecurity is, as we saw in a preceding chapter, the inevitable result of the multiple-party system.

Thus, from whatever angle we look at the problems of government, we are perpetually driven back to the importance of parties in the state. If party is the source of a cabinet's power, it can also be the source of its weakness, and, strong or weak, a cabinet always knows that a rival party, or several rival parties are standing on the doorstep, as it were, waiting with alternative cabinets, for a change in public opinion.

For good or evil, therefore, the cabinet system is that form of government which is most directly responsible to, and sensitive to, public opinion. Short of direct democracy, in its immediate dependence on parliament and in parliament's close relation to the electorate, it is the nearest approach to the faithful expression and representation of popular sovereignty. And that is why it tends to be the dominant pattern in the democratic organisations of today.

2. THE DECIDING OF POLICY: THE HEAD OF THE STATE

Every state has at its head a person who is both the representative of the state and the chief person in the government. This individual may be a hereditary monarch, or an elected president. The monarch may be a man or a woman but so far no woman has been elected to a presidency, though there is legally nothing to prevent this in the numerous constitutions in which both sexes have absolute equality of rights. Presidents are elected for terms that vary from four (U.S.A.) to seven years (France). They are chosen by the whole people in the United States, by parliament in France and Russia. The Swiss President is just one of the cabinet, acting as the head of the confederation for one year in his turn. Presidents can usually be re-elected, indefinitely in the U.S.A., for one term in France, not until after one term of interval in Lebanon and Syria.

King or President.—It is obviously futile to argue in the abstract as to the respective advantages of monarchy and republic. Each system suits one country and is unthinkable in the other. It seems, however, as if the days of powerful monarchs are over. King Ibn Saud is probably the only effective sovereign in the world today. In all other monarchies it has been the tendency to make the king the national symbol, outside all controversies and party politics, whose powers are exercised by his ministers in his name—probably by now the only way in which the hereditary principle and royal dignity can be preserved in democracies. It is much the same in fact with presidents of republics. We have seen that the Swiss President is a mere figurehead as such, only acting on a few formal occasions. Whatever real power he possesses comes to him as a cabinet minister. The evolution of France has made of the French President a republican counterpart of a constitutional monarch, who can only act on the advice of his ministers. The countersignature of a responsible minister is necessary to all his acts, and his only effective influence lies in the occasional selection of a prime minister.

The exceptions to the statement about the legal weakness of presidents are to be found in the oldest republic of all. The American constitution makes the President the real head of the government as well as of the state; he really chooses ministers who are responsible to him alone, and the national policy is his policy—as long as he can carry Congress with him. And even the opposition in Congress does not force him to resign. Nor can Congress provide an alternative executive; its resistance simply means that during the life of a hostile assembly little is done beyond routine administration.

Personal Influence.—This discussion of royal and presidential powers is, of course, limited to the legal and outward aspects of the positions. How much influence a king or president really exercises is quite another matter. No human being can ever be a complete 'rubber stamp' as Bernard Shaw shows in his witty and penetrating play, the 'Apple Cart', and the personal element can never be completely ruled out. The most constitutional of sovereigns will affect the course of national policies in two ways. First, he has the full right to be consulted, to advise, and to warn. He has an experience that none of his ministers possesses and wise ministers will take this into account. They have the last word, of course, but the king will have had his word. Presidents of republics are experienced statesmen, usually with many years of ministerial office behind them. They too have their right to their say, even if ministers finally decide, 'You cannot', as someone once remarked, 'always say "no". When you have said "no" to a king three times, you must say "yes" the fourth time, to be able again to say "no" on the fifth.'

Secondly the personality of the ruler, his likes and dislikes, his way of looking at things and men, is bound to colour the political atmosphere of his time. It is not for nothing that history is divided according to reigns and even in a republic the 'Septennate' of Loubet, or Poincaré or Doumergue or Lebrun has a definite connotation. The most constitutional or even ornamental of heads of state must therefore be included in any survey of the agencies of government. In effective power he certainly does not lead, and electorate, party, parliament and cabinet all count for more. But he counts for something, perhaps far more than the public knows or thinks, and one can agree with Bagehot, who says, after discussing the various ways in which a wise king can exert his influence and give the benefits of his experience, that 'such a king would have had a happy life. He would have passed a life in which he could always make his arguments heard, in which he could always make those who had the responsibility of action think of them before they acted, in which he could know that the schemes which he had set to work in the world were the likeliest of all things to be right—the ideas of one very intelligent man, at last accepted and acted upon by the intelligent many.'

3. THE EXECUTING OF POLICY:

ARMED FORCES AND CIVIL SERVICE

We have studied what may be described as five organs or agents which decide the collective policy—electorate, parties, parliaments, cabinet and ruler, and seen how each of these plays its part in its formation. We now pass on to the ways in which this policy is actually carried out and to the four agents of action or execution.

Cabinet and Head of State.—First come the last two already studied in their 'deciding' capacity and who reappear in their active role. The cabinet acts by giving the orders that put the whole machinery of the state into motion and control its various parts—armed forces, civil services, judicial services. And the head of the state plays there, as in decision, the essential role of final sanction, and of general influence which we have just been discussing; he may in fact be still more effective in appointments than in policy-making—partly because his longer tenure of power may give him a better knowledge of candidates for high office, partly because it is easier to yield to him on such questions than on more vital matters of state.

Armed Forces.—Coming to the more direct instruments of policy, we need say little of the armed forces. Most countries have adopted the principle of compulsory service, and the size and the respective importance in the national policy of land, sea, and air armaments are obviously technical matters which we can pass by here. The use of these forces creates, however, two problems, one concerns their use in foreign policy. Will these forces be used exclusively in accordance with international agreements and for defence on collective security only, or will they be limited to purposes of aggression and expansion? And what should then be the attitude of the citizen?

The second problem concerns their use at home. Are they exclusively for defence against external enemies, or are they to be relied on for the keeping of order? The use of the army in an acute emergency is practically universally admitted, but what constitutes an emergency? In some countries the army has been called on to put down strikes which, without such intervention, would have remained peaceful, or at least well within the scope of the ordinary police. In some countries, soldiers have been called upon to take the place of strikers in maintaining certain services. But this has never occurred without bitter resentment from the workers concerned, nor without creating a state of feeling that threatened to cut the nation in two, often straining almost to breaking-point the loyalty of the troops. And when this breaks, revolution almost inevitably follows. The more the army can be kept out of domestic issues, the better for all concerned.

The Civil Service.—This term covers the large number of officials necessary to run the machinery of government. This enormous mass, that goes into hundreds of thousands in a large state, is divided into the various departments or ministries, the number and features of which we shall discuss in a later chapter. At the top is the minister and the men immediately below who share with him the direct framing and execution of departmental policy; at the bottom the most junior clerks employed in the carrying out of ministerial orders; it excludes such workers as cleaners, drivers, messengers; typists are sometimes on one side of the line, sometimes on the other.

The problems of the civil service in the world of to-day are twofold. One concerns recruitment, composition and status, the other function. The former question need not detain us long. It is practically universally agreed that the civil service should be as far as possible a non-political body, providing the ultimate deciding agents with technical knowledge and experience, but not responsible for ultimate policy; that political influence should be reduced to the absolute inevitable minimum, and that some form of open competition is the only way of eliminating patronage and possible corruption in appointments. It follows that posts are held independently of political change, that the official is indeed the servant of the crown and of the public, and not of the party or the cabinet, and that he is therefore appointed either on a long-term renewable contract, or indefinitely on good behaviour, his removal for inefficiency or misconduct being only effected by a disciplinary committee of the services and not by the minister or any other political person. Promotion will not depend on favour or protection, but will be made in accordance with known rules, and usually based both on seniority and on efficiency. Merit rather than patronage will be the watchword. On all those points there is general theoretical agreement, even though the principles agreed on may occasionally be ignored. There is also agreement as to the needs of a good civil service—conditions good enough to attract a high type of intelligence, the duty of secrecy, the keeping of accurate records, the careful differentiation of function. This is important, as one mark of inefficiency is the ignorance of the proper department or section responsible for a particular matter, and its passing on from one to another because no one knows who is competent to handle it. Quickness in action is also much needed, and is only possible if the service is not too highly centralised, and adequate initiative is given all along the line.

Impartiality and impersonality are thus the two characteristics of a modern civil service. It must be no respecter of persons; it must be above suspicion; it must take its work seriously. The good administration of a state today is a complex and difficult matter, and nothing could be more naïvely wrong than the statements of an American President, Harding,[1] that 'government is after all a very simple thing'; on the contrary, it is more and more recognised that training for this work is necessary, and public administration is becoming an increasingly important subject of study.

The Sphere of Administration.—So much for the first problem. What about the second, that of function? This is more difficult. Is it possible to define clearly the sphere of administration, of action, as distinct from decision? Is not the manner of execution as important and decisive as the actual scheme? In simpler words, do not means matter as much as ends? If, therefore, we are estimating the actual effective power of the various agencies in the state, should not the administrative agent, the bureaucracy as it is often called, be placed very high on the list?

[1] Quoted by Frankfurter, 'The Public and its Government', p. 148. He also quotes President Jackson, saying a century earlier that 'the duties of all public offices are, or at least admit of being made, so plain and simple that men of intelligence may readily qualify themselves for their performance'.

Professor Mannheim in his 'Ideology and Utopia', distinguishes as follows the two aspects of socio-political life, which he terms 'Affairs of State' and 'Politics'. The former, he says, is a series of social events with a set pattern and recurring regularity. Its essence is routine. The latter is a series of events still in process of becoming, in which new decisions are necessary. Its essence is creativeness and struggle. The former is rational, the latter is irrational; by which Mannheim means that decisions in the administrative spheres are made according to rules and precedents that only need logical application, whereas in the other each decision is a new act, a new creation, and what is needed is imagination, initiative, ability to see things from a fresh angle.

This distinction is clear and helpful up to a point, but still leaves it difficult to draw an exact line. Administration has become so complex that the modern political or deciding agent can only lay down general rules or principles, and is obliged to leave a great deal to the interpretation and initiative of the administrator, who becomes in fact a deciding agent himself; the so-called 'executive' exercises 'legislative' functions; not only so, but many modern statutes confer on some committee formed of officials, or even on some one official, the power to adjudicate on certain disputes arising out of the application of the measure, so that the 'executive' becomes judge as well as legislator—surely a striking example of the breakdown of the Separation of Powers doctrine.

Bureaucracy and its Problems.—The enormous power of bureaucracy has become in fact one of the problems of the state.[1] These powers came from the wide extension of the scope of the government, and from the huge size of the modern state, both together necessitating many officials and inevitably leaving in their hands an authority which it becomes very difficult for either the government or the public to control—difficult for the government, for if no initiative is left to the official, who has to refer everything to a higher authority, the administrative machine becomes clogged and nothing will ever get done. (This is the constant complaint of centralised administrations like the French; officials must be

[1] See on this problem: Hewart, 'The New Despotism' and Laski's 'Grammar of Politics'.

given some freedom of action, and the risk must be run of this freedom being sometimes misused.) Difficult also for the public, who become the dependents of the officials as it were, and are too far from the centre of real responsibility to be able to defend themselves from administrative high-handedness. They are as the French call them 'les administrés', the subjects on which administration exercises its powers.

What is the remedy? Professor Laski, in an article on the subject in *Politics* some fifteen years ago, after laying down as an axiom that in 'A constitutional system must provide for the proper subordination of the legislature', stated three principles, 'the observance of which is desirable in any system of constitutional government in which discretionary power is conferred'. These principles are the threefold assurance, first that the powers taken by the executive do not exceed the original delegation of authority; second that those who are to be affected by the exercise of discretionary power shall be consulted about them before they come into operation; third that the legislature is fully informed of the uses to which such discretionary powers as it confers are put. 'This procedure', adds Laski, 'is the surest safeguard we can have against the dangers of bureaucracy. No public servant, not even a minister, ought ever to be so placed that his acts can escape a full and rigorous public scrutiny.'

Decentralisation and Democracy.—To these we might add two more possible defences. First, there should be some kind of appeal court against administrative decisions such as is found in France in the 'conseil d'Etat' whose function is precisely to hear complaints from the public against official misuse of authority—the procedure is very cheap and comparatively quick.[1] But far more important is large-scale decentralisation, putting more and more power into the hands of local bodies and officials who are nearer at hand than remote 'Whitehall' or Paris.

It may in fact be said that there can be little real democracy without local freedom, and that local freedom can be a useful corrective to excessive power at the centre. The history of English democracy is inseparable from that of English local life. France on the other hand, while establishing democracy

---

[1] If the plaintiff wins, he is reimbursed of all costs.

at the centre, failed to establish it locally, and the administration of the Third Republic, though nominally based on popularly elected councils, was in fact in the hands of officials scarcely less irresponsible than those of the *ancien régime*.[1] Decentralise— make the people manage their own affairs in their villages and towns; let them elect their own officials, or let these be appointed by locally responsible bodies—you will thereby decrease the sphere of possible arbitrary government and the dangers of officialdom, teach responsibility, prepare people for the duties of wider citizenship. It is worth some possible loss of uniformity, perhaps even of efficiency, for it will bring politics nearer to the unattainable but necessary ideal of government of the people, by the people, and for the people.

4. THE SUPREMACY OF THE LAW: THE JUDICIARY

The Functions of Justice.—Finally, we come to the part played in the state by judges and courts of law. We again are confronted by the impossibility of applying with any strictness the separation principle so often invoked, for the 'Judiciary' as it is called deals with many things beyond the strict administration of justice and application of the laws. It has executive functions, such as the management of trust funds, of various forms of private and public property, the issuing of orders or injunctions against officials and private individuals and it appoints all those who are employed in those activities. In some countries such as Britain disputed elections are settled by the courts, not by parliament or any other body concerned. Again, the judiciary makes law when it interprets an existing statute, for its decision becomes a precedent and therefore fixes the law for the future. Judge-made law is in fact necessary to fill up the gaps in formal legislation, which cannot possibly provide for every case in advance. And in certain countries such as the United States, courts can pronounce by 'judicial review' on the constitutionality of a law passed by the legislative authority.

On the other hand the judiciary has no monopoly of justice —we have mentioned the fact that some Second Chambers

[1] See Ferrat's 'La République à refaire' for a vivid description of this irresponsibility.

are final courts of appeal, that impeachment is part of most constitutions, that the head of the state usually enjoys a right of pardon, that modern legislation gives to administrative officials powers which are partly legislative, partly judicial.

Growth of State Justice.—Justice remains, nevertheless, the chief function of the judiciary; this includes broadly two main branches, dealing with law-breakers and settling disputes between individuals—criminal and civil law and courts. It is not so many centuries ago since it became definitely established that the only justice and the only law was that of the state. Private jurisdictions were usual in medieval days, and the grant of such a right over his territories was frequently a way by which kings rewarded the faithful service of some retainer. But gradually the royal justice absorbed as it were, all other forms—partly for the sake of order and uniformity, partly because of the financial profits derived; the king could not afford to let this source of wealth go to private pockets. This state monopoly of justice is now practically universal; ecclesiastical courts, however, administering ecclesiastical or 'canon' law on such matters as marriage, divorce, inheritance and offences committed by members of the clergy, still exist in some countries.

Together with the development of state courts went the gradual division of their work according to the nature and gravity of the cases, and the establishment of the rendering of justice as a definite profession distinct from other forms of administration. The fact that certain legislative bodies still exercise judicial functions, such as appeals and impeachments, is a reminder of the days when no distinction was made between the various branches of government.

Principles of Modern Justice.—It may be said that modern justice rests on a number of basic principles of almost universal application. There is one judicial system, and one law, both the creation of the state, and administered by its judges and other officials appointed for the purpose. Every member of the community is subject to that law, and is entitled to its protection. Justice must be administered strictly according to the law; there are no offences except those which are legally punishable; punishment must only be what the law lays down for a particular offence; and must always be the same for the same kind of offence; its object is not the vengeance of society upon the criminal but society's protection both from him and from his potential imitators. Some time ago we would have added that judicial torture had disappeared from all civilised countries; but the last few years have shown that it has not done so unless its use disqualifies a country from the title of 'civilised'.

It is also practically universally agreed that judges must be free from all interference. It is a crime for them to receive a bribe or for anybody to offer them one, or to threaten them, or bring any kind of pressure to bear on them. It is also wrong for the government to interfere, by trying to secure condemnations or acquittals; verdicts must be given in accordance with the facts and with the law governing the case, and not to suit the desires of politicians or other influential persons.

The Judges.—Justice must be free from politics and the justiciary must be independent of the government—these are the fundamentals of any civilised order. How are they secured? The answer is that they can never be absolutely secure, because in the last resort justice depends on the conscience of the judges and this can never be completely guaranteed. All that human ingenuity can do is to try and make the honest discharge of their duties as easy as possible.

First comes the selection of judges. An adequate legal training is the first condition—not merely the knowledge of existing law, and the techniques of the law court, but an understanding of the principles on which the law is built, and of the psychology that determines human conduct. To understand man is as important as to know the law.

In most countries judging is a profession on which a young lawyer enters, by competition or direct appointment, and makes it his career. It is, as it were, a branch of the civil service, governed by the same principles of permanency and independence. The weak point of that system is the problem of promotion. Even if it is in the hands of a board entirely made up of members of the profession, free from political or other interferences, it is difficult to guarantee that nothing but sheer technical merit, coupled with regard for seniority, will decide every case. But although this system has its defects, it seems preferable to the American system by which a large number of judges are elected and that on party lines; it seems difficult, in fact, to imagine a worse system, and the wonder is that the results are not nearly as bad as might be expected.

Judicial Independence.—Britain is alone in entrusting a great deal of her judicial work to unpaid amateurs, the J.P., appointed by the Lord Chancellor from among the residents in the locality thought to have the kind of standing and experience that would enable them, with the assistance of a trained lawyer as clerk, to decide the simple problems that make up some nine-tenths of the cases that come into court. The 'magistrate's Bench' has been for centuries a peculiar and successful feature of English justice. It has the advantage of doing without the host of minor judges that staff the lower courts of other countries. For the cases in which the Bench would be incompetent England uses a small number of County Court Judges, appointed by the Lord Chancellor,[1] as head of the judicial system, from barristers with a number of years of successful practice. In England, therefore, no man can choose judging as a career; he can only become a professional judge after a long period as a private lawyer; a judgeship is, in fact, a reward. The defect of the system is, of course, that various influences, often political, may come into play in the selection, though once selected the independence of the judge is secured by the fact that he cannot be removed by the government, but only by a vote of parliament petitioning the crown for his removal—a device which has never been used since it became law by the Act of Settlement in 1701.

The Search for Justice.—Such then are the characteristics of the judicial organisation of a democratic state—what happens to justice under totalitarianism will be studied in a later chapter. The whole story is one of man's efforts to place justice outside the reach of human prejudice and frailty—and on the whole with considerable success. An accused person knows that he will have a fair trial, according to the laws of the country; and in many cases the decision of fact will be entrusted to a jury of his fellow citizens, the judge only applying the law in accordance with the jury's verdict; as no-one can know beforehand who the jury will be, and as the jury will have no contact with the outside world during its deliberations, it is hoped that

---

[1] In theory by the crown.

it can act with complete freedom from any pressure.[1] The sentence once pronounced will be carried out with scrupulous exactness; the acquitted person can never be tried again for the same offence, even if new evidence come to light; the condemned person is certain not to be kept in prison one day longer than the duration fixed in the sentence; in fact, good behaviour will secure for him an earlier release. Sentence of death will be carried out as mercifully as is possible. No condemnation of an individual will involve his property or his family, though it may, in certain cases and in certain countries, give a wife or husband the right to ask for a divorce.

The judge on his side knows that the state will uphold his verdict. An appeal on points of law is, of course, possible to a higher court, but only within the judicial system; his decisions will not even be publicly discussed. Save in the most exceptional cases of partiality or incompetence, his position and salary are absolutely secure. He is asked to do one thing only—to administer the law, to do justice equally to all men without fear or favour. No wonder that the great American judge Holmes wrote at the end of his life that 'a man may live greatly in the law, as well as elsewhere; there as elsewhere his thought may find its unity in an infinite perspective'.

[1] It should be said that many experts doubt whether the jury really secures better justice than the single judge, or than a bench of three judges.

CHAPTER XII

SOME PROBLEMS
OF THE DEMOCRATIC STATE

I. THE DEFICIENCIES OF DEMOCRACY

WE appear to have assumed so far that everything was running smoothly in the most efficient and satisfactory of all democracies, but, of course, things don't turn out that way. Democracy has to face many problems and difficulties, and the question is whether its resources, material and moral, are adequate to meet them.

Dullness and Slowness.—The first of those problems is the contradiction between the fact that democracy is both slow and dull, while men like excitement and speed. It is slow; the democratic process needs the widespread, careful discussion of all important proposals and that takes time; nothing on a large scale can be rushed through, and in a large state the smallest plan becomes a large-scale undertaking. Democracy means patience, and people are by nature impatient. And democracy means long periods of quiet, unexciting living; it needs peace, and peace is less exhilarating than war;[1] it needs men who can stick to steady routine jobs out of the limelight; it is incompatible with quick and imposing results. How to persuade the electorate to accept and to stand by such humdrum plans and unpretentious living is one of the great difficulties of the democratic politician; he is at a constant disadvantage beside the advocate of an authority that can ride roughshod over opposition or criticism, that can easily mobilise all necessary resources and guarantee the rapid carrying out of grandiose programmes which flatter the pride

---

[1] The complaint that 'France was bored' with her pacific, unenterprising government was an important factor in the fall of Louis-Philippe in 1848. Many people wanted him to go to war with Britain over trivial disputes now practically forgotten. And the Crimean War was practically forced on a reluctant government by British public opinion.

of the citizen and promise him glory as a member of a go-
ahead community, or even of a nation of gods, with standards
of life made high at the expense of 'lower' peoples. The appeal
of the dictator to the human instinct for excitement and
corporate power is natural enough, and is not easy to with-
stand. And even when dictatorship has shot its bolt and
brought down the national edifice crashing into ruins, the
temptation is strong to attribute disaster to external causes, and
to promise that tomorrow a bigger and better dictatorship
will succeed where the earlier failed. France was not content
with one Napoleon, and it would be too optimistic to hope
that no second Hitlers or Mussolinis are not already waiting
for their 'day'. Democracy must make itself worth while, and
persuade its members that its processes as Laski says 'need not
be dull if you can grasp their real significance, nor slow if you
can realise that quickness is not compatible with permanency
of results'.

Democracy Face to Face with Hugeness.—In the second place
comes the problem of size. Even a small modern state numbers
several million people; four are well over a hundred million.
The smallest question of organisation becomes highly complex and technical; a decision on an apparently simple issue
involves huge numbers of lives with incalculable consequences.
The ordinary man feels helpless before the mere magnitude
of modern politics; how he can play the part, exercise the
responsibilities which are supposed to be his in a democracy?
What is the individual in the modern mass?

Some say 'representation'; but representation is only a
very partial solution. 'It allows too little', as Sheean says,
'for the ever-widening space that must come in large and
growing countries between the people and their representatives, and the evils resulting from the method of choice of
the candidates.' What happens in many cases is that the individual gives up what seems a hopeless quest and abdicates
before a strong government that will relieve him of the
responsibilities of self-government; in that sense, the fuller
the democracy, the heavier the demands it makes upon the
citizens, and therefore the greater the temptation to hand over
the job to a dictator. It is hard to believe that one who is only
one-tenth or one-twentieth of a million of the total people

really matters; to form a personal opinion on the innumerable issues of modern politics seems impossible. No-one can pretend that our systems of representation are really more than approximate, that the leaders are really, in any sense, chosen by the people, and that the people have had much share in the selection of the policies pursued. It is all done at second, third, fourth hand. Everything is a little out of date; a parliament represents, as far as it can represent, opinions of some time past—last year, two, three, four years ago. It cannot keep pace with a perpetually changing popular will. It is true, of course, that the members of parliament are themselves part of that changing will, but what guarantee is there that they change in just the same way and at the same speed? Parliament is essentially, as we saw, a conference of delegates of parties; what guarantees have we that distribution of these parties in parliament is now what it was at the time of the election? Obviously none.

Lack of Adequate Institutions.—This leads us to a third problem, the inadequacy of democracy's present-day institutions. In most countries parliaments and civil servants are hopelessly overworked. Parliaments came into existence at a time when the scope of government was strictly limited and when the numbers involved were small. The British Parliament, created in the Middle Ages, was originally meant for an agricultural state of some three or four million inhabitants, without armed forces of any importance, without colonies (the dependencies in France were the possessions of the Crown as a French Duke, not as King of England), without any foreign trade. Now the same body, practically identical in size and legal powers, administers a highly industrialised country of nearly fifty million people, with world-wide possessions, dependent for its life on its foreign trade. And the day is still limited to twenty-four hours and the life of man is still three score years and ten.

The trouble with all institutions is that they are by their very nature rigid and difficult both to adapt and to change. They have often been devised with great trouble; to alter or replace them is no easy matter. And what security is there that the alteration will really improve the instrument, that a new one will be better than the old? Change is always a leap in the dark and, therefore, dangerous. People forget that institutions are not ends in themselves but tools for certain purposes, which should be discarded if the purpose is no longer achieved; any proposal for institutional change always causes a mass of opposition, some well grounded and judicious, but much of it blind and prejudiced, afraid of innovations which might destroy the existing balance of power in the state.

Democracy has not yet developed its own institutions; it is still working on systems inherited from the past, and devised for very different social, political and economic circumstances. It is clear, however, that it will have to create them if it wants to survive.

The Unfitness of the Masses.—This leads us into yet another problem, that of the unpreparedness of the masses for responsible self-government and its consequences. 'Save for great occasions like war and revolution', writes Laski, 'the multitude is enfolded in its private life, content for the most part that initiative in thought and policy should rest elsewhere. So long as life flows smoothly upon a fairly even keel it watches public affairs as a drama in which it is not expected to play an active part.' And, he goes on to say, 'the inertia of the multitude is the foundation of public wrong, and the effort required to stir it from its somnolence lies at the root of the distortion of public opinion.'[1] Democracy must be participation, otherwise it is passive and negative, and the problem is, as Cole says, 'of finding democratic ways of living for little men in big societies'.[2] So far we have failed to do so, but it is probably the crucial problem of today.

2. DEMOCRACY AND GROUPS

Geographical and Functional Groups. One solution is to break up the masses into smaller elements through which both interest and responsibility can be diffused and grasped by the 'little man'. The first step is obviously administrative

---

[1] 'The word democracy does not contain enough positive content to stand alone against the forces you dislike—it can easily be transformed by them.' T. S. Eliot, *Times Literary Supplement*, November 4, 1939.

[2] 'Democracy Face to Face with Hugeness.' *Christian News Letter*, July 16, 1943.

decentralisation as a way of relieving pressure on the central machine, following the general principle that any function which can be, must be discharged by the inferior or more localised organ,[1] as likely to be in closer contact with the issues concerned and to give better opportunity for service to the ordinary people on the spot. Local bodies are, as we said earlier on, the natural training ground for national politics.

Administrative decentralisation, however excellent as far as it goes, does not go far enough. It still belongs to the category of officially-created and controlled organisation. The 'something more' which is needed may be found in functional as distinct from geographical groups, representing the spontaneous attempts made by citizens to come together for the carrying on of some common purpose. Although the family is the creation of nature, not of man, it becomes in some countries almost an organised unit for the defence of the property and welfare of its members. More specifically functional are bodies such as Churches, trade unions of all sorts, and others charged with the protection of some definite professional interests.[2] Lastly come associations for the carrying on of some activity or propaganda, humanitarian, cultural, technical. As Bentley says, 'Associations correspond to desires —for health, wealth, sociability, knowledge, beauty and rightness.'

The Role of Associations.—The essential features of those groups is that they represent a definite integration of the citizen with them; they are, in Dewey's words, 'social forces whose interactions with one another may offset if not control the dread impersonality of the sweep of the immense forces whose power and consequences the individual has no power of affecting'. They stand for the principle that no one body claiming to represent the community as a whole will by itself adequately safeguard the right of the individual to realise

---

[1] 'It is an injustice, a grave one and a disturbance of the right order, for a larger and higher organisation to arrogate to itself functions which can be performed efficiently by smaller and lower bodies.' (Encyclical *Quadragesimo Anno* of Pope Pius XI.)

[2] The Transport Commission proposals of 1931 were submitted to five transport associations, four motoring associations, four trade unions, the Association of Chambers of Commerce, the Federation of British Industries and the National Federation of Iron and Steel Manufacturers.

himself. They are, in that sense, if not rivals, at least complementary influences to that of the state, and stand in direct contradiction to the old French idea that 'it is never lawful for anyone to suggest to the citizens any interest coming between themselves and the common interest, and to try and separate them from the public weal by any sectional outlook'.[1]

The following passage from Taine deserves quoting in spite of its length. 'They (the old-fashioned centralising politicians) are suspicious of any collective undertaking. They will not admit that the social body is made up of distinct specialised organs, all equally necessary and natural, each adapted by its particular structure to a definite and limited use, each one spontaneously produced, formed, kept up, renewed and stimulated by the initiatives, the reciprocal affinities, the free play of its constituent cells, the individuals.

'According to them there is one organ of a superior character, the state, in which alone reside intelligence, reason, knowledge of first principles, calculation of consequences. The state knows, therefore, better than all other organs what is good for them and has, therefore, the right and the duty not only of inspecting and protecting their activities, but of controlling them, of directing them by encouragements or repressions, so as to give them the form it wishes.'

The Free Group in History.—The primary fact about groups is that they exist, have always existed; and lie at the very roots of any interpretation of history. Who could understand the past without an appreciation of the work of religious groups and corporations, from the most primitive medicine-men to organised Churches, using the term in the broadest and not only in its Christian sense, or economics without realising the importance of guilds of all kinds? And how could one ignore the significance of the family as a factor in social origins? No-one can understand the development of Anglo-Saxon communities in particular without realising the incalculable influence of their innumerable free associations.

Conditions of Healthy Group Activity.—So far so good. The groups we have been surveying have obviously fulfilled functions in social evolution, and there can be no reasonable denial of the right of citizens to organise to try and secure

[1] Le Chapelier Law on Associations, 1791.

support for their aims. But there is one essential condition for
the healthy functioning of such groups, and that is that both
their purposes and their methods should be ready to stand the
light of publicity. Their membership should be known, their
policies and ways avowed and defendable before public
opinion. All groups unfortunately do not fulfil this condition.
All through history, and including the present time, large
group forces are at work secretly, or at least unobtrusively,
trying to use their influence for the advancement of policies
that will not always bear public discussion. These forces are
usually economic, mostly standing for the activities of private
citizens working for their own advantage. Farming, armaments, liquor, and especially banking and finance,[1] just to
name a few, have been accused at various times of working
behind the scenes and pulling strings, by fair means and foul,
for the realisation of their particular interests. 'The general
tendency of those who wield economic power—financial or
commercial—is to hide their effective strength, and make it
inconspicuous by process of dispersion', says Pierre Maillaud,
and he speaks of the 'elusiveness of modern economic feudal-

[1] 'In theory the people was the sovereign and the people suffered, com-
plained, sometimes kicked against the pricks without being able to utter a
clear unanimous thought, which it could not conceive owing to its lack of
political or economic capacity. In fact the sovereign had virtually abdicated
and parties interpreted its alleged will. . . . The parties themselves although
theoretically but groups based on common opinions and open to all, actually
defended the interests of different classes, not always clearly defined but distinct enough for those interests to conflict. And above all parties, above
them because most derived their sustenance from her, smiling at their vain
babblings as long as they did not affect here essential interests, there was
working the most formidable and most thoroughly organised of all real
powers (*puissances de fait*), the true ruler of the regime—Finance.'
'By what was an apparent paradox, Finance was the real sovereign of
French democracy. Her power was all the greater that it was made up of the
accumulation of a mass of small savings, the cleverly drained savings of the
most economical nation of the world, so that her advocates had the cool
audacity to say that Finance was democratic. She exercised over public
affairs an unquestioned control. She manipulated the inner workings of the
political machine, both domestic and foreign, so as to prevent the erection of
an obstacle to her policy; possible checks were the public authorities and
the press, and these she watched, controlled, maintained; those outside her
authority were helpless. So much had financial feudalism or oligarchy
become the driver of the political machine that the working class no longer
troubled to distinguish between the bourgeois middle-class and the republic
proper. In their opinion democracy had become plutocracy.' (Guy-Grand
' la Démocratie', pp. 12-13.)

ism; the trouble is', he adds 'that the growth of anonymous power in the economic field is a contributory cause to the spread of anonymous political power.'

The Problem of Pressure Groups.—This anonymity, this secrecy of operation,[1] is due to the fact that many of these 'pressure groups', as they were called, are really trying to by-pass, as it were, the democratic process—endeavouring to get their own way irrespective of public consent.

We have there, in fact, one of the perpetual difficulties of democracy—not so much the avowed enemy outside, of whom more later, but the man inside who takes advantage of the liberty of action given to him by a free society without any intention of being bound by its rules of open discussion and majority decision—the man who means to get what he wants whatever the rest of society may think or do.

Ultimate Value of Groups.—In one sense, therefore, the free functional group which was defended as a method of solving democracy's problem of the little man in a world too big for him is also the origin of many of democracy's troubles. It will obviously try and guard against the danger of under-ground subversive action by constant systematic enquiry and wide publicity; but it is evident that there can be no complete protection against the danger. The advantages of free group work would seem, however, to outweigh the dangers, and we would agree with Mr. Harvey Fergusson when he insists that 'instead of such pressure-groups being a threat to demo-cracy, they are really democracy's greatest hope; a great variety of organised forces, forming a complex pattern of interaction, is the best safeguard against tyranny, exploitation and the splitting of society into two rigidly opposed classes. . . . Only group organisation can realise for the mass of men the conditions of true freedom—an individual experience, a way of life, an opportunity to develop one's capacities and talents, to choose one's work and become one's self.'[2]

Groups and Freedom.—Free grouping provides in fact the

[1] 'In the modern state real power is in the hands of the big industrial trade unions, the steel and coal cartels, which use national policies, both domestic and foreign, for their own aims and profits. But they no more wish to be seen than those autocrats of old, who were all the more feared and venerated that they remained hidden.' (Paul Louis, 'Le déclin de la société bourgeoise').

[2] Review of Harvey Fergusson's 'People and Power' in the *New York Times*

answer to the question asked by Mannheim in his 'Man and Society' as to the conditions of real freedom and healthy common life: 'How, where and why do people meet? How are power and influence, risk and responsibility distributed? Do men act spontaneously or under orders?' There lies the real defence against regimentation, militarism, apathy, paternalism—men coming together to get something done, without waiting for the government either to tell them to do it or to do it for them. That is the key to democratic freedom.[1] The whole story of education in Anglo-Saxon countries is a most striking instance of the spontaneous action, either of the Churches or of associations of individuals, who to this day manage their own affairs, undisturbed by the later development of schools under official control, and left free to use at their discretion the grants now supplied by the state.

3. RULING CLASSES AND LEADERSHIP

The Problem of the Ruling Classes.—Necessary as groups are, however, we must not forget the essential fact of politics that ruling is inevitably the work of the few. 'The masses', says Ferrero, 'are always passive and stagnant; it is impossible to convert to an extreme idea millions of men and women whose education, temperament, profession and orientation are different. Extreme ideas are always the property of small selected homogeneous minorities, according to the community of interests, passions and enthusiasms.'

In one sense all societies are managed by oligarchies; they all have their 'ruling class'.[2] The question is, what kind? Military? Priestly? Hereditary? Landed? Moneyed? Democracy answers (none of these, but a ruling class selected for its intellectual and ruling fitness).

The character of its ruling class is, in fact, a distinguishing feature of every society. For every society *has* its ruling class, and a change in the one is expressed by a change in the other. A century ago the English ruling class was trained in the older

---

[1] Remembering, however, that, as Lord Lindsay puts it, 'there is a certain amount of tosh in all associations. . . . To understand human associations it is as necessary to take into consideration their falling short of the purposes which inspire them as to remember that they are actually inspired by these purposes.'   [2] See Mosca's 'Ruling Class'.

public schools and universities; no political career was possible
without a private income and some influence and connections.
Our present ruling class still has room for some representatives
of the older regime; not only the Conservative but even the
Labour party has its men from Eton and King's, Winchester
and New College. But trade union, and municipal council,
county school, technical college and 'provincial' university,
together with the generalising of the competitive system also
serve as recruiting grounds.

Democracy and the Ruling Class.—The ruling class, however,
is still there, and the only difference democracy makes is to
offer the ordinary man greater opportunities of entering it,
of influencing it and keeping in touch with public opinion and
desires, in other terms, democracy establishes a much closer
relation between the rulers and the ruled. But it does not do
away with the difference between the two.

It follows that even in a democratic state the ruling class
will still have to face the temptation of every ruling class, to
develop interests of its own, different from and often opposed
to those of the rest of the people. Under the domination of
soldier or priest or hereditary aristocrat, the temptation is
obvious enough; under that of merchant or landlord it is less
evident, since their prosperity must be bound up to some
extent with that of the country as a whole.[1] And when the
ruling class is widely recruited from many elements in the
nation, is neither hereditary nor identified with any particular
interest, its temptation is the more subtle one of making of its
administrative power an end in itself; of creating rules for the
sake of rules and of justifying its own existence by an over-
zealous 'throwing one's weight about'. And there is always the
'unofficial' ruling class of the controllers of economic power,
and of ecclesiastical authority, of the educational and military
leaders—whose influence behind the scenes needs, as we saw,
constant watching and checking.

It can be said in a general way that the power of the ruling
class, both legal and extra-legal, will bear a direct relation to the
degree of political maturity of the community as a whole.
A wide-awake democratic society with powers widely

[1] We are thinking, for instance, of the sacrificing of agriculture to industry
in Britain in the middle of the last century.

distributed both functionally and geographically, such as Switzerland, will be more fully independent and really self-governing than a highly centralised state like France, however intelligent its members, or than the politically inexperienced societies of the South American and Asiatic world. Again, states in process of evolution will obviously be more dependent on their ruling classes than old and stable societies. 'Tell me what your ruling class is like, and I will tell you where you stand in the line of political and social development' would be a fair summary of the subject.

Leadership and the Common Man.—Free association, then, meets to some extent the problems of personal participation in collective life by breaking up the mass into a large number of small units in each of which the individual can realise and express himself. But another solution lies in the opposite direction—in the same individual realising himself by identification with his fellows in their collective life.

The giving of a unity of purpose to a large number of isolated separate persons, and welding them into a living whole, is the work of leadership.

We discussed in an earlier chapter the importance of leadership in the formation of political societies, and some of its essential characteristics. We defined it then as being the possession both of certain outstanding qualities, such as courage, imagination, clear vision, perseverance, will-power and understanding of one's fellow-men, and of a certain elusive quality which makes the rank and file accept and follow him in whom those qualities are to be found.

Leadership must not be confused with a domination based on discipline and unquestioning obedience. This, as Pigou rightly remarks in his 'Leadership or Domination', is its antithesis. Leadership is freely accepted, and can be equally freely rejected; it is the deliberate recognition of a man's knowledge of the road to be taken and of his moral right to urge others to follow him. This kind of leadership 'involves treating democracy with a new respect, offering scientific schemes of a far-sighted and far-reaching order, commanding them by the method of reason, and asking that they should be judged on their merits alone.'[1]

[1] Manifesto on 'Democracy and Leadership', *Manchester Guardian*, February 14, 1934.

Types of Democratic Leadership.—There are, in fact, two distinct types of democratic leader, the one who carries the people on to the immediate task of today, and the one who, looking further ahead, sees the task of tomorrow. One is statesman, the other prophet. The former is concerned with urgent issues that cannot wait; the latter is more concerned with 'the definition of the ultimate values towards which the society should move', the discovery of 'the essential issues of a state or generation, and in season and out of season proclaiming their meaning as they see it to their contemporaries.'[1]

The essential difference between the two is that the statesman must, quite rightly, put action first and therefore offer himself for political office. He is a Chatham, a Lloyd George, a Disraeli, a Lincoln, a Kemal Pasha, a Stalin. The prophet on the contrary must 'rigorously maintain his aloofness from power'. His business is to proclaim the truth, whether pleasant or unpleasant. He must therefore practise self-denial and independence as well as the other qualities of political leadership.

The Great Leader.—Both types of men are indispensable to democracy. Without it politics become a matter of petty affairs and personal rivalries, uninspired and uninspiring. There are no ideals, no breadth of vision. And where there is no vision, the people perish.

The great leader on the other hand gives life to the bare bones of politics. He challenges every individual to make his contribution to a common cause and offers a meaning to the existence of the ordinary citizen. The essential difference between him and the competent politician is twofold; he does not flatter, but on the contrary is able to utter unpleasant home truths, and get them accepted, and to inspire his followers with capacity for sacrifice. This last may well be described as the hallmark of leadership.

Of course this does not mean that every citizen will respond to the challenge. The imperfections of human nature mean that in all societies there must be indifferent elements, careless of any general welfare and only intent on their own affairs. Nor will they be transformed into co-operating citizens by integration into groups which they will probably never

[1] Laski, 'The Elite in a Democratic Society' (*Harpers Magazine*, 1933).

join. That is inevitable, and we may as well admit both the fact and that nothing can be done about it.

What both free groups and inspired leadership can do, however, is to give every man his chance, both in the free association in which he can take a leading part, and in the larger collective action, in which his part, though smaller and less thrilling, will nevertheless give a meaning to his membership of the community. It is probably impossible to do more.[1]

4. THE CONFLICT BETWEEN THEORY AND PRACTICE

The Corruption of Democracy.—Finally we come to a problem already raised in our first chapter but to which we must return, namely the difficulty of reconciling the theory and the practice of government. Here is a country, whose institutions, on paper, seem an almost perfect expression of the democratic ideal. Its constitution provides for universal suffrage, a sovereign parliament, a responsible body of ministers, a freely chosen head of the state, an independent judiciary, legal guarantees of individual civil rights. What more can anybody want? But look at the actual working of the constitution, and what do you find? Most of the electors being uneducated, some indeed illiterate, adult franchise is a mere farce. Many do not really know for whom they are voting, or why; others vote as they are told to do by their clergy and landlords; those who might try and exercise an independent judgement are bullied, illegally disfranchised, sometimes beaten up or physically prevented from getting to the polls; dead voters are 'resuscitated' for the day of election, and the voting boxes are filled at the last moment with papers for the official candidates. In such a country—and there are many like it in the world of today—elections have never been 'free' in any sense of the term.

---

[1] 'Initiative and responsibility, the feeling of being useful and even indispensable, are vital needs of the human soul. Man needs to have to take decisions concerning major and minor problems involving interests not directly his own but with which he feels concerned. . . . In any person with any strength of mind the need for initiative goes as far as the need for command. An intense local and regional life, with many educational and social movements, will give to anyone not totally unfit the opportunity of exercising command during certain periods of his life.'—(Simone Weill, 'l'Enracinement', p. 20).

As to political office, this goes to rival cliques of wealthy influential people, who use their tenure of power for their personal ends; the civil service is full of their nominees and the spoils system reigns. If the law happens to provide for competitive examinations, these are 'rigged' so as to secure the success of the 'right' candidates. Judges may do their best to administer justice, but know they dare not apply the law to any who are 'in' with the government. Bribery is to be found among high and low. The big folk can ignore regulations which are ferociously applied to the small fry. The same holds good of taxation. As to freedom of the press, it doesn't exist. Newspapers are suspended and their editors sent to prison on the slightest excuse of 'disturbing order' by criticising the powers that be; the arbitrary arrest and imprisonment without trial of 'inconvenient' people are of daily occurrence.

And between those travesties of free democracy and the genuine article there are innumerable intermediate stages. Few countries can deny that their practice and their theory do not fully coincide; it is indeed difficult, not to say impossible, to secure the complete elimination of bribery, of inefficiency, of influence due to birth or wealth. The fact is that the corruption of democracy which we have been describing has been a stage in the political evolution of all countries, even of those who can now claim a very fair degree of achievement. When Walpole said that all men had their price, he spoke from direct knowledge of English eighteenth-century politics, and the condition of our civil service before its reform a hundred years ago presents an unbelievable picture of gross neglect of duty, nepotism and backwardness. Nor would the France of Napoleon III or the United States of Grant give one a much better impression.

All of which goes to show that the high sense of public spirit which alone makes real democracy possible is a lesson that takes a lot of learning and of constant re-learning. And this education in the right ways of common living is perhaps the biggest task facing a would-be democratic society, for no law can secure respect for law; this can only come from the citizens themselves. But the example of more evolved countries shows that the lesson *can* be learnt, and it is true, in that sense at least, that a people has the kind of government it deserves.

Some Other Problems.—This survey of the problems confronting democracy at the present time could obviously continue almost indefinitely. We could study the danger of leadership turning into personal tyranny, the disintegration of social ideals into the pursuit of material prosperity, the temptations to mental and physical idleness, both for the individual and for the group. And any student of politics could easily add to this list. The fact is, that as soon as some problems are solved others appear. This for two reasons, first, because men are imperfect, and no political system will do away with the evils inherent in the tangles and shortcomings of modern society—and of man himself, secondly, because man strives for perfection, and is therefore never satisfied; life consists in asking fresh questions, making fresh advances and thereby raising fresh problems. No democratic society can ever rest on its oars, for its work is never fully done.

CHAPTER XIII

THE DUTIES OF A DEMOCRATIC STATE

HAVING studied the machinery of the State, we must now ask the question. 'What is all that machinery for? What is it to do? In other words, what are the proper functions of the State? What is to be the range of its activities?'

I. SOME GENERAL PRINCIPLES OF STATE ACTION

Can we, first of all, lay down any general principles by which to test these activities? It is, of course, no answer to say the state must act for the general welfare or common interest; there is no form of state activity, down to the most ruthless and tyrannical, which has not been defended on that ground; and it is also obvious that no interference would be tolerated that did not claim the general welfare as its justification.

State Action and Freedom.—It may be well to remind ourselves of two facts laid down in an earlier chapter, first, that the freest possible development and creative self-expression of its members is the primary end of the state, and second that all state interference is an interference with their freedom. Therefore, all interference must be justified in relation to that primary end—in other words, it must be proved that the limitation of the freedom of citizens helps ultimately to secure for them more freedom than abstention would guarantee. This is the first criterion.

Bearing this in mind, we might next remark that the respective spheres of society and of each of its members can be roughly defined by stressing what must be, in all circumstances, the main specific contribution of each to the common work. Society has what may be termed a monopoly of permanence; it goes on for ever while the individual comes and goes: the latter's share is strictly limited in time and space: he only sees a small part of what society can see as a whole scheme. Again the latter has a fund of knowledge and experience which no single person can have. The individual on the other hand will contribute an experience which may be limited but is essential; he can tell how exactly the common action affects him personally: he can appraise and criticise. He is also the indispensable agent, both the subject and the object of a common action which must be based on a mutual relation and what may be called a balance of power. Too much individualism results in haphazard, unconnected, unrelated small-scale effort; as in the pioneer days of early time, it is everyone for himself or his group, family, or village. Too much social control, and the individual loses initiative, self-reliance; he is no longer interested, and collective action becomes the depersonalised inhuman all-embracing machine of a totalitarian state.

The question to be always kept before us then is the maintenance of this happy balance, in which each partner will get the fullest opportunity of giving of his best along the lines for which he is best fitted.

The State and Opinion.—Our first obvious conclusion will be that if there is one department of life from which the state is automatically barred, it is the formation and expression of opinion, especially religious opinion. This also has been discussed before in another connection; and we have seen that the community, no less than the individual concerned, suffers from any attempt to restrict this liberty, for without freely-thinking persons there is no community. The reason for this was stated some seventy years ago by Thomas Hill Green, when he laid it down 'that the state cannot interfere with any act, the doing or not doing of which is only valuable because of the motive for which it is done or not done'. Anything of the soul and of the mind derives its value exclusively from the reasons which prompts the action; 'compulsory religion' is a contradiction in terms. Beliefs can be neither enforced nor prohibited. And we are left with what we may call 'Green's Law', that 'the only acts which the State ought to enjoin or forbid are those of which the doing or not doing, *from whatever motive*, is necessary to the moral end of society', that end being the formation of free creative personalities. We may reinforce this principle with that enunciated by Professor Hocking, that state action must be 'readily defensible before the common judgement', from which it follows that it would be a mistake to imagine that state action can be on a higher level than the intelligence or the morals of the ordinary citizen; 'it cannot act well', adds Hocking, 'where prompt speculative inventiveness is needed nor where there is required a notable heightening of the level of conscience'.

He draws a further conclusion, in which Green would certainly have concurred, that 'the state must not supplant the normal actions of its members'. In other words, whatever can be entrusted to private initiative should be left to it. Democracy was built up on the spontaneous initiatives of religious and social groups—the congregation and the voluntary association. Nothing should be done to discourage these; the state should only come in when the matter in hand is either altogether beyond the capacities of private collective action, or belongs to a sphere that must obviously be the monopoly of the state.

Essential State Duties.—First among these would come the maintenance of public order, which includes the definition of citizen rights and the punishment of things done in excess or violation of those rights, that is the repression of crime. We saw in an earlier chapter that justice had gradually passed from private to collective hands; we may lay it down then that the making and administering of law are certainly primary state functions. This will not, however, help us to decide exactly in what disorders consist, and what are proper subjects for legislation; the agreement is only on the fact that these matters cannot be left in private hands.

In the second place it is agreed that only the state can enter into relations with other states by peaceful intercourse or war; it has a monopoly of collective defence and policy. This is so evident that we need spend no time in discussing it.

In the third place, it is also obvious that the state must be in sole control of the common resources; that it alone can decide what the community will spend, and on what it will spend it; and how much money will be collected. There are, however, the deepest possible differences of opinion on these points, and we shall return presently to these problems: how much of the collective wealth should be actually taken over by the state, what are proper objects of collective

expenditure, by what methods shall the money be collected
and on what basis will the burden be shared by the citizens—all
of these are part of one of the biggest issues involved in state
activity, namely the relation of the government to property.

This three-fold task—justice and order, external relations
and defence, and what Merriam calls 'the fiscal allocation
of the national resources for the general good', may be described as a universally agreed basic minimum for any state
at any time. Without these, there is no state in the modern
sense of the term. It is, however, equally true that no modern
state stops there. The least interfering of all now has a range of
activity which a century ago would have seemed like a distant
dream to the advocates of collectivism and a nightmare to the
defenders of *laissez-faire*.[1]

Education.—Of those newer activities some are in fact
practically universal. Education is one. There are few states
that do not feel responsible for the 'procuring and dissemination of knowledge' as Lord Lindsay calls it.[2] National state-
controlled systems of education, from infant school to university, exist in almost every country. Curiously enough this
has come about, mainly in the last hundred to a hundred and
fifty years, from two absolutely different causes. France and
Prussia were the pioneers of state education on the ground that
the state could not leave the making of citizens to private
hands; it must mould the young to the proper shape, give them

[1] The main issue of European politics is no longer whether greater
social security and economic equality shall be aimed at, nor whether those aims
shall be sought through extensive nationalisation of the main industries and
through social and economic planning. It is whether those aims shall or
should be pursued, this planned reconstruction should proceed through democratic Parliamentary methods, which shall safeguard civil liberties and
individual freedom, or through the methods of totalitarian collectivism and
the machinery of the single-party state. It is in short an issue of liberty and
not of equality. Are Freedom from Want and Freedom from Fear to be
sought in reconciliation with Freedom of Expression and Freedom of Worship, or at the expense of these Freedoms?' (*The Times Literary Supplement*,
October 12, 1948, p. 68).

[2] But as recently as 1928 an industrialist could write: 'The chief impediment to British agriculture is the legislation which forces children to go
to school, where they get no wages, and forbids them to work until they
are over fourteen years old. If they were allowed to work they would
get plenty of wages and would grow up to be strong and clever men and
women, who could get schooling in winter evenings and on Sundays.'
(Quoted in the *New Leader* for May 25, 1928.)

the right point of view, exclude dangerous ideas and risky experiments. In other countries, especially the Anglo-Saxon, state education came from the inadequacy of private enterprise, the need for greater expenditure, in a word, from social necessity, not from the pressure of political uniformity; it claimed that no citizen could really be free 'unless provided with the chance of mental development'. In other terms, one approach was from the danger of educational freedom, the other from the need of educational opportunities in the name of freedom. And this difference of approach has resulted in wide differences of educational policy, uniformity being the aim of the one, variety and experimentation of the other.

Welfare.—It is again very generally admitted that the state has a definite responsibility for the physical welfare of its members. Disease must be fought, hygiene must be developed, the quality of medical services guaranteed by oversight of the medical profession; in industry, hours of labour must be limited, conditions of work in shops and factories must be fixed and supervised, compensation for accidents enforced; in the general interest motor cars must be inspected, their speed limited, their drivers licensed; bakeries, slaughter houses, dairies, all come under some kind of control; building can only be carried out under certain conditions. It is in fact impossible to make a complete list of those departments of collective life in which the state interferes to say what may and may not be done, and in some cases what must be done, in order to maintain the health and physical security of its members.[1]

Rules of Daily Business.—Again, the most extreme opponent of state action will admit that the modern state must lay down an enormous number of rules as to how the everyday business life of the community shall be run. It must establish a uniform system of weights and measures, grant licences for the proper carrying out of certain occupations so as to guarantee the competence of its representatives, decide the conditions under which most of the community's work will be done (factory laws, inspection of premises of all kinds), fix the rules according to which commercial undertakings may be established (partnership and company laws) or may be ended (bankruptcy laws).

[1] And as Tawney remarks, 'Health is a purchasable commodity'.

9

These activities may so far all be described as protective—
the collectivity defending itself against the intellectual and
physical disintegration of its members, and for that purpose
going so far as to protect them against themselves—against
the results of their ignorance, or their foolishness, or their
carelessness, preventing them for instance from sacrificing
their health for the sake of higher wages by working excessive
hours. (We have already noted that many labour laws were
resisted by the workers as involving a loss of the potential
wages of themselves, their wives, and even their children.)
And we are also so far on solid ground, in the sense that
objection to these activities has to all practical purposes disappeared; there is no movement in any progressive state
for the repeal of this protective—sometimes called 'grand-
motherly'—legislation.

2. THE STATE AS A DIRECT AGENT IN ECONOMIC LIFE

A very different situation is created when we find the state
moving forward, as it were, to take its place as a direct sharer
in these activities. It is no longer a controller, it is an actor.
The modern state—and not necessarily a 'Socialist' state—
owns and runs buses, tramways, aeroplanes, railways, shipping
lines, canals, harbours, dockyards, electricity and water-
supplies. It monopolises postal services, and usually telegraph
and telephone as well. All roads and streets are its property.[1]
In some cases the state appears as a competitor to private
enterprise; in others it excludes it by establishing a monopoly.

The defence of state management and ownership is usually
based on the plea that the activities involved are too important
to be left in private hands, that profits arising from essential
public services, which everyone is bound to use, should go
to the public, that it may be necessary at times to provide them
at a loss, either the taxpayer or some more remunerative
undertaking making up the deficiency, which private enterprise obviously cannot do, since profit is its *raison d'être*.
And this again is, generally speaking, accepted—with occasional grumblings and protests perhaps, but accepted nevertheless. The state as manager seems to have come to stay.

[1] It is unnecessary to distinguish between state and municipal ownership;
in this connection both are forms of collective control.

Nationalisation.—Far more controversial is the industrial 'nationalisation' on which certain states have entered. By this is meant the taking over by the state not of a service which by its very nature is monopolistic, such as telephones or even railways, but of a department of production hitherto a field of the activities of many rival firms. Here the deliberate intention is to destroy the competition on which the industry has been built. The extreme instance of this is, of course, Soviet Russia, to which we shall return; but lesser instances abound within states which have not followed Russia in monopolising the whole industrial productive and distributive process. Such instances would include the state monopoly of armament manufacture, of matches and of tobacco in France, of the buying of cotton and wool, of coal mines, of road transport in Britain—countries in which nationalisation is only partial and exists side by side with free enterprise in some other department of production, and in which distribution remains free, sometimes within the limits of rationing and fixing of prices. The essential feature of the system is that the state thus controls the whole output of particular commodities, decides how much shall be produced and of what quality, thus substituting its decision for the play of supply and demand.

In this field controversy rages. Every extension of state activity is resisted, and in many cases opposition parties are pledged to the reversal of nationalisation policies wherever possible. But one of their chief criticisms is precisely that reversal of policy is impossible; to give back to free enterprise an industry that has been nationalised is like trying to get an omelet back into its component eggs—it just can't be done. Hence the need for extreme caution and careful preliminary enquiry before nationalisation policies are embarked upon. In all this the nationaliser replies that competition is wasteful, that he is bringing down prices, that the workers in nationalised industries feel they are working for the community and not for some one's private profit; and to those who complain of the slowness and inefficiency of state action he replies that the state must use the same kind of agents as private enterprise, that in any given country prevailing standards are bound to be much the same in private and public affairs, so that private enterprise is not likely to be remarkably efficient, quick and honest in a country where the administration is slow, lazy, wasteful, and corrupt.

Economics.—But we must now face a question which must have been for some time in the mind of any intelligent reader. By far the greater part of the activities we have been describing are definitely not political but economic, and one wonders whether the state has wandered from its primary existence as a political agency. It is indeed a fundamental question, for much of our modern organised life depends on the reply we give to it.

We would answer by asking once more another question, an old one, which is basic to our problem: what is the state? What is its *raison d'être*? It is to act for the collectivity in all those matters which the collectivity, through its representatives, decides to bring under its control. The state is the servant of the community; its purpose, in a phrase already quoted, is to make it more truly a community; and for that it must direct—help those forces that work towards better common living, check those that work away from it or against it.

It follows from this that we do not trouble ourselves to ask whether a particular activity is political, or economic or social. Is it an activity in which the community is vitally concerned? Is it to its interest to leave it to private hands or not? Is it something that should be encouraged or discouraged? Its exact nature is irrelevant; the only relevance is its relation to the common life.

Apart from this, however, the fact remains that at no time in history has it been possible to make a sharp distinction between the political and the economic; the difference may be useful for purposes of classification but it has no essential meaning. All life is based on a material setting, on the production and distribution of wealth. The most apparently non-material of human activities—religious, cultural, artistic, depend on being financed by groups of individuals, which means the community must be prepared to set aside, or at least to allow the setting aside, of the necessary part of its resources. It could easily prohibit such expenditure if it wished; and apart from that some communities may well be too poor to have anything to spare for anything of no immediate material gain.

Economic Aspect of Politics.—It is especially obvious that many of the ordinary activities of the state have an economic aspect, or may have economic consequences or may be connected with economic policy. Taking the question of crime, for instance, it is interesting to note that in most countries offences against property are dealt with more heavily than offences against persons: wife-beating and cruelty to children will be punished by a few months imprisonment; theft or arson by long periods of hard labour. We see there a survival of less civilised centuries, when life was cheap and property so sacred that the theft of any article worth more than five shillings was punishable by hanging. The problem of prison reform is complicated by economic considerations; one of the great difficulties is to find suitable occupations for prisoners, but for them to produce economically useful commodities involves competition with normal manufacturers. Disarmament raises the problem of work for the thousands employed in arsenals, and govern-ments have found it difficult to choose between their desire to save the money spent on ships and their desire to provide work for the government dockyards. In fact if we consider with care the consequences and implications of the varied activities of the modern state we shall soon perceive that few, if any, of them may be said to be free from all economic connections.

Just as a man's livelihood is the basic factor of his existence, so the basic factor in any society is 'the way it earns its living', as Tawney puts it. Political activities rest on a foundation of economic activities, which will go a long way towards determining the nature of the particular state, by what class of men it will be governed, and in whose interests politics will be run. 'Economic conditions', as Dewey says, 'are an essential part of the culture that determines the actual turn taken by political measures and rules.' It is important, for instance, to differentiate between highly industrialised countries like England, in which the agricultural interest plays virtually no part, and one like Bulgaria in which 80 per cent. of the people are peasants. Economic considerations are of primary importance in foreign policy and a self-contained country can ignore international trade and run certain risks which cannot be easily faced by one dependent on its foreign trade for its food supply.[1]

[1] Compare the foreign policies of France and of Great Britain, for instance.

3. THE STATE AND ECONOMIC FORCES

The State and Economics in History.—At no time in history has a state been able to leave economic life alone. The maintenance of legal slavery was the state's control of the chief source of labour, and many a war has been fought for the express purpose of making prisoners to be turned into slaves. The economic causes of state expansion, for the seizing of some particular source of food in times of scarcity, the control of some commercial route, the monopoly of some profitable trade need no elaboration. In medieval days state interference with economic life went to the length of prescribing what kind of cloth should be woven in some particular town, of imposing the use of woollen shrouds for burial, so as to encourage the woollen as against the new cotton industry. The control of exports and imports included sometimes complete prohibitions, sometimes bounties, shipping regulations—a most elaborate network of laws, supervisions, inspections, going far beyond what we are used to in normal times. Medieval society was in fact a rigid socio-economic-political group, in which a man's political rights and duties were fixed by his social and economic status.

This medieval rigidity was broken by the superseding of land by trade and industry as the main source of wealth and power. The new economic activity broke the bonds of medieval restriction. For one thing, the landlords as a governing class had one single interest; the new industrialists had not, and wanted freedom to expand and experiment each in his own way. For another, industry and commerce needed mobility of labour, and objected to a legal system tying down a man to a particular farm. They only wanted state intervention to defend their interests against their competitors from other countries ; at home they wanted a free hand. Hence the policy of *laissez-faire* or non-intervention, which marks the modern period—the eighteenth and nineteenth centuries in particular.

This could not and did not last. The new economic forces, while enormously increasing the total wealth of the community, failed in two ways. First, they tended to treat labour as a commodity to be used exclusively for profit ; second, they failed to tackle the problem of distribution and left large sections of the working population in a state bordering on chronic destitution. Slowly the community realised it would have to act for the protection of large numbers of its members and therefore of itself. Hence the growth of what we have already described as protective social legislation.

Forces of Modern Industrialism.—But the enormous expansion of modern industry and commerce, the coming of new techniques, showed that economic forces were playing an entirely new part in human life. Industrialism had released huge forces—'a direct control over material resources, markets, employment, credit, price, competition, the stimulation of demand—forces swifter than the political, more variable, more elastic, protean and multi-centred' (McIver) and it became clear that these forces would become dominant unless they were held in some sort of check. Economic and technical development was in fact creating a civilisation to which the political categories of the past were largely irrelevant. 'The new conditions incident to the extraordinary industrial development of the last fifty years', says Senator Root, 'are continuously and progressively demanding the readjustment of relations between great bodies of men, and the establishment of new legal rights and obligations not contemplated when existing laws and limitations were introduced.'

The problem of state action in economic affairs is therefore both old and new. It is old, in so far as it has never been possible to isolate these from the rest of the community's activities. 'The frequent implicit assumption', says Merriam, 'that there is a well-defined economic domain, exclusive and self-regulated, into which government should not enter, a self-regulated system of economics which if left alone will automatically produce the greatest flow of utilities for society is a fallacy disproved by the last century,' to which one could add that, as a conscious belief it was only held for a brief period in history. *Laissez-faire* is a short-lived episode, sandwiched in between the regulation of the medieval state and the protectionism of early modern times, to which the world seems to have returned. 'Political Science and Political Economy are inextricably inter-woven', says Nash, 'and the only measure of independence which they had was only valid during one restricted period of man's life, the rise and heyday of a capitalist economy based on the independence of business activity from all government control, except the furnishing and guarantee of the legal framework of private property.'

New Problems.—It is also true, however, that we are now confronting a situation which is new in a number of ways. The first is the hugeness of present-day economic forces— huge because of the scale on which they operate, because of the actual size of the productive machine in men and equipment, of the total amount of the product, of the extreme complexity and delicacy of the financial organisation on which it rests. The wonder is not that economic accidents happen but that they do not happen more often, and that when they do occur they are due less to faults in the system itself than to distur-bances from outside, wars in particular.[1]

The problem is new also because these forces are to a great extent blind.[2] We mean by this that they are largely un-organised, unrelated and in a sense purposeless. Each industry works largely on its own and from its own point of view, and so does each firm within the industry; no-one is much concerned to take a broad view of the industry as a whole and in relation to other industries; the sole test of success or failure is inevitably the profit or loss balance shown by the books. Each one may see his own little bit of the economic field, but is blind because he is really working in the dark.

The anonymity of economic forces is a third new feature. It is not for nothing that limited liability companies are called in French 'sociétés anonymes', for no one knows who they really are. 'It is the general tendency, of those who wield economic power, industrial, financial and commercial', says Pierre Maillaud, in 'The English Way' 'to hide their effective strength and make it inconspicuous by process of dispersion,' and he speaks of the 'elusiveness' of what he terms 'modern economic feudalism'. But such anonymity is dangerous;

---

[1] Wars have, of course, economic causes, but modern wars are primarily wars of nationalism, and nationalism is not a primarily economic phenomenon.

[2] One of the chief purposes of political society is to take cognisance of the fact that economic forces are blind, and yet strong, and that it is the function of the state to direct or limit the determination of forces, whether or not economic in character. (Wilson, 'The State in Theory and Practice.')

dangerous in itself, because whatever dare not operate in the open is thereby open to suspicion, and dangerous because it helps to spread anonymity in other fields, and 'the growth of anonymous power in the economic field is a contributory cause to the spread of anonymous political power, and to the building up of an anonymous machinery that may render democratic institutions inoperative'. The state cannot afford to let those nameless forces operate freely; 'it must track them to their retreat by building up bureaucratic machinery of investigation and control', for the security of its own institutions which depend on the light of open discussion and interaction; there is in fact a most striking contrast between the publicity of democratic politics and the secrecy of much of the contemporary economic life.[1]

Need for Social Control.—In the same way the hugeness and blindness of those forces mean that they need some kind of oversight, some adjustment to each other and to other aspects of national activity. All this comes to saying that the state must either exercise over economic forces enough control to keep them, as it were, in their proper place, or allow them to become in fact the real effective power—which is the aim of any free government, since those forces will be under no authority and be able to use their powers irresponsibly. If it is true, as has been said, that the modern state is essentially an economic state, it follows that the social control of economic forces is an essential function of the modern state.

The situation today is, in fact, the realisation of the fallacy of the old-time assumption, quoted by Whitehead, that 'industry would so develop as not greatly to disturb the orderly run of society'. It has disturbed it in 'a variety of ways, by creating conflicts of interest between unrelated and unassociated groups, by reducing the personal creative activity of workers to mere mechanical occupations, by wasting much of society's resources in unprofitable expenditure and production of little social value. Hence the need for new integrations, in which men will feel they are employed in worth-while

---

[1] 'The problem is not whether there are economic movements which elude human control, for obviously there are. It is whether the public possesses adequate guarantees that those which *are* controllable are controlled in the general interest and not in that of a minority.' (Tawney.)

9 *

occupations and will be able to relate their lives to understood and accepted ways of life.'[1]

4. THE STATE AND PROPERTY

The new economic development has created a number of new problems into which the community had to interfere. Some are problems of supply of essential services either too complicated for private enterprise, or too important to be left to the uncontrolled policies of the suppliers. Some arise out of rivalries of economic groups, whose conflicts are dangerous to common stability and security. Some consist in necessary adjustments of claims and counterclaims between employers and employees. And the manner of these adjustments is full of controversial points and policies, so that party programmes became largely plans of economico-social readjustment. From whatever angle we approach the problem, it is evident that state interference with private enterprise in the production and distribution of wealth becomes, in some way or another, interference with private property, its acquisition and use.

Defence of Property Rights.—Few individual rights have in modern times been as unquestionably assumed as the right of private property in all its numerous forms. (We say 'in modern times' because the idea of unrestricted private property rights is of comparatively recent growth.) The right of the individual to make money as he pleases, to use it as he pleases, and to dispose of it after death as he pleases is one of the foundations of the modern industrial order; and any restriction of that right by the state has only been carried through with the utmost difficulty, and that only when it could be conclusively proved that such restriction was so overwhelmingly in the material interests of the community that insistence on the individual right was in this case an infringement on the property rights of others. Even now the cry of 'property in danger' is used with much effectiveness against any schemes of economic reorganisation.

A current defence of property rights is the assertion that wealth being the creation of individual efforts, the individual's

[1] Berle and Mears, 'The Modern Corporation and Private Property', quoted by Russell, 'Power', p. 23.

enjoyment of it should not be interfered with. But this is surely making a number of assumptions that beg the point at issue. Are there no limits to such 'enjoyment'? Has the community no right to demand that such enjoyment shall be directed along socially useful channels? Further, how many people own wealth that they have really 'created'? Certainly not inherited wealth, nor wealth obtained by unearned increase of value, such as a rise in the value of land, or a sudden boom in certain stocks. Much wealth is created by the work of others, and is not owned by its real creators. Lastly, and this is still more fundamental, is any wealth at all really 'created' by individual effort? Take the wealth produced by a successful business: who is its creator? the actual founder who has the intelligence and the ability certainly plays an important part, but he is by no means the sole creator of that wealth. Alone, he would have been helpless; society helped him at every stage— not only by the direct loan of capital (which is retributed, and that often excessively) not only by the labour of the employees (which is also retributed, more or less adequately) but by the existence of a complex machinery of credit and exchange, of the innumerable agents society has organised for the carrying on of economic life.

Wealth a Social Creation.—'The accumulation of property', writes Benjamin Franklin, 'must be an effect of the protection afforded to it by the joint strength of society in execution of its laws. Private property is a creature of society, and is subject to the calls of that society, whenever its necessities shall require it, even to its last farthing; its contributions therefore to the public exigencies are not to be considered as conferring a benefit to the public, entitling the contributors to the distinctions of honour and power, but as the return of an obligation previously received, or the payment of a just debt.

'The important ends of civil society, and the personal securities of life and liberty, these remain the same in every member of society; and the poorest continue to have an equal claim to them with the most opulent, whatever difference time, chance or industry may occasion in their circumstances.'

In other words, wealth is partly an individual, but mainly a social creation, and society may well declare that 'the individual is entitled to a reward for his own productive effort, and the community is entitled to receive the benefit of the co-operative aspect of that effort'.[1]

Limits to Property Rights.—There is, of course, no modern society which recognises an unlimited right of private property. Individual wealth is taken directly by taxation of all kinds, indirectly by all measures which control the acquisition and use of wealth: usury laws, factory acts, adulteration laws, tariffs, etc. But modern societies, however much they may interfere with private property, assume that such interference is only to be defended in case of exceptional necessity, and that, unless that necessity be proved, the individual's freedom remains unimpaired to hold uncontrolled whatever he has been able to acquire without actual breaking of existing laws. The idea of property needing any kind of moral, or even economic, justification is alien to current conceptions. 'I can do what I like with my own', and 'my own' is whatever I have been able to acquire lawfully, however morally or socially indefensible my methods of acquisition may have been.

The result of such an attitude has been the creation of appalling inequalities in wealth, and the appearance of theories denying in varying degrees the validity of private property. The declaration 'I can do what I like with my own', is met by Proudhon's outburst that 'Property is theft', and the widespread influence of Communist doctrines of all kinds forces one to formulate some coherent theory of property.

Social Role of Property.—Private property may be said to meet two essential and legitimate needs—self-expression and security. The propertyless man is, to say the least, hampered in his desire to express himself; there can be no fullness of life without the control of those things that make up the material background of our daily intimate life. A system of society which did not allow us to decide how we would spend our own share of wealth, however small, would not be tolerated for long by the great masses of men. But most people nowadays have so little wealth that all they have goes to the meeting of immediate needs—food, clothes, shelter, so that only a small margin is left through which personality can really be expressed.

Further, to most people property means security and is

[1] 'Industry and the State' by four Conservative M.P.s, 1924.

sought for as such. Men cling to wealth for what it will bring now, but also for what it will bring later, to them or their descendants. They see in it a defence against ill-health, unemployment, poverty in old age. This is natural enough but it is clear that only few enjoy this security through their own property.

Private property, in a word, is neither right nor wrong in itself; it has to be encouraged in so far as it is essential to the creation of true social values; it has to be perpetually subjected to the double test of function and use. The duty of the state will be therefore to secure for each citizen those material conditions which will give him the fullest opportunity possible of a full life, and will apply that test to every possible intervention or non-intervention. It will grant the individual economic freedom, as long as that freedom is not interfering with the freedom of his neighbour—and no longer. It will not tolerate any economic system in which men are mere tools, sacrificed to profit, and will deny that the community can possibly benefit by such a system.

Problems of Distribution.—The problems connected with property are so numerous that only a few can be discussed here. First of all we will mention those involved in the inequalities of its distribution. No society has ever succeeded in eliminating these but the glaring contrasts between extreme wealth and extreme poverty are largely a result of modern industrialisation. One of the chief results of this contrast is the social and political instability which it causes, and twenty-three centuries ago already the Greek philosopher Aristotle attributed revolution to 'the disproportional increase in any part of the State. When the rich grow numerous, or properties increase, the form of government changes to oligarchy or government of families.' 'From difference of degree and kinds of property', wrote Madison over two thousand years later, 'ensues a division of society into different interests and parties', and a little later his fellow-American, Daniel Webster, declared that 'a form of government is determined by the nature and distribution of property, and disturbances arise principally from the conflict of groups resulting from variation in the form and distribution of property', and he added that 'universal suffrage is incompatible with great inequality of wealth, and that the freest government would not long be acceptable if the tendency of its laws were to create a rapid accumulation of property in a few hands, and to render the great mass of the population dependent and penniless'. And these Americans were only echoing their seventeenth-century Puritan forefathers, such as Winstanley's 'Wherefore that there is such wars and rumours of war? Only to uphold civil property of Honor, Dominion and Riches. Property and single interest divides the people of a land and the whole world into parties, and is the cause of all wars and bloodshed and contention everywhere.' 'Equality of estates (property) causes equality of power, and equality of power is the liberty not only of the commonwealth but of every man', says Harrington, 'the rich artificial thieves doe rob the poore and that under a feigned show of justice, and a seeming holinesse, and when they have done it most impiously they say and affirm that God's Providence hath made them rich and those whom they have robbed poore, for they say that God's Providence makes rich and poore.'[1] Rightly does Professor Tawney conclude that it is really the difference of economic and social structure that determines the difference between states.

Dangers of Economic Inequality.—Economic inequality has other dangers than direct revolution; it creates between classes of society such differences of culture, of health, of what mainly gives meaning to life that Disraeli could speak a century ago of the 'two nations' in England. Here are some illustrative statistics. In the city of Glasgow the death rate is twice as heavy in an industrial as in a residential area, the infant mortality rate three times, the death rate from phthisis and other respiratory diseases five times, from infectious diseases fifteen times. The figures for Manchester were much the same.[2] About that same time Professor Clay calculated that half of the British national income went to one-twentieth of the population the remaining nineteen-twentieths having to be satisfied with the other half.[3] And if we take capital instead of income we

[1] Quotations from Petrogorsky, 'Democratic Ideals in the Seventeenth Century'.

[2] Figures for 1927. They have certainly improved since, but the contrast cannot have disappeared.

[3] In the United States the Brookings Institute came to the conclusion, just about the same time, that the richest 1 per cent. of the population received as much of the national income as the poorest 60 per cent.

get an even more glaring inequality which Tawney brands in these scathing words: 'Where conditions are such that two-thirds of the wealth is owned by one per cent. of the population, the ownership of property is more properly regarded as the badge of a class than as the attribute of a society. But,' he goes on to say, 'in conditions in which ownership is centralised and diffused, the institution of property is a principle of unity. It confers a measure of security and independence on poor as well as on rich, and softens the hardness of economic contrasts by a common similarity of social status. But in the conditions most characteristic of an industrial society its effect is the opposite. It is a principle, not of unity but of division. It sharpens the edge of economic disparities with humiliating contrasts of power and helplessness—with differences not merely of income but of advice, civilisation, and manner of life.'

The State and Redistribution of Wealth.—The problem of state interference with property is therefore many-sided. That the state must evidently take in taxation what it needs to carry out its duties is admitted by everybody. But is it the duty of the state to try and minimise inequalities of wealth by deliberate transfer of wealth from some sections of the population to others? This is, of course, what happens whenever the state deliberately taxes wealth by such devices as exempting low incomes and putting a supertax on high incomes, the tax going up to over 90 per cent. on the rich. There is a further shift of wealth whenever the state provides from the funds thus obtained services which, though nominally available to all, are really only used by the less fortunate—free schooling, insurances, etc. These mean in fact a very appreciable addition to wages.

Here are some interesting figures for Britain in 1937. Of income tax 68 per cent. came from incomes over £10,000, 30 per cent. from incomes between £10,000 and £125, and 2 per cent. from incomes below £125.[1] Of the benefits provided by those taxes, nearly half went to incomes below £125 and less than 1 per cent. to those over £10,000. The writer from whom we are quoting, Dr. Barna,[2] calculated

[1] But these highest incomes only paid 3 per cent. of indirect taxes, the lowest 14 per cent. and the middle incomes 83 per cent., since these fall on consumption.

[2] In his, 'Redistribution of Incomes Through Public Finance'.

that about £250 million were annually redistributed by state action. 'But', adds the reviewer of the book in *The Times Literary Supplement*, 'this is no more than 5 or 6 per cent. of the national income, and the group below poverty line could have been completely removed by a more effective redistribution of the national resources.'

Modern Taxation.—This, it is true, was a dozen years ago, and war taxation has certainly shifted a greater proportion of the national income, while war and post-war high employment and new insurance schemes have gone a long way to diminishing the number of those living near the margin of destitution.[1] But there is, naturally, a great deal more to do along that line—if we want to move in that direction. Some people, of course, do not, and consider that interference with property has gone far enough; but in the main the old complaint that the state has no 'right' to carry out those policies of redistribution, and that high taxation is 'robbery and confiscation' is not often heard nowadays. There is widespread agreement that 'only the state can accumulate for social ends that large element of wealth which does not depend on the energy of living individuals' as Hobhouse puts it.

Criticism today is directed not so much against the principle of state action towards property as toward its effectiveness. Does it not tend to discourage initiative and therefore diminish the total collective productivity? Is not the state in fact engaged in killing the goose that lays the golden eggs? But the whole science of modern finance is precisely knowing how far to go and when to stop; it is in fact the technique of the best and wisest disposal of the national resources—in a word, it means wise planning.

[1] In 1936, Lord Boyd-Orr, the great food expert, calculated that 30 per cent. of the population of Britain was under-nourished. In order to be properly fed the British people should have had 30 per cent. more meat, 40 per cent. more butter, 55 per cent. more eggs, 80 per cent. more milk, 87 per cent. more vegetables and 124 per cent. more fruit. A building enquiry made at the same time showed that there was a need for 15 million new dwellings if overcrowding was to be eliminated, but that most available steel went to skyscrapers for office blocks because there was greater profit to be made that way than in building working-class homes.

5. THE STATE AND PLANNING

What is Planning?—Everybody talks of planning nowadays —but what exactly is planning? It was defined by Sir Stafford Cripps in the House of Commons in November, 1946, as 'the laying-out of all national resources in the national interest to a nationally desirable end, and the organisation of the necessary methods, by the use of all the means that the people in a democratic society are prepared to give to the government.' 'It includes', he went on to say, 'six principal elements: choice of what is to be produced, the supply of the necessary labour, the supply of materials, the supply of capacity, the supply of the best location and the supply of finance.'

And Sir Stafford Cripps' definition can be completed by what Mr. Herbert Morrison had stated a few days earlier to be 'the five stages of planning'—making up one's mind to plan, getting the necessary facts, devising alternative plans, choosing between these and deciding what is to be planned and what is to be left unplanned, and finally carrying out the plans, and adjusting and devising so that things happen in the right way and at the right places and at the right time.

The Need for Planning.—Why are we all planners nowadays? Because of the inability of a non-planned economy to meet the needs of the modern world. Inequalities of wealth we have already noticed, and in their present form these are intolerable in a professedly democratic society. Monopoly has too often replaced competition and deprived society of the advantages of the competitive system without removing most of its drawbacks. More than anything else, however, is unemployment the disease of our time which the system has failed to cure and which must demand the attention of other doctors— i.e. of other economic systems. In fact, it is probably true to say that democratic planning has become the only alternative to Communism, which is one hundred per cent. planning.

Unemployment.—A book like this cannot enter into the problem of unemployment. It is enough to remind readers that in the fifteen years or so preceding the war no industrial country had less than one-tenth of its workers unemployed, and usually a much larger proportion. What unemployment means in physical and moral distress we cannot attempt to describe here. It is enough to say that the consciousness of not being wanted, of having no place to fill in the active life of one's community is one of the keenest forms of suffering an individual can have to face. Even war may well appear preferable to a state of things in which there is no incentive for self-expansion or self-development, in which a man in the fullness of his powers is nothing but an idle mouth to feed, in which life has nothing to offer, no effort to demand.

Nor must we forget the cost of unemployment to the community. The American depression meant a loss in goods and services to the amount of 350 billion dollars. This amount is more than double the capital stock of all the corporations in the United States. It is enough to build 350 river valley developments the size of the Tennessee Valley Authority. It is enough to pay in full for 70 million homes at $5,000 each, more than three times as many as would be necessary to eliminate all the slums in the United States, both urban and rural, and the same would be true of Britain and Germany, the two other chief sufferers from the plague of unemployment.

The chief feature of the period between the two world wars was the complete failure of free enterprise to prevent large-scale unemployment, whether in Germany, Britain, or America. This being so, and security of employment being the dominant demand of the age, for that, if for no other reason, there seems to be no escape from some degree or form of planning; and the only question is 'Who is to do the planning?' The problem in other terms is the use of the economic process for the purpose of general welfare and not for the advantage of one section of the community, the owners of the machinery of production. That is *the* problem of today.

Planning and Techniques.—Planning has in fact become necessary because of the size of society and the complexity of the new techniques which are perpetually appearing. 'Inventions create new possibilities of organisation, administration, education and social co-operation, which make it easy to influence human behaviour and pave the way to totalitarian forms of government if man cannot control them and use them for freedom. This is where planning comes in—the awareness of a situation as a whole, the capacity to see things in relation to each other—the habit of thinking in terms of whole social situations made necessary by the size and complexity of the modern scene.'[1]

Planning is necessary whenever technique goes beyond the human scale—it may do this either by excessive monopolies, by competition to the death, by equipment being either defective or too rapidly renewed and by the overlapping of problems creating difficulties beyond the scope of existing organisation.

Assumptions of Planning.—Planning, like every human system, rests, of course, on a number of assumptions—i.e. of unprovable bases of opinion which must be taken for granted. One is that there must be in the present world an over-all social control which only the state can exercise. Another is that while there is a wide sphere in which such control is needed, there must be a clear recognition of areas of self-activity into which the state will not ordinarily penetrate, but will strive to foster and protect. A third is the need for the control system to be carefully reorganised in terms of modern science, technology, and education. A fourth is the need for the adequate recognition and protection of value systems, other than political, in the framework of political association. Lastly, it is necessary to co-ordinate with great care national and local policies, and public, quasi-public and private plans.

But behind all this lies the fundamental assumption, as Mrs. Wootton says, that 'objectives do exist which are for the benefit, if not of all, at least of so overwhelming a proportion of the community that it is safe to work for them even at the cost of some restraint of freedom of action, and that it is possible to determine those objectives with a reasonable degree of accuracy'. It also assumes that 'the people on whom

---

[1] This involves in particular any policy that restricts production for fear of a glut. Everybody over a certain age will remember the deliberate destruction of foodstuffs during the 'economic blizzard' of 1929-33. But as late as 1942 the Federation of British Industries, in its 'Report on Post-War Reconstruction' expressed its fear of an over-abundance of raw materials. 'It might be solved by a drastic curtailment of production of the primary productive countries.' The Report adds, however, somewhat naïvely, that 'a policy of artificial scarcity of essential raw materials and foodstuffs does not seem a sound basis on which to build a more prosperous world'. No indeed!

lies the duty of making decisions for the benefit of all will in fact continuously pursue those objectives'.

Planning is, of course, a matter of degree—nowhere is nothing or everything planned. The difference between a planning and an unplanned society is in the emphasis, and particularly on the deliberateness and publicity of planning. It is in planning by the organ representing the community—'the conscious and deliberate choice of economic priorities by some public authority'.

Planning and the Citizen.—How will planning affect the citizen? First as producer, it will undoubtedly limit his choice of work. We already have some indication of this by the fact that unemployment benefit may be conditional on either moving to another district or accepting to be trained for a new job—although no-one is actually compelled to fall in with those changes. It will certainly involve the closing of certain occupations or their limitation by some kind of test, but as Mrs. Wootton remarks 'to close the doors of an occupation to people who have never followed it is a very small infringement of freedom'. Planning is obviously incompatible with the overcrowding of certain occupations, with shortages of workers in others; the equilibrium may be restored by attracting people by higher pay, or by eliminating candidates by means of insistence on vocational tests.

What about the citizen as consumer? It is clear that the old law of demand and supply can no longer be the only factor in determining production. Capacity to purchase an article will no longer ensure its manufacture if the resources of the community are needed to produce something more socially useful. Selling on points and rationing are obvious instances of limitations to the consumer's freedom.

Planning must also take into consideration the fact that consumer demand is only an indication of capacity to buy, not of real need, and may involve the supplying of certain things below cost price by means of subsidies; without these the whole of our war economy would have collapsed.

Another limitation on the consumer's freedom will be in the sphere of investment, i.e. in his freedom to save rather than to spend his money. It is evident that the total amount of employment in existence in any country at any time is made up of the expenditure on goods and services by two elements, the citizens and the government; unemployment arises when people do not buy enough and the government is unwilling or unable to make up the deficiency; if the mass of the people do not buy enough to maintain full employment, and yet are buying all they can, then wages are too low, and too much wealth is going to those who can afford not to buy and prefer to invest. But since it may be laid down as a general principle that some investment is necessary, there must usually be some governmental expenditure to maintain full employment.

Planning and Private Enterprise.—None of this, of course, need involve Socialism. Private enterprise can, as it were, be given its head, the normal price-system be allowed to work freely, and only if the level of unemployment tends to fall does the government outlay set to work the resources which private enterprise is not using. It does so by such undertakings as slum clearance, road building, afforestation, etc., or direct payments to consumers such as pensions, family allowances, unemployment benefits, food subsidies, etc. The Roosevelt New Deal is an excellent example of considerable planning under capitalistic private enterprise. 'From the point of view of creating employment, expenditure by the rich is just as good as expenditure by the poor and there is a good deal of scope for promoting expenditure without making any attack on the existing distribution of income. New Deal planning may be framed in such a way as to solve the problem of unemployment without disturbing the capitalist system in any way.'[1]

Planning in fact may be looked upon both as a checking and as a restoration of competition.[2] In those essential services which cannot be a matter for rivalry without damage to the community, there must be the establishment of a control that will eliminate competition based on profit making. In other words, wherever monopoly is practically inevitable by the nature of the undertaking, state control seems necessary. But whenever rival services can be offered without damage,

---

[1] Joan Robinson, 'Socialist Planning', in the *Political Quarterly*.

[2] 'Competition, the beneficent private war which makes one man strive to climb on the shoulders of another and remain there.' (Sir Henry Maine, quoted by Tawney, 'Equality' p. 140.)

the state may well step in to guarantee real competition— to prevent practices which may become monopolistic, to ensure that competition shall be fair, that the quality of the goods shall be guaranteed, that competition shall not be at the expense of the people engaged in the work, whether in wages or conditions of labour. The prevention of industrial abuses, the arbitration of industrial conflicts, 'keeping the ring and seeing fair play' may well be as important a part of planning as the establishment of public ownership or the use of taxation to redistribute wealth, or restriction in the use of land.

All this planning involves, of course, drastic intervention with private property rights. 'Social planning', says Niebuhr, 'is possible only by the rigid circumscription or total abolition of the rights of property. It is implicitly assumed that modern society fails to plan its economic processes by lack of intelligence. The fact is that the interests of powerful and dominant groups, who profit from the present system of society are the real hindrance to the establishment of a national and just society!'[1]

6. PROBLEMS OF PLANNING

Limitations.—The dangers and drawbacks of planning are numerous. The first is perhaps the fact that it can only be carried out by each state within its own frontiers, and stands therefore in direct opposition to the co-operation between states which, to many, appears more essential at the present time. Even Socialism, which used to pride itself on its 'international' outlook, is now becoming intensely national, because the state unit, being the area in which Socialism has to be established, must be defended at all costs for the sake of the Socialist experiment.[2] Russia offers the striking instance of the building up of a new Communist patriotism, using for this the traditions of the old Tsarist devotion to the Russian fatherland. And yet the urgent need of the world is to transcend those state boundaries in every aspect of human activity.

A second difficulty is that 'Planning is the result of fear and insecurity, and what men do when they are afraid is apt to be

---

[1] 'Nature and Destiny of Man,' p. 213.
[2] See Borkenau, 'Socialism, National and International'.

hastily and imperfectly conceived'.[1] Planning assumes danger—danger of scarcity; it is a philosophy of emergency, of crisis, as the Germans would say, and as such can only have a relative validity.

Last but not least is the fact that it involves greater concentration of power in the hands of the state—and power once given cannot easily be taken back. It is not only a matter of merely economic organisation; the line cannot easily be drawn, and economic power easily becomes general control over the whole life of the community. The example of Russia is again significant in this respect.

Planning and Freedom.—And this brings one to what is really the central problem of all planning. Is it compatible with individual freedom? 'Britain', said Mr. Morrison in October, 1946, 'is the first great nation to attempt to combine large-scale economic and social planning with a full measure of individual rights and liberty.' Can she succeed?

Only the future can answer the question, but we may quote here in conclusion, a striking passage from a review of Professor Mannheim's 'Man and Society in an age of Reconstruction'[2].

'Planning may be described as the last of three decisive stages in human thought—chance discovery and invention being the first two. This third stage comes about with advance from the deliberate invention of single objects or institutions to the deliberate regulation and intelligent mastery of the relationships between the objects.' This is not incompatible with freedom, for the true background of freedom has always been conformity rather than chaos. 'The liberal age could give its whole attention to the propagation of the idea of freedom, for it could build on the foundations of the traditional conformity it had inherited from the old community culture of the Middle Ages.' Our search for freedom involves, therefore, a search for a new conformity: 'Identification with other members of the society, collective responsibility and the necessity for possessing a common background for our attitudes and behaviour.' This must be achieved within the framework of free parliamentary institutions. 'We must insist', the

[1] Mitrany, *Commonwealth Review.*
[2] In *The Times Literary Supplement.*

reviewer adds, 'that the technical problems of society cannot
be solved by tactics and class warfare alone. There is a terrible
destiny in store for generations who are brought up to believe
in the false alternatives, democracy and planning.'

Planning and the Old Liberalism.—The fact is that, just as
man must learn to live in peace with members of other states
if he wants to survive, so he must learn to reconcile the essentials of his individual freedom with life in a planned society.
'While planlessness', says Mannheim, 'is anarchy and chaos,
yet planning must not do violence to the spontaneous forces
in society.' How completely dead are the old conceptions of
economic *laissez-faire* is shown by what happened to Mr.
Walter Lippmann. His book 'The New Society' is a defence of
the liberal tradition, in which he argues that large-scale planning
is incompatible with democracy, and that even the policy of
'gradual collectivism' is driven inevitably toward the
aggrandisement of the sectional interests of 'pressure-groups',
toward divisive nationalism, and toward power-politics and
the menace of 'total wars'. Yet his list of what even a liberal
state must undertake, includes: 'Large social expenditure
on eugenics and education; the conservation of the people's
patrimony in the land and natural resources; the development
of the people's estate through public works which reclaim
land, control floods and droughts, improve rivers and harbours
and highways, develop water power, and establish the necessary
facilities for transporting and exchanging goods and services;
providing the organisation of markets by information, inspection and other services; insurance and indemnification
against the risks and losses of technological and economic
change; and many other things, such as providing the
opportunities for recreation which would not otherwise
exist in specialised and congested communities.'

In the same way Professor Fisher, whose 'Economic
Progress and Social Security' breathes, as a reviewer said,[1]
the spirit of nineteenth-century liberalism, argues nevertheless
that, in order to promote labour mobility, social insurance
should be all inclusive; he advocates family allowances,
bonuses for mobile workers, better housing amenities, an
educational policy which gives 'a larger number of people an

[1] In the *New York Times.*

opportunity to acquire higher types of skills', a reduction in direct taxes on business, and above all perhaps, the breakdown of monopoly; and he conlcudes by saying that if the fruits of increased productive efficiency are to be enjoyed, there must be more or less continuous transfers of resources of production for the expansion of old or the opening up of new fields for employment and investment. To the extent in which these transfers are successfully resisted, the achievement of higher standards of living is postponed, and the risks of insecurity, by reference to which resistance is often defended, are usually increased. The creation of conditions in which transfers will be less difficult and resistances less likely to be successful should, therefore, be a major objective of public policy. What more can the most enthusiastic planner demand?

One essential fact which emerges from this discussion is the enormous importance of business and the business man in modern society. The times are past when a political philosopher like Aristotle could dismiss the economic side of a community in the contemptuous term 'Banausia', which the dictionary defines as 'handicraft, the life and habits of a mechanic, hence vulgarity and bad taste'—an occupation no self-respecting person would take up. There was in his day no realisation of the economic basis of all common life and therefore of the important part played by its representatives. We know better now. 'The behaviour of a community', says Whitehead, 'is largely dominated by the business mind. A great society is a society in which its men of business think greatly of their functions. Low thoughts mean low behaviour, and often a brief orgy of exploitation; low behaviour means a descending standard of life.'

Conditions of Planning.—What are finally the conditions for successful planning?

First and foremost, to realise the risks involved. Planning is a delicate instrument, double-edged, boomerang-like in its effects. Too much of it, or using it in the wrong place, may simply paralyse productive processes and diminish instead of increasing the total wealth.

Secondly, to realise the need for the most careful selection of the planners. So much power is put in their hands, so disastrous would be the result of their mistakes, that everything must be done to secure the right man in the right place—a thing easier said than done.

Thirdly, to simplify election issues. The electorate is easily bewildered, very apt to think the problems are really beyond it. If we believe that in fact they are not, but that most political questions are capable of being presented in their essentials as simple alternatives, parties must spend much time and care on their presentation. No hasty last minute posters and addresses will serve the purpose.

Fourthly, we must decentralise, that is, let each problem be dealt with in the smallest area compatible with efficient handling, so that the voters should be to the greatest extent possible deciding on issues and men with whom they are familiar; the more 'local' the consultation, the lesser the margin of irreducible error, the greater the probability of knowledge based on direct experience.

And lastly there must be an educated electorate, by which is not meant book learning, necessary as it is, but the capacity to judge, the power to let reason predominate over emotion and prejudice, to see through shallow argument and self-interest. This is no easier to achieve than the other conditions, but without them planning will be either ineffective or tyrannical, or run for the benefit of the few and not of the community.

7. THE SOCIALIST CHALLENGE

We said a moment ago that the central problem of planning was its compatibility with individual freedom. But many people are more concerned with the question of planning's adequacy to meet the needs of today and consider that a more complete collective control of economic life has become an absolute necessity. They are Socialists.

Socialism and Planning.—Planner and Socialist have some assumptions in common. They agree that free enterprise fails to deal adequately with the problem of distribution, and creates both inequality and unemployment; they further agree that in a time of scarcity it is necessary to husband resources, prevent waste, and therefore lay down the general lines of a programme of production, which in fact may well be much the same in a planned and in a moderately socialised economy.

Justice or Efficiency.—Where does the difference lie? It is in the difference of inspiration. The planner is primarily concerned with the efficiency of the economic system, the Socialist with its justice. No doubt many planners are conscious of the injustices of our present system, and many Socialists of its inefficiency, but we believe the difference of starting point is both real and important. The planner looks at the interests of the community, the Socialist at the plight of its masses; the two may travel for some way along the same road, but points of departure and arrival are not the same. A planner may end in a totalitarian state of a Fascist pattern; a Socialist may end as a Communist; without reaching those extremes, their ideals may be realised in very different types of state, the one authoritarian, the other equalitarian.

It is the injustice of the present order that has inspired Socialism, from its French pioneers, St. Simon, Fourier and Proudhon, to Karl Marx and its present representatives in all countries. It was a reaction against the glaring inequalities which we have already mentioned—inequalities that were even more marked in the earlier days of the industrial revolution, when many literally sweated and starved to keep a few in luxury. It was a revolt against the exploitation by man of man and of child, in field, factory, mine and workshop. It was a protest against the building of an economic and social system on the incentive of profit not service, believing that an injustice was thus perpetuated against human nature. It was opposed to the principle of competition, believing that the perpetual semi-conflict at home was one of the chief causes of war outside.

The Moral Aspect of Socialism.—The Socialist challenge to the existing order was therefore primarily moral, and the waste and inefficiency involved formed only a secondary consideration. It was also the assertion of the rights of a class which, it declared, had never obtained a fair deal anywhere, the class composed of the workers on which the system depended. At one time in history this class, the proletariat, was chiefly made up of slaves; then of half-free or nominally free agricultural labourers; finally of industrial urban workers. This class, urged the Socialist, had always been deprived of its share of the product of its labour, denied the opportunities

open to the possessing minorities by effective participation
in the affairs of the community, for political power without
its economic counterpart was only a delusion and a snare.
No constitutional reform, no change of regime, not even improvements in social conditions would avail anything as long
as there was no change in the system by which the few owned
and controlled the capital necessary for production, and thereby
the whole productive and distributive machine. Community
ownership and control, production for general use and not
for private profit, abolition by a juster distribution of the
glaring contrast between wealth and poverty, social security
for all—so far all Socialists went, and have always gone together.

Socialist Evolution.—For the realisation of this programme
all that was apparently needed was organisation and patience.
The traditional Socialists, represented mainly by the French and
English currents of Socialist thought, believed in the peaceful
realisation by constitutional means of the workers' aims, in a
free classless democracy in which the workers, having obtained
a majority in representative assemblies, would be able to
establish the control by the community of the instruments of
production and distribution. They believed in the ultimate
readiness of the possessing class to yield, both because of the
justice of the workers' claim and because of its inability
to resist with any hope of success the overwhelming predominance of numbers. The vote, trade union organisation,
education, would ultimately secure, not indeed a paradise, but
an adequate guarantee of comfort and welfare for all. What the
more extreme or Communist answer was we shall see later.

This Socialism made slow but fairly steady headway in most
industrialised countries, especially in Britain, France, Germany,
Belgium, Italy, and Scandinavia. Strong 'Labour' parties were
able to enforce, even before the First World War, large programmes of reform, and some cabinets actually had Socialist
ministers. But Britain in 1945 was the first major country
to put into power a homogeneous Socialist ministry, pledged
to a complete programme of socialisation.

It is therefore too early to speak of the success or failure of
what we may term 'Constitutional' Socialism; only some years
hence will it be possible to pronounce on the practical working
and results of a socialised economy, combined with a great

deal of free enterprise in minor productive and distributive processes, and with maintenance of democratic methods, including freedom of dissent and criticism.

Problems of Socialism Today.—It is only possible here to offer a few remarks on the general position of Socialism in the world today. First, it must be noticed that it was greatly helped by the establishment during the war of large-scale semi-socialised planning. The aim was not Socialism but in its results it went a long way along the road. A society at war could not tolerate waste, production for sheer profit and not for need, the misuse of resources and of labour. And the inevitable maintenance of many controls after the end of hostilities paved the way for their integration into the permanent pattern of the national life.

The success of war-time controls removed the old-time objection that Socialism was impracticable. It did not, however, remove the objection of high costs. In war time price is a minor factor; in peace time it is all important. A devastated world, short of goods of all kinds, is still prepared to absorb our socialised production; but the problem of competition with other economic systems in more normal times remains. Another objection is that of the creation of a huge bureaucracy, expensive and often slow, apt to think of itself as an end and not a means. We need not, however, go back to this problem already dealt with in an earlier chapter; but we must remember that it *is* a problem.

A third consideration is that Socialism does not really solve the question of the relation of the worker to the employer. It is true the employer is now the community and not an individual or a company out for profit, but this does not automatically guarantee satisfactory conditions of work, or adequate wages; strikes of state employees have occurred. The problem of establishing genuine democracy in industrial production is still there, and must be solved if the socialised machine is to work harmoniously and efficiently.

Fourthly, it must be noted that Socialism does not guarantee honesty any more than efficiency. As Bernard Shaw says, 'many Socialists believe that socialist government is incorruptible. It is in fact far more corruptible than unsocialist government, from which it differs in employing the power and riches of the state to develop agricultural and industrial production instead of letting them alone, and confining itself to police work and to those indispensable services which are in their nature incapable of making commercial profits or are beyond the resources of private capital'. Clearly such an enormous extension of state power and activity carries with it a formidable extension of its possible abuse.

Lastly, even more than other forms of planning Socialism must face the problem of freedom. Planning, after all, may take more risks there; it is out for efficiency, nor personality. But Socialism dare not neglect the issue. It must be able to prove to the worker that its controls will not make him any less of a free man; otherwise, whatever its practical results, it will have betrayed its initial principles and failed to achieve its essential purpose. 'Socialism', says Cole, 'means four closely connected things—a human fellowship which denies and expels distinctions of class, a social system in which no one is so much richer or poorer than his neighbours as to be unable to mix with them on equal terms, the common ownership and use of all the vital instruments of production, and an obligation upon all citizens to serve one another according to their capabilities.'

Problems of Adjustment.—In the last resort, however (and from any point of view), the relationship between the state and the managers of the economic machine are, in a would-be free society, bound to be a matter of constant and delicate adjustment. 'Industry on the one hand asks for independence, and on the other for co-operation', as Whitehead remarks, and it is perpetually passing from one of those attitudes to the other. One day it demands protection—against foreign competition, for instance, or against what it terms the unfair competition of certain rival agencies; the next it cries out against any form of interference. The state on the other hand must maintain a balance; it must not direct over-much, and yet 'must drive into economic practice the truth that all capital use is a matter for public interest'. The fact is, as Frankfurter says, and not only of economics, that 'the paradox of both distrusting and burdening the government reveals the lack of a conscious philosophy of politics. It betrays an unresolved inner conflict about the inter-relation of the state and of society.'

CHAPTER XIV

THE UNFREE UNDEMOCRATIC STATE

ALL we have said so far has assumed the need for preserving individual freedom. But not everybody would agree with this assumption. 'Whoever said freedom was a good thing?' asks Seeley at the end of a lecture, and the authoritarian state challenges the would-be free state with the assertion that 'liberty is a dream and not even a good dream'.[1]

I. THE THEORY OF COMMUNIST AUTHORITARIANISM

Communism as a Complete Way of Life.—We are all familiar with the existence of two forms of authoritarianism, the Communist (Russia) and the Fascist (Italy, Germany, Portugal, Spain).[2] They both have much in common, but their starting points are entirely distinct. Both historically and dogmatically Communism has its roots in Socialism. The essential difference between them has been defined as that between a tendency and a body of fixed dogmas. Communism is such a complete system of doctrines and life that it has been termed[3] 'a religion of the most imperious quality, claiming to reveal to man the meaning of his existence, to answer all fundamental questions set by life' and indeed, Communism, as everybody knows, is held by its leaders—we were going to say by its high priests—to be incompatible with any religious system that would claim a prior loyalty. This atheism, professed by all consistent Marxists, is not a necessary consequence of the social system but is presupposed as its very principle, its starting point. Marx, in a word, 'was an atheist before he was a Communist'. His Communism is not economic but metaphysical and philosophical. Man is alienated from himself

---

[1] The original phrase was applied to perpetual peace by Marshal von Moltke, Bismarck's contemporary.

[2] One should probably add several of the South American Republics. Pétain's France went a long way along the same road. Kemal Pasha's Turkey also, but with many mitigating differences.

[3] By Laski in his 'Communism'.

and his work by private property, as he is alienated from himself by the idea of God into which he projects his own essence, and by religion.

'By the abolition of private property Communism will mark the return of man to human life, the emancipation of Communism into its necessary corollary, the religious emancipation of atheism.'[1]

We insist on this dogmatic and all-pervading character of Marxist Communism because it is central to its faith and essential to its understanding. We may divide its message into several elements, and some people may feel able to accept some of its tenets and not others, but to the Marxist there is no choosing between the various parts of what he sees as an indissoluble whole—with him it is all or nothing.

The Essentials of Marxism.—Critics have distinguished in Marxism four essential aspects—a philosophy of history, a theory of social development, a strategy of revolutionary propaganda, and an economic theory.[2] The last we shall leave aside, with the remark that its central thesis, the labour theory of value, is rarely defended nowadays.

The first three, which constitute what may be called politico-social Communism, rest on the basic belief that among the forces that have made history, the economic is the most fundamental—not indeed the sole one, but so much the most important that it tends to become a primary first cause. This being so, the system of economic production prevailing at any given time, and the property system that goes with it, is the essential factor in any community. It is property that sets the dominant ideas and principles of a society, that determines men's positions in that society, so that 'men broadly think and act in terms of an experience made and unmade by their class position'. 'In the social production of their everyday life', wrote Marx, 'men enter into certain relationships independent of their wills, inevitable and determined. These relations in production correspond to a certain degree of development of their material production forces. The sum total of these relationships forms the economic structure

---

[1] Cornu, 'Karl Marx'.
[2] See Hook's 'Towards the Understanding of Karl Marx', Laski's 'Communism', and Lindsay's 'Karl Marx's Capital'.

of society, the real basis on which arises a juridical and political superstructure, and to which correspond certain social and determined forms of consciousness.'[1] And his disciple, Engels, adds the comment that 'Marx was the first to discover the great law of historical development, law according to which all historical struggles on the field of politics, religion, and philosophy or any other ideology are in fact only the more or less accurate expression of struggles waged by social classes.'

The Economic Interpretation of History.—Rightly interpreted the 'economic interpretation of history', as it has been called, is in many ways the most solid part of Marxism. It brought into the scope of historical criticism a whole series of factors which historians had tended to neglect; since Marx, no reputable historian will dare ignore the economic factors of any situation, even if they be not immediately apparent; he will especially enquire to what extent the desire to maintain or to obtain economic advantages may not affect men's ways of thought, how far economic wishful thinking may not be at the basis of many philosophies or institutions. He will not ignore other factors, however, or deny their reality—any more than did Marx himself, who, on being told what was being presented by some of his followers as his teaching on historical determinism, is said to have remarked 'then I am not a Marxist'.

The economic interpretation of history is a richly suggestive approach to historical questions, a light which has illuminated many obscure events and solved many a problem. But like all principles it must be used with caution; it must remain the historian's servant and never become his master.

The State and Economic Power.—Returning now to Marx's description of the political structure built on an economic foundation, it follows that 'the state will be controlled by the owners of economic power'.[2] 'The state is a special organised public power of coercion, which exists to enforce the decision

---

[1] 'Critique of Political Economy,' 1859.

[2] 'It is an illusion', writes Spender in ' Forward from Liberalism'', that within a liberal democratic state it is more than remotely possible to establish any form of government, Communist, Liberal, Socialist or Conservative, irrespective of the interests of the people who own all the landed property, the capital and most of the circulating wealth of the State'.

of the group which controls the government'—and which does this because it controls the society's property system. Its purpose is primarily to keep this system whole, to protect it from the attacks of the unpropertied, who would like to change it in their favour, and to maintain intact all the social and political privileges which property gives. In the agricultural old days the propertied groups who controlled the state were the landowners; in an industrial age they are the owners of capital, the bourgeoisie, as the city-dwelling business middle classes are termed. It is the bourgeois capitalist, and those who depend on him, who organises the modern state so as to preserve his real monopoly of power; political concessions can be safely made as long as the balance of economic strength is left unchanged.

The Class War.—Politics is thus largely a war between social-economic classes; as a system of production alters, the champions of the old are thrust aside by those of the new, and at the same time the class in power is engaged in maintaining its position against the dispossessed or 'proletariat'. 'The class war is a fact of history', says Marx, 'which is inbred in the very nature of our system; there is no need to advocate it, and it is futile to deny it. But responsibility for it is on the side of those who selfishly keep to what they have', and Marx would have echoed these words of Leonard Wolff, 'the real cancer in modern society is the refusal of the minority to share civilisation and its advantages with the majority'.

The reality of the class war is thus basic to Communism. But what exactly is a class in Communist thought? It is not just a functional group, a unit of society co-operating in its common purpose. The class does not admit of a general purpose; it is characterised by a common economic interest antagonistic to the economic interest of other classes; it is, says Maritain, 'an independent totality, refusing any common ground for public good. Marx's stroke of genius', he adds, 'was his "secessional" conception of the class-war, ignoring the links of nation or religion'.

What causes the predominance of class loyalty? Partly the common experience of low wages and falling standards of living, the feeling of common separateness from other more prosperous classes. Partly also the existence of organised parties, 'the agencies by which socio-psychological obstacles to class consciousness are removed'. Partly also the obvious opposition to proletarian interests of the state and of other groups.

A keen consciousness born out of a sense of class-solidarity is therefore essential to the success of Marxism. Everything must be done to make the proletariat all the world over increasingly aware of its common sufferings, its common aims, its ultimate common victory. 'Workers of the world unite', transcending all barriers save those created by your common fate as 'the cursed of the earth'. Class must be introduced or emphasised in every department of human activity. And this not only for the proletariat, for the more class conscious other classes will be, the more class conscious will the workers become. Thus 'each class develops ideals and programmes involving hardships for others, philosophies and outlooks congenial to its claims and selects facts to support these'. And in any country, at any given time, the dominant ideals and culture will be those of the dominant economic class.

The Dictatorship of the Proletariat.—It may be observed that this 'class' interpretation of life can be accepted without its Marxist conclusions. The specified Marxist element is the putting forward of the proletariat as the class which is entitled to supersede the others and become in its turn dominant, and in the method by which this will be achieved.

This change will never come about peacefully—that is the illusion of Socialism. 'I have been driven to the conclusion that no class ever voluntarily abdicates from power. I have come to learn that the private ownership of means of production makes it impossible for the democratic idea to transcend the barriers of class without the capture of power by the working class— men broadly think in terms of an experience made and unmade by their class position, and taken generally all our institutions and their workings are conditioned by the property relations of any given society.'[1] So wrote a prominent Socialist some ten years ago, and it would be futile to assert that the years since have invalidated his judgement.

Since peaceful change is out of the question, the proletariat must prepare for the capture of power and the

[1] 'Why I am a Marxist', by H. J. Laski in the *New Republic*, 1939.

establishment of its 'dictatorship', until such time as all opposition will have died out and the free classless society having been established, the state as a power of coercion will have withered away. This entails the advocacy of revolutionary tactics and the discrediting of all alternative methods.

'Revolutionary tactics' does not mean perpetual violence, but rather the keeping up of disturbed conditions, the prevention of any stabilisation that might make the worker contented with his lot and make the bourgeois feel secure. The revolution will arise not in a clear sunny sky, but in stormy weather and therefore all that encourages this must be encouraged—strikes and wars in particular.

The Meaning of Force.—What about the use of force? This has no value in itself, but must be related to alternatives; it must liberate new productive activities. The problem is its intelligent use. One thing is certain, that the possibility of its need can never be set aside—you cannot base a policy on the abstract possibility of a peaceful victory. Dictatorship is force—and the dictatorship of the proletariat is justified because the alternative is not freedom but the dictatorship of the bourgeoisie. But if revolution is essential for any fundamental change, it has its necessary conditions, and cannot occur anywhere at any time. A revolutionary-minded political party can make itself ready, but it cannot produce the needed situation. There must be first of all the background of a highly developed capitalist system of production, with a powerful class of capitalist magnates and a large working class, forming the majority of the people, suitably disciplined and organised, and engaged in an active class struggle with the employers. The critical situation when the workers must act will arise when three further conditions are fulfilled. First, the breakdown of the forces of production and distribution by the excessive disparity between the share of the workers and their production, causing acute unemployment, the stoppage of credit and an economic crisis. Second, the lack of immediate political homogeneity among the ruling classes, as a result of war or of some other calamity, leading to divisions, disorder, etc. Third, the spontaneous manifestation of class consciousness and struggle, by strikes, riots, and the disintegration of the habit-pattern of blind obedience. 'Revolution', said Lenin, 'is only possible when the masses do not want the old regime and the rulers are unable to govern as of old. There is nothing automatic about it.'

Marxist Strategy.—The essence of Marxist strategy is to be always prepared, never to be discouraged by past failure but to be ready to seize the opportunity when it comes. It was in this that Lenin's genius lay, to have seen in the autumn of 1917 that the revolutionary fruit was ripe for plucking although most of the theoretical conditions were not fully realised. And while the Marxist prepares and waits he must realise that his gravest danger does not come from the capitalist enemy but from the Socialist half-friend; with the former, he knows where he stands; there can be no peace with him, and no-one can ever take him for anything else than a foe; but the latter is to be feared because he also appeals to the worker in his sufferings, in his sense of injustice, but denies the revolutionary remedy and seeks to turn the workers away from the only road that can bring victory, to compromise, concession and therefore defeat. Hence the bitter attacks of Marxists on Social Democratic and Labour parties.[1] Hence also the insistence on the strictest orthodoxy, the bitter feuds over what often appear minor points of doctrine or strategy; Marxist dogma can brook no heresies.

2. THE PRACTICE OF COMMUNISM

Soviet Russia.—Turning now to Marxist practice, we must remember that Soviet Russia is so far the only completely Communist state in existence with any length of life behind it, and that many of its aspects are not necessary applications of Communist principles. It is by no means certain either that Russia really is a Communist state as Marx dreamt of it, or that a Communist state need be as ruthless and autocratic as the regime set by Lenin and continued by his successor.

Soviets and Party.—With this word of caution in our minds we may note first that the Russian system is based on an elaborate organisation of representation, compatible in theory with complete democratic practice and with the existence of several parties, all accepting the general principles of Communism

[1] See in particular Trotsky's attack on British Labour.

but differing in the methods of its applications and in loyalty to leaders. Russia is in fact a one-party state, but that is not inherent in Communism, for within Communist orthodoxy there is room for considerable variety of interpretation, as recent Russian history shows.[1]

Freedom.—In the second place, Russia does not pretend to have established freedom in our western sense of the term, if by that is meant the right to criticise and weaken the regime and the government. This is probably due mainly to her rulers not feeling secure enough to face such opposition. But one must not forget that the Russians have never known our kind of freedom, and therefore do not miss it. Finally they would argue they do have the kind of freedom that really matters, namely economic equality and freedom from the exploitation of an employer bent on profit. And to the Communist 'freedom is really purely collective' says the Russian philosopher Berdyaev. 'Freedom of thought and conscience is impossible because it assumes that there is a spiritual principle in the individual which is not dependent on the community, which Communism cannot admit.'

Functions of the Communist State.—In the third place stands the claim of the Communist state to be all-inclusive in its operation. But here again we must distinguish. It is not inherent in the Marxist conception of the state that it should control every form of culture, every intellectual activity. Even if there be such a thing as 'proletarian art' it can be of many forms, and it is difficult to imagine Marx laying down the law on painting and music with the same sense of infallibility as some of his present-day disciples. On the other hand the rigid state monopoly of large-scale production and distribution, industrial and agricultural, including all foreign trade, is in the regular line of Marxism, which in fact could not be realised without it. The elimination of the profit motive, the establishment of community control, the assigning to the individual of his place in the economic process—all this is solid essential Marxism, as are the Five Year Plans.

Economic Basis of Communism.—In other words we would be inclined to say that the enquirer into the true nature of

[1] All the victims of the various 'purges' claimed to know better than anyone else what Marx really meant.

Communism can disregard to a great extent the fact that Russia is an authoritarian police state but must take her economic organisation as its correct expression. As to Communism being 'successful' in Russia or not, such a question can scarcely be answered. What is the criterion of success? What would the alternative have been? And its 'success' or 'failure' in Russia is no guarantee to its 'success' or 'failure' elsewhere. There again, what would the alternative have been? The one point to bear in mind is that, as we saw, Russia did not appear in Marxist eyes to be the proper field for a Communist revolution and experiments. Britain, France, Belgium or even Italy would have been in theory far 'better', in so far as their people were more politically mature, far better organised and with more experienced leaders. A Communist revolution in one of those countries[1] would have been, to a Communist, a far better test of Marxist principles and tactics. But the curious fact is that the countries on which Russia has been able to impose a Communist regime have all of them been agricultural countries, and not the kind that any Marxist would select for the experiment.

Three Systems in Communism.—Our conclusion on Communism would be therefore that the student must distinguish with great care between three quite different systems. The first is the actual philosophy of Marx himself. The second is the interpretation of that philosophy given by his disciples, by Lenin especially. The third is the policy followed by the present rulers of Soviet Russia.

With the last we cannot be concerned now. It may drown the world in blood and destroy civilisation in a third world war. Or it may be content with its dominant influence in eastern Europe and northern Asia, and accept to live peacefully side by side with Socialist and capitalist systems. Or it may be much weaker in reality than it appears and suddenly collapse in inner feuds and rivalries. Who can tell? For the present one is tempted to dismiss it in the words of a recent writer in *The Times Literary Supplement:* 'When on February 25, the students

[1] This is not altogether imaginary. Between 1919 and 1922 a Communist revolution seemed very near both in France and in Italy, and Mussolini's seizure of power in the latter was thought by many people to have been only the clever forestalling of seizure of power by the extreme left.

of Prague marched to the Presidential palace to show their
loyalty to the political ideas of Masaryk and to express their
abhorrence of the Communist *coup d'etat* they were halted,
according to one account, by a detachment of security police
and workers' militia under the command not of a uniformed
officer but of a civilian wearing a leather jacket. It was pre-
sumed (so the account went on) that this was an official of the
Ministry of the Interior.

'The man in the leather jacket sits behind the desk of
government in many European capitals, and his power greatly
exceeds that of the civil servant in the subfusc suit. When we
first had a clear sight of him, perhaps in the Spanish Civil War,
we covered his energy and brutality with a romantic cloak;
he was a genuine though uncouth democrat. Since then
English opinion has swung desperately between the poles of
admiration and horror; but now, except for a minority of
obtuse and corrupted clerics, the view, formed unwillingly
under pressure of events, is coming to be that the man in the
leather jacket is the "Neanderthal man" of Mr. Koestler's
political morality play, a creature lacking conscience and
bowels of compassion, inveterately hostile to western civilisation, the grave-digger, not of capitalism as his own mytho-
logy asserts, but of free societies everywhere.'

What Marx Really Taught.—We shall not spend any time
either in discussing Lenin, and how far his ruthlessness and autocracy was really what Marx meant by the dictatorship of the
proletariat. For obviously we cannot tell. But it is worth while
making some assessment of the actual teaching of Marx.[1] In
doing so we shall venture to make use of an illuminating
article in *The Highway* by Dr. P. Ford, entitled, 'What is
Living and What is Dead in Marx'.

Dr. Ford rules out Marx's philosophy and psychology,
now out of date, and his labour theory of value as now dis-
credited. Many of Marx's economic predictions have been
shown to be false, such as his belief that the condition of the
workers would go on steadily deteriorating and that the ill-paid
black-coated workers and small shopkeepers, fighting chain-
store and monopoly capital, would throw in their lot with the

---

[1] All students should read the 'Communist Manifesto of 1848'. It is short,
clear, and the authentic voice of Marx.

proletariat—whereas they are usually the most passionate defenders of the existing bourgeois order. He did not foresee the rise of new classes of technicians and managers, neither employers nor proletarians, often still uncertain as to their position in the social struggle. Marxist tactics again split the working classes in Germany, France, Italy, Spain and helped the establishment of totalitarian regimes. And finally his 'economic interpretation of history' is certainly over-rigid and narrow.

'Well', asks Dr. Ford, 'when these criticisms have been made, what is left? All that matters', he answers. First Marx drew attention to a whole body of new material about economic life which is slowly finding its way into the teaching of history and the social sciences. The significance of economic changes in affecting the strength and interest of different classes, the importance of institutions which prevent men from having access to jobs and to the world's productive resources, the paradox that property in the instruments of production, which once guaranteed the spinner or weaver against the exactions of his rulers, now perpetuates the dependence of workers on those who inherit property—these considerations have been brought to prominence in our social studies largely by the widening influence of Marx's work. His criticisms of parliamentary democracy in an inequalitarian society are part of the common stock of ideas of social theorists. Marx was not the first writer to point to these facts, but he was the most learned and the most able, and it is largely because he worked them into a coherent theory that their significance has slowly been recognised. Though in his view of history he was undoubtedly too exclusive, the theory of class struggle is a major key—though only one of the keys—to understanding the life of our time. In terms of tactics it may perhaps be conceded that it is the most important key.

3. THE THEORY OF DICTATORSHIP

The Communism whose aims and methods we have been studying, primarily from their economic aspects, becomes as a political force the denial of the democratic doctrines of

10 *

freedom and majority control. 'As long as the proletariat needs the state,' wrote Engels, Marx's friend and disciple, 'it needs it not in the interests of freedom but in order to crush its enemies, and when it becomes possible to speak of freedom the State as such will cease to exist.' Freedom and state are in fact incompatible terms.

Communism, Fascism, and Freedom.—Communism and Fascism have in common the negation of the fundamental principles on which democracy rests. They begin with the community, not with the individual, and consider that the claims of the state, as representing the community, must always have precedence. They deny that the power of the state should be limited by appeal either to individual rights or to fundamental laws: law is the will of the state; and the state can know nothing higher than itself. They deny that the government should be in any way responsible to public opinion, or indeed to anything or anybody—the non-accountability of government is in fact one of their fundamental concepts. And they deny that any part or aspect of either collective or individual life can be outside the normal complete and continuous control of the state, which is charged with authority over the whole, the totality of what goes on within its borders—political, economic, religious, cultural. The state is both authoritarian and totalitarian;[1] as was wittily remarked, 'whatever is not forbidden is compulsory, whatever is not compulsory is forbidden'.

The Old Absolutisms.—So far in one sense there is nothing very new in all this, and totalitarian regimes are merely a type of that absolute state which, in Lippmann's words, 'claims the right to a monopoly of all forces within the community to make war, and peace, to conscript life, to tax, to establish and disestablish property, to define crime, to punish disobedience, to control education, to supervise the family, to regulate personal habits and to censor opinion'.[2] After all, absolutism in some form or another is the oldest type of government, whether we go back to the rule of the

[1] On dictatorship, read Cobban's 'Modern Dictatorship'. It can scarcely be totalitarian without being authoritarian, but an authoritarian state is not necessarily totalitarian. The benevolent despotism of the eighteenth century was compatible with a great deal of toleration.

[2] In his 'Preface to Morals'.

father as head of the family group or to that of the military conqueror. It is against various forms of these autocracies that democracies slowly vindicated their rights and few of them have survived the attack.

The old absolutisms, resting usually on heredity and divine right, have in fact disappeared one by one, and, with the transformation of the Japanese empire, King Ibn Saud of the Hedjaz is the only monarch of the old order still in power. The new systems have no religious or hereditary basis and justify themselves by appeal to another concept, old in one sense but 'modernised', that of dictatorship.

Dictatorship in History.—What is dictatorship? It has been defined as 'the government of one man who has not primarily obtained his position by inheritance but either by force or by consent, usually by a combination of both. He must possess absolute sovereignty, exercising it arbitrarily by decree rather than by law'. As we said a moment ago, its essence is non-accountability, and, we may add, absence of any limitation of duration.

The term is borrowed from ancient Rome when, in an emergency, unlimited powers could be conferred on one man by the Senate. But it had three conditions which modern usage ignores; it was an exceptional device, not a normal method; it was limited to a short period, usually six months, never more than a year; at the expiration of that time the dictator had to give an account of his mandate.

Various rulers elevated to absolute power by special circumstances, William of Orange, Cromwell, Danton, Robespierre, have been called 'dictators'—not by themselves, but by later times. But the first real dictator of modern times, the man who really established the pattern, was undoubtedly Napoleon I. He came to power in a crisis but made his rule permanent, and laid down the principle of what was in fact a new type of authority, absolutism based on a mixture of general consent and sheer power. 'My position', he once said, 'is entirely different from that of the old sovereigns. Nobody contested their legitimacy, nobody thinks of replacing them. Everything is different in my case; within and without my dominion is founded on fear'. And his nephew, Napoleon III, defined the system before giving it himself a fresh application, when he wrote[1] of his uncle's rule 'the imperial system has a democratic basis since all power comes from the people, and its organisation is hierarchic, since there are in society the different grades necessary to stimulate all capacities'. And he systematised this new type of 'popular autocracy' by the plebiscites which marked his assumption of power and the various changes he gradually introduced in its practical workings.

Similar governments were set up in South American republics during the nineteenth century, usually as the result of some military revolt. But in its present form dictatorship appeared in Russia with Lenin in 1917, to be followed shortly after by Kemal Ataturk in Turkey, then by Primo de Rivera in Spain and by Mussolini in Italy. Later on Poland, Greece, Portugal, Germany, Yugoslavia, followed suit; Spain returned to the system after a brief experiment of democracy and even France succumbed to the infection in 1940. Still more recently authoritarian regimes of the Communist type have been set up in Bulgaria, Hungary, Rumania, Yugoslavia and Czechoslovakia. But Russia and Germany may be said to present the standard pattern of the Communist and Fascist systems.

The Origins of Modern Dictatorship.—Before studying their principles and practices it may be worth noting how very similar they are in their immediate origins. In no case, save the shortlived 'Vichy' experiment in France, did dictatorship emerge in a country with democratic traditions, with a strong sense of personal freedom and individual responsibility in politics. Where democracy had appeared, it had been a plant with no deep roots, alien to the soil. In every case dictatorship was born of disillusion and despair; military defeat, economic crisis, breakdown of old traditions, apparent lack of any decent alternatives—the 'nothing could be worse, nothing to lose' attitude; and this coinciding with the existence of a man or group of men with a definite programme, a clear plan of action and a complete freedom from any 'inhibitions' of morality, humanity and decency. That is not to say that all dictatorships or authoritarian regimes have shown the same characteristics as Nazism; even Italian Fascism has cleaner hands, and neither Kemal Pasha nor Salazar deserve to be bracketed

[1] In the 'Idées Napoléonniennes.'

with Hitler; but the fundamental principle of the overpowering rights of the state, and the refusal of any considerations that could impede its action except those of expediency were essentially the same.

Present Characteristics: 1. *No right of Criticism.*—The first characteristic of all those regimes has been the absolute denial of any right of opposition or criticism. You differ, literally at the risk of your liberty and life, and the concentration camp has been from the beginning inseparable from those regimes. Occasionally indeed, a form of popular consultation is resorted to, plebiscite or election; but the option of a 'no' is not really given and the choice offered to voters is only between competitors equally devoted to the system. To Fascist and Communist alike opposition is treason. The regime being identified with the welfare of the nation, to oppose it is to set yourself against the national will and interest. There can be therefore no freedom of press, or meeting or association; the preacher in the pulpit must abstain from criticism,[1] the teacher in the school must present all subjects, history especially, in the manner laid down by the authorities for the glorification of the regime. Not education only but all culture and science is to be its handmaid. We have all of us been both shocked and amused at the 'purges' of literature, music and painting in Russia, so as to secure the true Soviet spirit in art, proletarian culture being apparently something different from bourgeois. But Germany proclaimed that she 'renounced international science, renounced the international republic of learning, renounced research for its own sake. History was taught and learnt, not to say how things actually happened but to instruct the German people from the past.'[2] As a German physicist said, 'I shall be told that science is and remains international. That is false; science, like every other human product, is racial and conditioned by blood.'

2. *Nationalist Tendencies.*—In the second place, being born of defeat, totalitarian regimes have been expressions of the will of national regeneration and reconstruction, have tended to

---

[1] When in Germany in 1936, however, we heard two courageous sermons from a Lutheran pastor who, without actually condemning the Nazi regime, did not hesitate to criticise as unchristian its racialism and its attempt to control the churches. [2] At Göttingen University, 1937.

become identified with the more extreme doctrines of national independence and complete self-sufficiency, with the right of domination over other 'inferior' nations. It is noteworthy that nationalism in its modern form was born in Prussia after her defeat in 1806, and received a new expression in defeated Germany after 1919,[1] while Fascism was born in an Italy who, while technically victorious, felt frustrated in her victory. And Russian Communism, although based originally on the predominance of class-links over those of nation, gradually identified the Communist revolution with Russian nationalism and restored the old national heroes to their former position in history and public admiration.

It is, of course, evident that this nationalism rejects the rights of other nations. 'What we really believe is that with the rapid developments of science and technique, mankind has entered the phase of its puberty, a phase of radical, global experiments with total disregard of the individual, his so-called rights and privileges, and other liberal mumbo-jumbo. . . .

'Wipe out those ridiculous winding boundaries, the Chinese walls which cut across the fields of energy; scrap or transfer industries which were heedlessly built in the wrong places; liquidate the surplus populations in areas where they are not required; shift other populations, or whole nations, to spaces where they are really wanted and to the type of production for which they are best fitted. Wipe out any disturbing lines of force which might superimpose themselves, that is the influence of the churches, of overseas capital, of any philosophy of the past, religion, ethical or aesthetical system.'[2]

3. *Worship of the State.*—But, and this is their third characteristic, however strongly nationalist, modern authoritarians are primarily worshippers of the state. It is the state which matters. As Gentile, one of the prophets of Fascism says, 'the higher personality is only a nation in so far as it is a state. The nation does not exist to generate the state; it is created by

---

[1] 'We start very consciously with the conviction that we have been placed in the arena of the world in order to work out moral perfection not only for ourselves but for all mankind. We cannot grant that the preservation of some small insignificant nationality as a political unit is as important for the development of mankind as the growth of those world nations who are the standard-bearers of culture.' Dr. Rohrbach, 1912.

[2] Koestler's 'Arrival and Departure'.

the state, which gives to a people conscious of its own moral unity a will and thereby an effective existence.' The state is to be Fascist as Mussolini put it, 'all-embracing; outside it no human or spiritual values can exist, much less have any value. Fascism is totalitarian, and the Fascist state, a synthesis and a unit inclusive of all values, interprets, develops and potentialises the whole life of a people. Everything within the state and nothing outside it.'

The basic conception may be described as unity through uniformity. Fear of diversity, dread of those differences which democracy calls vital and valuable, horror of the 'non-conformist', of him who wants to walk by himself, to think for himself, belief in a complete plan of life laid down by the state.[1] It involves the conception of a mould into which human nature can be poured and fixed, the acceptance by the great mass of mankind of ways of life imposed on them, or at least which they feel incapable of realising by their free initiative.

4. *The Single Party.*—If in the fourth place we come to methods of government we find that all authoritarian regimes, to right or left, have adopted essentially the same technique. The leader or dictator who stands at the head obviously cannot do everything; he must rule through an 'elite' or selected ruling class, and this class is the party which is the basis of the system.

Totalitarianism, which denies party politics because they assume differences of opinion when unity is wanted, was in fact born of the party system, by one party breaking its rules. These rules are, as we have seen earlier, agreement to abide by majority decisions, not to use force to have your own way if a minority and belief in liberty of propaganda in appealing to a free public opinion. But first the Communists in Russia, then the Fascists in Italy, later the National Socialists in Germany, and the other day the Communists in Czechoslovakia, refused to accept their minority status and forced themselves into power, not necessarily by immediate violence, but by a

---

[1] Authoritarian doctrine is primarily a negation of the liberal doctrine that the variety and conflict of spiritual forces enriches and ennobles life. . . . On the contrary it distrusts spontaneous forces in conflict among themselves, tries to prevent or cuts short the conflicts, prescribes the course to be followed.' (Croce.)

distortion of constitutional practice and rules. Then once in power they proceeded to suppress other parties, to refuse free elections or free expressions of public opinion, and established a regime which gave them a legal monopoly of power.

Membership of the party thus became a necessary condition for the holding of any office of importance, the doors into the party being closed, left ajar or flung wide open according to circumstances, but membership having rigid qualifications and heavy duties. The conception of a 'one-party system' is, of course, a contradiction in terms since the existence of one party implies that of others, a part being always smaller than the whole; but this distortion of the meaning of 'Party' was neither the first nor the last trick played.

The party then is the new ruling class, based on strict orthodoxy to the party dogma, on strict loyalty to the leader and on strict obedience to all orders received by superiors in the party. But the party is large, and effective power is in fact in the hands of an inner group, made up of the original founders and dominant figures, with the addition of selected reliable henchmen—a practically self-perpetuating committee, that originally chose the leader and would in fact choose his successor.[1]

A Three-fold Dictatorship.—Totalitarianism rests in practice on a triple dictatorship—that of the party as regards the mass of citizens, that of the inner group as regards the rest of the party, that of the leader as regards inner group, party and nation. Whatever we may think of it ideally, it cannot be denied that it has proved an effective form of government: so far only war and defeat has brought it to an end—after eleven years in Germany, after twenty-two years in Italy; in Russia it is now thirty-one years old and still apparently going strong.

4. THE THEORY OF 'FASCIST' AUTHORITARIANISM

The Fascist Theory of the State.—We have studied so far those functional characteristics of authoritarian regimes which

---

[1] It should be noted that both Fascism and Nazism came to an end under their original leaders, although the inner group had undergone some important changes. But the change from Lenin to Stalin in 1924 led to the gradual elimination of practically all the original Communists and to the building up of an entirely different 'inner group'.

are common both to their Fascist and Communist forms, but this parallel obviously breaks down when we consider their doctrinal origins and their avowed aims. It is evident that they are deeply rooted in different philosophies of the state. Turning first to Fascism we may remark, with Professor Catlin, that it is 'idle and superficial to deny that Fascism is a doctrine. Fascism is a very definite theory, that denies the all-sufficiency of the economic thesis about the founts of power, and substitutes a thesis of personal power as old as the ancient opponents of Plato and their theories—'Power', they say, is its 'own justi-fication.' And the official 'Dottrina fascista' declared once that 'Fascism is now complete, not only as a regime but as a doctrine.'

It is true that we have on the other hand the statement of Mussolini that 'Fascism has never attempted to clothe its complicated and powerful mental attitude with a definite programme, but has succeeded by following its everchanging individual intuition. Everything I have said and done these last few years', he adds, 'is Relativism by intuition. If Relativism means contempt for fixed categories and men who claim to be the bearers of external objective truth, then there is nothing more relativist than Fascism. We Fascists have always ex-pressed our complete indifference towards all theories; we have had the courage to discard all traditional political theories. It is sufficient to have a single viewpoint, the nation. From the fact that all ideologies are of equal value, that they are mere fictions, the modern relativist deduces that everybody is free to create for himself his own ideology.' But such state-ments need not be taken too seriously; no system can endure for long without a basic philosophy and both Fascism and Nazism, and indeed all authoritarian regimes, have a perfectly clear and definite political philosophy; we can question its validity but not deny its existence.

Historical Origins of Fascism.—As a theory, modern authori-tarianism was born of opposition to the French Revolution and its doctrines. 'We are irreducibly anti-modern', writes a young Fascist, echoing the words of Joseph de Maistre, who may be described as the first modern authoritarian. His point of view may be simply summed up as opposition to the Revolution and all it stands for. 'There is a natural antipathy between the French Revolution and virtue', he wrote; 'and to its heralds and prophets'; while 'Rousseau deceives even when he is speaking the truth, anyone who is attracted by the writings of Voltaire may be sure that God does not love him' and he dismisses the essential principles of 1789 by the assertion that 'The order of societies, however obtained, is always more important than the freedom of individuals; society is based on natural differences not equality.'

The words 'however obtained' are significant; there can be no limit on authority either as to extent or as to means. 'The sovereign must be able to choose how to rule. You may not forbid him to use certain methods which circumstances may suggest—a father cannot promise never to open or always to open his son's letters.' It is therefore futile to speak of individual rights; 'The concentration of all rights in the rulers is the only basis of social order; the rights of the ruled mean anarchy. Social order will always be incompatible with the permanent freedom of each to question afresh daily the very bases of society.'

Obedience Based on Faith.—What then is to be the basis of political organisation? It is to be obedience, based not on reason, but on 'faith'—believing spontaneously and without previous demonstration in the dogmas proclaimed by a competent authority, which is the essential condition to enable the establishment and the maintenance of a real intellectual and moral unity of mankind.

In politics, the less you think the better. 'The cradle of man must be surrounded with dogmas, and when his mind begins to awaken he must find all his opinions already made, at least on everything which influences behaviour. There is nothing so important as prejudices.'[1]

The Fear of Reason.—This fear of reason, which characterised early authoritarian doctrines, is one of its modern features too. It was a much later disciple of de Maistre, another Frenchman, Charles Maurras, who wrote that 'what matters is the worship of habits which will be all the stronger for being unconscious. It is almost blasphemous to try and bring them to consciousness; one of the disasters of our times is that the citizen should be expected to have a deliberate personal opinion about matters of state,' and all Hitler did was to intensify this disregard

[1] Maurice Barrès, 'Scenes et Doctrines du Nationalisme'.

of reason and insistence on emotion. He defined his own position as 'going with the assurance of a somnambulist the way which Providence has sent me', confirming another Nazi slogan, 'one must think with one's blood and not with one's brain'. As the Nazi leader, Krieck, said, 'There has arisen blood against formal reason, race against purposeful rationality, honour against profit, unity against individualistic disintegration, martial virtue against bourgeois security, the folk against the individual and the mass'.

The 'Leader-Concept'.—This rejection of the rational is nowhere more clearly seen than in the leader-concept which is at the bottom of authoritarianism. 'There is', as Dr. Cobban says, 'no aspect of modern dictatorship for which it is more difficult to find a comprehensive explanation in rational terms.' Hitler as leader of the party, and later as leader of both party and state, demanded of all Germans: 'You must fuse your wills with mine', while Goering could say in the Reichstag after the 'Rohm Purge': 'And if abroad it is believed today that chaos threatens Germany, the German people responds with the single cry "We all approve always of what our leader does." 'I do not become the follower of a leader because I have tested his political or economic programme, have felt it to be right and on these grounds declare my allegiance. 'Where real leadership exists, I have trusted myself to a leader whose purpose I only see in part. I give him my whole trust. He has captured me. He may lead me now, either to death or to life. All later decisions must issue from the dark womb of the future and be born in pregnant night.'[1]

The Leader Born out of Despair.—This queer mysticism finds, of course, a partial explanation in the circumstances which attended the birth of the regime. 'The leader is the product of despair. He rises in an age of mass-democracy as a substitute for shattered institutions. Thus his rise is partly explained as due to the weakening or disappearance of political institutions, the breakdown of the ruling class and the undermining of an accepted code of values. Above all he comes when men have persuaded themselves that government is something external to themselves, when, weary of the effort needed, they deliberately evade the responsibilities and difficulties of the

[1] From an article in the *New Statesman.*

discipline of self-government. It is at such a time that the primitive urge for a personal leader wells up again in civilised man and makes nonsense of the generalisation that when society reaches an advanced stage of civilisation its members discard personal symbols and can express loyalty to an idea through an institution instead of a person. But the dictator is merely accepted as a symbol; he is not the main feature of the modern dictatorship. It is the idea of the totalitarian state which has been fertile in creating the myth of the modern dictator, and in the due course of its development it has made the dictator often its own fashion.'

Psychology of Leader-Worship.—In a short survey such as this one hardly knows how much space and importance to give to this 'leader principle' which is at the basis of modern dictatorships. Is it a passing phenomenon deserving little consideration, or a new and permanent factor in politics?

It should be noted that leader-worship is certainly a product of modern mass-movements, craving for a personal embodiment. The dictator's infallibility—'Mussolini is always right' was a slogan to be found all over Italy—was the reflection of the infallibility of every one of the followers who trusted implicitly in him; and belief in his divine inspiration identified the believer with the divine guidance. 'Our champions, and first and greatest the Duce', said the Fascist party in 1926 'have been urged and inspired from on high—from those heights which are in every man, and from which springs the creative flood of will.'

It has been also rightly remarked that 'leadership' is often to use Freudian terms, a 'Father-substitute'. This was particularly marked in the case of Pétain, whose extreme age gave his paternalism some apparent justification. 'I speak to you as a father', was a favourite expression of his, and exhortations to a child-like attitude towards him was frequent among his followers, but perhaps 'childish' in this connection would be better than 'child-like'. Fatherhood eliminates any suggestion of equality; the child's attitude is a mixture of love and wholesome fear, and the closeness of the link enables the follower to make his own the virtues and exploits of the leader.

But the instinct of 'follow my leader' is anterior to those

mystical identifications. As Carlyle wrote a century ago, 'find in any country the perfect man, raise him to supreme place and loyally reverence him—you have a perfect government for that country—no ballot-box, parliamentary eloquence, voting, constitution building or other machinery can improve it: what he tells us to do must be precisely the wisest, fittest that we could anywhere or anyhow learn—the thing which it will, in all ways, behove us with right loyal thankfulness, and nothing doubting, to do'. All of which is a somewhat elaborate way of saying that many people are happier if they can abdicate their responsibility to someone who will do their thinking for them—provided, of course, that it corresponds in a general way with prevailing impulses, prejudices and emotions. 'Leadership', says Griffith, 'is temporarily successful in so far as it brings to a focus and renders articulate the relatively unformulated but insistent desires of the individuals. It should coincide with the inner nature of man, and its means should give to the persons concerned a sense of creative participation in attaining the ends.'[1] It is here, by the way, that Nazism has been particularly successful. Hitler summed it up in a few words, 'authority from above as the result of leadership conscious of its responsibility, confidence and discipline from below'. But Shelley's lines remain true:

> The man of virtuous soul commands not, nor obeys ;
> Power, like a desolating pestilence,
> Pollutes whate'er it touches, and obedience,
> Bane of all genius, virtue, freedom, truth,
> Makes slaves of all men, and of the human frame
> A mechanised automaton.

Methods of Propaganda.—These appeals to the subconscious and irrational are also seen in the methods of totalitarian propaganda—symbolism, demonstrations, slogans, 'bread and circuses'. It has been rightly described as 'the rape of the masses', as the 'creation by totalitarian regimes for their own ends in their respective communities of a system of conditioned reflexes which reverses the evolutionary order of things' as *The Times Literary Supplement* puts it. It is based on the

[1] 'O for a dictator—a dictator to do our own bidding'—Meredith, 'Diana of the Crossways'.

idea, to quote the same article, that 'most people have common-place minds dominated by herd emotions'. They are 'un-enlightened and short sighted' and the result is that 'the intelligence of the political animal has failed under the assault of flagrant falsities and half-baked retrogressive theories'.

It is in fact a curious paradox that one of the most intel-lectual and educated of peoples—perhaps the most—should have used all its powers of organisation to stop thinking. Why have idiotic notions of race, of race purity and race superiority triumphed over the evidence of biological law? Why have dictators been able to blot out the idea of liberty, and with it the creative impulse of human culture, over so large an area of Europe? Why, briefly, has the intelligence of the political animal failed under the assault of flagrant falsities and half-baked retrogressive theories? The answer is simply that, for their own ends, the totalitarian regimes have created in their respective communities a system of conditioned reflexes which reverses the evolutionary order of things. 'Without any understanding of Pavlov's theory, Hitler has in fact applied it with unexampled ingenuity to a peculiarly suggestible people. The absolute reflex he has worked upon is, of course, the combative instinct; the forms of excitation he has adopted include all the pictorial and symbolical devices of Nazi propaganda, from the omnipresent swastika to the pageantry of the party rally; the conditioned reflex thus created by the "physical violation" of the masses exhibits the political and social aspect of the Nazi process of Gleichschal-tung. In other words, by the use of a sufficiently bold and elaborate technique of mass persuasion, people—or at least the German people—can be made to believe anything, or at any rate almost anything.'[1]

In his 'Study of History', Toynbee advances an interesting explanation of such phenomena as the emergence of Nazi barbarism. 'Around every centre of higher civilisation', he says, 'there tends to grow up a zone of lower culture, which is to some extent dependent, or parasitic on its civilised neigh-bours, while at the same time possessing a higher degree of mobility and a greater aptitude for war', and he gives as instances the Bedouins in the Arab civilisation, the Mongols

[1] From an article in the *New Statesman*.

in the Chinese. 'Every ultimate advantage', he goes on to say, 'was on the side of the barbarians, for every fresh invasion increased their warlike efficiency, whereas the destructive effects of warfare on the higher civilisations were cumulative. But our barbarians are from within.'

Varieties in the Fascist Appeal.—A curious feature of the doctrinal appeal of totalitarianism has been its extraordinary capacity to do so to very different kinds of people on very different grounds. Along one line it obviously played the game of the bourgeoisie, and has indeed been described as 'essentially the reaction of the middle class in danger of proletarisation'; it has been the ally of big finance and big industry without whose help it would soon have crashed in bankruptcy. It put all labour under control, forbade strikes and proclaimed a crusade against all forms of left-turning action. And yet it obtained a vast measure of proletarian support, offering the people certain material advantages, such as cheap holidays, free shows, and far more than this, the removal of unemployment by work, on armament for example, doing all this by appealing to mass hatred of minorities, to the instinct of national expansion. And the conclusion is that authoritarianism successfully double-crossed both bourgeoisie and proletariat, at least for a time, though we cannot tell how long this deception would have lasted in more normal circumstances.

'Fascism is a social and spiritual phenomenon, with a vision of the world proper to a social group. Isolated members of that group can react against that vision and escape from it altogether, while it may yet attract minds of different social formations, but in the main we can define Fascism as a social and political movement, born on a vision of a world, born in certain milieux of the European bourgeoisie after the First World War, prepared by numerous and deep changes in the social and economic structures, and by an intense ideological preparation at work since the middle of the nineteenth century.

'What sort of a world-vision was the bourgeoisie to build? Traditional religion was no longer tenable; Marxism offered a creed that ruled out the very essence of bourgeois existence. Something new was needed, built on the only remaining realities that were still compatible with middle-class existence:

nationalism and a belief in the elite or natural racially
designated governing classes.'[1]

Fascism and the Bourgeoisie.—The concept of 'bourgeoisie',
of governing class and privilege is essential to Fascism—using
'bourgeoisie' as the class opposed to the working class. And
the 'small bourgeoisie', or lower middle class, however far
it be from the upper middle class in wealth and material
position, has nevertheless the same vision of the world—
it hopes one day to regain the privileges it has lost, or to attain
to privileges it has never had, and lives in the fear of either
slipping back into the unpropertied mass from which it has
painfully climbed, or of being cast down into it for the first
time by gradual impoverishment and loss of status. Having left
the proletariat, even if only to be the hanger-on or butler
of the upper classes, the lower middle class becomes the cham-
pion of the existing order, the defender of the haves against the
have-nots to which they belong, nearly, but not quite. And
'privilege' is two things—what I have, and what others
haven't got, and the lower down the scale of privilege, the
larger looms this latter point of view. As long as I do not
belong to the have-nots, I may hope one day to be a real 'has'.

The Appeal of Nazism.—The fundamental articles of the
National Socialist creed are a reflection of Hitler's reactions to his
bitter experiences in the capital of the Austrian empire during
the years before the First World War. The roots of that creed
are planted not in German idealist philosophy but in the doss-
houses and night shelters of Vienna. And to those experiences
one must add the experience of the War—and of Germany's
defeat, the companionship of the trenches and the loss of that
common life. Man felt himself alone in a shattered world, and
the only trade which he had mastered was, often enough, that of
the soldier. 'The meaning of life is to kill' (Ernst Junger). 'If
men wish to live, they are forced to kill others' (Hitler). The
German republic proclaimed toleration, international concilia-
tion, the dull, drab tasks of reconstructing a society which had
lapsed into chaos. And in place of that uninspiring programme
the National Socialist offered to men fighting—the job which
they understood—and above all offered to them a Gemeinschaft
—a new companionship, a sense of 'belonging' which gave

[1] Royan, 'Dans la Pause du Fascisme', *Revue Socialiste.*

once again some meaning to life. National Socialism held out to them fanaticism in place of reasonableness, a flaming hatred in place of toleration, and the hope that out of this new-born sense of personal community there might at length be created a 'Volksgemeinschaft'—a community of the whole German people. It is this note of passion which one must recover if one would understand the compelling force of National Socialist propaganda. It offered men a new faith: 'The Programme of the Party is the confession of faith of a new religion. Even the smallest minority can achieve a mighty result if it is inspired by the most fiery, the most passionate will to act.' (Hitler.)

Racialism.—It will have been noticed that we have said nothing of the part played by the racial basis in German dictatorship. The reason is that it may be said to be incidental, not essential, the proof being that other forms of dictatorships of the right were entirely free from it; and we are only concerned with the fundamentals of authoritarianism. All we need say about racialism here is that it went to reinforce the Nazi rejection both of reason and of freedom. 'The racial conception of the world corresponds to the innermost will of nature because it re-establishes that free play of forces which leads to progress which leads to natural selection. Strife is always the means of developing the species and is consequently a primary condition in its progress.' (Hitler.)

Collective Egotism.—It is difficult, if not impossible, to express an unprejudiced view of Fascist totalitarianisms; the harm they have done to the world is still too recent. If one may express a personal opinion, its ultimate condemnation lies in its proclamation as final of an egotism, which is not less wrong for being collective rather than individual. Three centuries ago the French philosopher, Pascal, referred to 'the hateful ego', and Foerster, the German Liberal, rightly condemns totalitarianism as being, 'the collective hateful ego put forward as a political ideal'. And when Scotza, chief of Fascist youth, tells one that 'not to hate, or still worse, to love our enemies, is a form of cowardice that no cause can accept', he is only joining hands with the Communist, Bukharine, writing in the *Pravda* (March, 1934) that 'the Communist victory will be preceded by a class hatred with regard to capitalism. That is why Christian love which applies to enemies is the worst enemy of Communism.' It is unnecessary to say more.

Fascism and Communism.—Returning to Communist totalitarianism, it is evident that both its theory and its aims differ widely from those of Fascism. If the latter is born of despair, the other is born of hope; if one is fighting a rearguard action in defence of privileges, the other is leading a frontal attack on those privileges in the name of social justice. The emancipation of the proletariat may be a narrow and limited purpose but neither its original inspiration nor its first prophet were unworthy of a great cause.

The distortion of this cause, both in theory and in practice, is familiar history. It is doubtful in fact whether what prevails in Russia can be called either Communism or Marxism; it is certainly authoritarian totalitarianism and therefore belongs to this chapter, just as the economic and social aims of Marxist Communism belongs to the chapter on Socialism. In contemporary practice, single party control, individual dictatorship, ruthless repression of individual freedom in action and thought, submerging of the person in the group—all these are as characteristic of Moscow today as they were of Berlin or Rome. Still, there are many who will feel that whereas Fascism was never anything but a shocking perverted manifestation of collected egotism gone mad, early Communism was really moved by a desire to solve 'the unsolved riddle of social justice'.

5. THE PRACTICE OF 'FASCIST' AUTHORITARIANISM

Before concluding we may note by the way that modern techniques have enormously increased the ease with which a government can act—plane, radio, telephone, motor car have revolutionised the conditions of administration; revolts are either virtually impossible, or certain of success if the revolutionaries can seize certain key positions.

The Authoritarian State.—From the point of view of constitutional law, the authoritarian state stands outside ordinary classifications. It denies such categories as division of powers, objective law, distinction between state and society, between state and government; all powers are fused into one, that of the

leader, who delegates as he wills. Law is simply the leader
interpreting the will of the nation, and 'legality' is a meaningless
term if by that is implied any rule that might hinder the state
or any of its agents. 'Over and above the legality of today we
are required to prepare that of tomorrow' said the Fascist del
Vecchio, while Goebbels declared that statutes and rules of the
National Socialist outlook, the thought of the German people
reduced to its primitive and original formulae—all this was
only confirming the statement of the German academy of law
that 'Courts shall punish offences not punishable under the
code when deserving of punishment according to the underlying idea of a penal code or to a healthy public sentiment,
of which the judge is a representative.' The German academy of
law considers the common welfare the sole standard of its work;
'service to the vital necessities of our people, not service to
theories, is the idea of the German guardian of law'. We are
far from the concept of an independent judiciary, guardians of a
legal system aiming at the protection of citizens from the
arbitrary invasion by the government, or of law independent
of the wishes of the rulers of the moment. As to Russian
Soviet conception of law and justice the trials and purges are
evidence enough.

Totalitarian regimes are obviously based on the human
desire for order and fear of anarchy, but are a misuse of that
desire. They are a misuse, as are all systems that claim infallibility and exclusiveness in truth; in eliminating the disorders resulting from excess of freedom, they eliminate freedom
itself and refuse to admit even its relative value.

The Individual in Fascism.—'There is no freedom of the
individual any more than freedom of the classes. What does
freedom of the individual mean? Nature continually forces
man to do things which do not please him. There is but one
form of freedom, the freedom of the nation. And this freedom can only be guaranteed if every individual is prepared
to do his part in sacrificing for this freedom. Freedom of the
nation means above all securing of a rule of conduct for life.'

Thus spoke Hitler, and we see in those words that refusal to
look beyond his limited viewpoint. Since freedom has its
dangers, we do away with it altogether. But the real fact is that
authoritarianism, both of right and of left, is the standing

evidence of that fear of freedom which we mentioned in an earlier chapter. There are many men as we said who do not want freedom because of the responsibility involved. They want to be told what to do and what to think, and gladly run to authority for shelter and orders, and it is true enough that 'there are militarist and capitalist conceptions of the social order, or of national greatness, which would fit in with slavery far better than with modern freedom'.

The success of authoritarianism has frightened many people who fear that any measure of intelligent deliberate planning and control may open the door to the totalitarian evil. And it is true, that, as Edwyn Bevan says, 'The danger before us is not anarchy but Despotism, loss of spiritual freedom, perhaps a universal world totalitarian state. . . . Anarchy can be but a phase because it is essentially weak, and in an anarchic world any firmly organised group with rational organisation and scientific knowledge could spread its domination over the rest.'

Then the world would enter upon a period of spiritual petrification, a terrible order which would be death for the higher activities of the human spirit. It would be more rigid than the petrification of Rome or China because the ruling group would have much greater scientific means of power. 'It cost Europe 1000 years of Barbarism to escape the fate of China', says Macaulay. But there would be no barbarian races to break up a future world totalitarian state.

'In such a state, while philosophy and poverty would languish, scientific research might go on with continuous fresh discoveries.'

No one can deny the reality of the danger. But a danger which is seen can be guarded against. The essential thing is to preserve intact the ultimate responsibility and accountability of those in power to the considered opinion of the majority.

CHAPTER XV

AND NOW, WHAT NEXT?

THIS book has been written with a double end in view. Some of its readers will be passing on to a fuller survey of the subject, and these chapters will merely have introduced them to the variety and complexity of the problems that lie ahead. We can only hope that they will find that this introduction has been both clear and full enough. Others will not be carrying their formal study beyond this and some of the additional reading suggested in the bibliography. But there will in fact be very few days when they will not be making their own contribution to the art of government. On every issue of the time they will be expressing their ideas and thereby helping, consciously or not, to build up that public opinion which, in a free society, will determine the lines on which its affairs will be run. And at intervals they will vote, and perhaps be candidates for office. We trust we may have been able to clarify some of the issues, and to help such readers towards the intelligent fulfilment of their civic duties and responsibilities.

And it may be as well to remind both 'Specialist' and 'Ordinary' citizen, of some of the lessons we have learnt in our common study, that they may apply them when verified by experience and correct them when found wanting.

THE SIX LESSONS OF POLITICAL SCIENCE

The Law of Change.—One dominant fact that stands out is the fact of perpetual change. 'Panta rhei', everything 'goes on rolling', like Ole Man River in the negro song, and we have to be perpetually adapting both ourselves and our institutions to this unending process of which we ourselves are part. 'Political history', says Professor Schlesinger, 'is a record and analysis of man's efforts to resolve the problems of change within the social framework.'

But a three-fold caution is necessary here. In the first

place we must remember how slow is the working-out of consequences, how important the 'time-lag' between cause and effect. Man goes on speaking, and all the more thinking and feeling, in categories that no longer correspond with reality. Neither in his private nor in his collective life does he 'take in' things quickly. Stages in economic and intellectual evolution overlap, and the new by no means drives out the old at once, not even when they are obviously incompatible.[1] Change may be logically inevitable but it is rarely immediate. Together with this goes acceptance of the limits of possible deliberate change. 'A leader', says Merriam, 'can only function within a set of predetermined and generally understood lines of authority, some automatic, some deliberate.' This is shown by the inability of either revolutions or dictatorships to achieve more than the partial realisation of their aims. And we must remember thirdly, the terrific force of inertia to be found in the ordinary man which no political scientist dare neglect. Man is by nature an 'accepting' animal, who finds it easier to say 'yes' than 'no'. He will put up for centuries with the most trying and difficult of conditions, without any outward manifestation of protest or revolt. The would-be reformer will always find this exasperating fact his biggest obstacle, far more serious than direct opposition. 'Why bother?' is the grave of many a hope of social and political improvement. It is, in fact, amazing what the public will stand, and the problem for politicians is to see precisely how far this 'standing' will go. It certainly goes a long, long way, and yet some day the break comes; but why 'so far, and no further' remains a puzzle; that is why revolutions take governments by surprise.

The Law of Compromise.—Our second conclusion is that, just because political science is not a science, its solutions of the problems of collective life are tentative and imperfect. 'If you try to set forth in a catalogue what will be the exact settlement', once wrote Mr. Winston Churchill, 'you will find that the moment you leave the area of pious platitude you will descend into the arena of heated controversy.' As a consequence of this, you rarely get in politics neat and tidy complete

[1] See, for instance, the survival of slavery almost to our own time, or our reluctance to grasp the implications, both for good and evil, of the discovery of atomic energy.

answers to your questions. On the contrary, to quote another politician, Lord Eustace Percy, 'present-day politics tends to take the form of continual attempts to patch up temporary compromises between rigidly organised interests and rigidly limited minds'.

Compromise is in fact of the very essence of politics, and must be accepted as such. But compromise rightly understood is not the cowardly abandonment of principles but the inevitable give-and-take, the willingness to consider other people, without which there is no orderly common living. As John Morley puts it in his famous essay on the subject—an essay which every student should read—'the interesting question in connection with compromise obviously turns on the boundary which divides wise suspense in forming opinions, wise reserves in expressing them, and wise tardiness in trying to realise them, from unavowed disingenuousness and self-illusion, from voluntary dissimulation, and from indolence and pusillanimity'.

One lesson then, which we must keep in mind, is that in a free society no one individual, group, or nation, can expect to have it entirely his own way, and that when this does happen, it is disastrous for everybody concerned. Man is innately too selfish and too ignorant to be entrusted with much power over his fellows, and a satisfactory settlement of any issue is usually one that fully satisfies no one.

The Imperfections of Man.—This human selfishness and ignorance accounts for a third fact of common life; the extraordinary contrast between man's technical knowledge, powers of organisation, control over his physical environment, and material power over his fellow-man, and the poverty of the results achieved in creating a good life for the masses by the elimination either of want and destitution or of wars and dangers of war. It would seem, as Mr. Hay puts it in his 'Salt and Leaven', that man is incapable of understanding and satisfying the real needs of persons. 'The art of managing and manipulating other men has been carried to an extraordinary level of efficient subtlety; the capacity to appreciate and comprehend persons has made no such advance. There is antagonism as well as disparity, for the more the techniques of mass-manipulation and organisation are perfected, and the more widely they are applied, the less will those who practise them be able to give understanding consideration to persons as such, for you cannot truly respect what you are habitually managing, controlling, and manipulating.'

Man is unfit for much power over his fellows because he is not disinterested enough to study their needs without constant references to his own desires and interests. And the tragic fact is that he cannot carry into his social organisation the principles of altruism and self-sacrifice which he often does apply in his private relations. 'Moral Man and Immoral Society', wrote Dr. Niebuhr in a singularly penetrating study, which we recommend to our readers. 'There is the constant and seemingly irreconcilable conflict between the needs of society and the imperatives of a sensitive conscience.' The reason for this conflict is that 'group-relations are in terms of power, not ethics, and while an increase in social intelligence and moral goodwill may mitigate the brutalities of conflict, it cannot abolish conflict itself. Power can only be challenged by power.'

The Dualism of Human Nature.—One would like, of course, to dismiss this notion as cynical and exaggerated, but its essential truth is bound up with that dualism in human nature and relationships which we saw to lie at the very roots of our study. Man is both social and individual, co-operative and selfish; we may try and enlarge the field of solidarity and point out the waste and folly of struggle, but the imperfection inherent in him makes inevitable numerous manifestations of his self-regarding instincts. The element of conflict cannot be eliminated without revolutions in human nature of which so far there have been no signs.

This, of course, does not mean to say that we must give up all attempts to moralise politics and 'mitigate the brutalities of conflict'. It can be done, at least to some extent, by never forgetting the humanity of the opposing forces, by refusing ever to treat them as impersonal machines or mere means to ends, and by translating all our actions into terms of individual lives, while remembering at the same time that it is individual lives that we are trying to protect from exploitation by unscrupulous and aggressive power. 'What we have somehow to do,' said Lord Lindsay in a broadcast in May 1948, 'is to combine goodness and cleverness . . . to learn to harness the scientific mind to the service of the merciful heart. And we can learn how to answer this new challenge of our time from some of the countless men and women who are meeting it already (I know lots of them), who are putting knowledge and administrative skill in the service of goodness, and are learning to use organisations and yet to treat men and women as individuals.'

The Complexities of Politics.—There is the problem, and it is no easy one—which leads us to our fourth conclusion, that the more one studies politics, the more one realises what a difficult art it is, and how far removed from the easy complacency of those who think it is simple. The infinite complexity of man and his affairs baffles us, and our equipment is so inadequate. And one of our obstacles is that we are so hidebound and obsessed by prejudices, by assumptions which we are incapable of challenging. 'There are certain doctrines', wrote T. E. Hulme in his 'Speculations', 'which for a particular period seem, not doctrines, but inevitable categories of the human mind. Men do not look on them merely as correct opinions, for they have become so much a part of the mind, and lie so far back, that they are never really conscious of them at all. They do not seek them, but other things *through* them. It is these abstract ideas at the centre, *the things which they take for granted*, that characterise a period. It is these abstract things at the centre, those doctrines felt as *facts*, which are the source of all the other more material characteristics of a period.' And with this we may couple Burnham's words that, 'the laws of political life cannot be discovered by taking men's words and beliefs at their face value'.

It follows that those who really help in the progress of their day and generation are those who can discern what are the beliefs universally taken for granted, bring them from the unconscious into the light of reason, and either challenge them when false or restate them as truths consciously and deliberately accepted.

'The Faithful Living of Hidden Lives.'—And seeing the complexity of our problems and our inadequacy to face them, we may well wonder at times that things are no worse, and that there has been real advance, in spite of periods of retrogression. The explanation lies surely in a striking phrase of George Eliot's in 'Middlemarch': 'that things are not so ill with you and

me as they might have been is half owing to the numbers who lived faithfully a hidden life and rest in unvisited tombs', owing to the mass of devoted, common, ordinary people who did their daily duty faithfully and obscurely, being content to be put down as having loved their fellow-men.

The Position of the Individual.—And this brings us to a fifth point often made in these pages. In his 'Political Thought, the European Tradition', Professor Mayer distinguishes four problems of politics: the meaning of liberty, equality and other great abstractions; the relation of churches and other groups to the state; the question of property in its different aspects; the conditions of peace and international intercourse. But putting aside the last as outside the scope of this study, the other three are really all one, and resolve themselves into the one basic problem of the relation of the individual to the state, whether one of conflict, or one of co-operation, or one of independence. And the answer will obviously vary according to the nature of the particular state under observation, and of the opportunities it offers to its members for creative, co-operative activities, to the degree of liberty given to their free initiatives, to the feeling it gives them that the state exists for their welfare and not for the pursuit of aims in the benefits of which they have no share. And we may conclude with Weldon that 'there is a genuine and irreducible difference in fundamental beliefs between those who attach primary importance to the self-determination of the individual and those who acknowledge the superior reality of the state'.

The Problem of Values.—And lastly we come to the underlying reality of it all. Politics is ultimately and supremely a matter of values. What matters most to man and for man? But to this political science can give no answer. It supplies us with no standards by which to judge, and yet judge we must. Every act of our lives is a choice involving conscious or unconscious judgements as to what is good for us and for society. But what will be our criterion of goodness? This must depend on our general view of the universe, and the answer is to be found in ethics and theology, not in our political field.[1]

[1] The Ancient Greeks could see no difference between Ethics and Politics, nor could the medieval mind distinguish between those two and Theology. Perhaps it was right.

Dr. William Temple, later Archbishop of Canterbury, once gave the following definition of education.[1] 'The aim of education,' he said, 'is to enable men and women to assist or resist the tendencies of their age in the light of the fullest knowledge and the highest ideals possible.' Political science can supply the knowledge, the raw material, for our education in the art of social relationships. But the ideals it cannot provide. Belief in the individual is rooted in certain unprovable assumptions about man and the universe; those assumptions will not meet with universal acceptance. And we must leave it at that.

We insisted at the beginning on the importance of politics to the ordinary man and we hope the book has confirmed this significance. But we cannot conclude without reminding ourselves and our readers that politics is not everything. The real answers to the problems of human life lie outside parliament and polling-booth, and the lines of Dr. Johnson are as essentially true now as two hundred years ago:

> How small of all that human hearts endure
> That part which Kings or Laws can cause or cure.

[1] In a lecture given in Bristol nearly forty years ago. The lecture was never published, but permission to reproduce the quotation from our notes was given by Dr. Temple soon after.

BIBLIOGRAPHY

AND SUGGESTIONS FOR FURTHER READING

I. GENERAL WORKS

A. *Introductory*

BARKER, Sir Ernest. *The Citizen's Choice* (Cambridge University Press), 1937

BOWMAN, E. F. *Introduction to Political Science* (Methuen), 1927

COLE, G. D. H. *Social Theory* (Methuen), 1920

GARNER, J. W. *Introduction to Political Science and Government* (American Book Co., N.Y.), 1910

GETTELL, R. G. *Introduction to Political Science*, Revised edition (Ginn, Boston), 1922

GINSBERG, M. *Sociology* (Home University Library), 1934

JENKS, E. *The Ship of State* (Duckworth), 1949

LASKI, H. J. *An Introduction to Politics* (Allen and Unwin), 1931

LEACOCK, S. D. *Elements of Political Science* (Constable), 1921

MABBOTT, P. J. *The State and the Citizen* (Hutchinson), 1948

SEELEY, Sir John. *Introduction to Political Science* (Macmillan), 1896

SMELLIE, K. B. *Civics, The How and Why of Self-government* (Bell), 1939

B. *More Advanced Works*

BARKER, Sir Ernest. *Reflections on Government* (Oxford University Press), 1942

CATLIN, G. E. C. *The Science and Method of Politics* (Kegan Paul), 1926

—— *A Study of the Principles of Politics* (Allen and Unwin), 1930

GARNER, J. W. *Political Science* (American Book Co.), 1928

GETTELL, R. G. *Political Science*, Revised edition (Ginn, Boston), 1949

HAINES, C. G. *Principles and Problems of Government* (Harper), 1926

LASKI, H. J. *The State in Theory and Practice* (Allen and Unwin), 1935

LORD, A. R. *Principles of Politics* (Oxford University Press), 1921

MCIVER, R. M. *Community* (Macmillan), 1917

—— *The Modern State* (Oxford University Press), 1926

—— *The Web of Government* (Oxford University Press), 1947

MCLEOD, W. *Origins and History of Politics* (Willey Social Science Series, N.Y.), 1931

MERRIAM, C. E. *Systematic Politics* (Chicago University Press), 1945

SIDGWICK, H. *Elements of Politics* (Macmillan), 1920

SPENDER, J. A. *The Government of Mankind* (Cassell), 1938

WILSON, F. G. *Elements of Modern Politics* (McGraw Hill), 1936

WILSON, T. Woodrow. *The State* (Harrap), 1919

II. WORKS DEALING MAINLY WITH THE THEORY OF POLITICS

ALLEN, C. K.   *Democracy and the Individual* (Oxford University Press), 1945
BOSANQUET, B.   *The Philosophical Theory of the State* (Macmillan), 1920
BURNS, C. D.   *Political Ideals*, 4th edition (Oxford University Press), 1929
DEWEY, J.   *Individualism, Old and New* (Allen and Unwin), 1931
GREEN, T. H.   *Principles of Political Obligation* (Longmans), 1895
HOBHOUSE, L. T.   *Elements of Social Justice* (Allen and Unwin), 1921
—— *The Metaphysical Theory of the State* (Allen and Unwin), 1922
HOCKING, W. E.   *The Lasting Elements of Individualism* (Oxford University Press), 1937
—— *Man and the State* (Yale University Press), 1926
LASKI, H. J.   *Authority in the Modern State* (Oxford University Press), 1919
—— *Problem of Sovereignty* (King), 1917
LEACOCK, S. D.   *The Unsolved Riddle of Social Justice* (Lane), 1920
LLOYD, R.   *The Glorious Liberty* (Longmans), 1946
MANNHEIM, K.   *Man and Society in an Age of Reconstruction* (Kegan Paul), 1940
WARD, P. W.   *Sovereignty* (Routledge), 1928

III. WORKS DEALING MAINLY WITH THE PRACTICE OF POLITICS

A. *General*

BENTLEY, A. F.   *The Process of Government* (University of Chicago Press), 1908
BRYCE, Lord.   *Modern Democracies* (Macmillan), 1921
CORRY, J. A.   *Democratic Government and Politics* (University of Toronto), 1946
FINER, H.   *The Theory and Practice of Modern Government* (Methuen), 1932
FRIEDRICH, C. J.   *Constitutional Government and Politics* (Harper), 1937
LASKI, H. J.   *A Grammar of Politics* (Allen and Unwin), 1925
LASSWELL, H. D.   *Politics, Who Gets What? How? When?* (McGraw Hill), 1936
LINDSAY, Lord.   *The Modern Democratic State* (Oxford University Press), 1943
MARRIOTT, Sir J. A. R.   *The Mechanism of the Modern State* (Oxford University Press), 1927
ROBSON, W. A.   *Civilisation and the Growth of Law* (Macmillan), 1935
SAIT, E. C.   *Political Institutions* (Appleton Century, N.Y.), 1938

B. *Particular Countries*

BEARD, C. A.   *American Government and Politics* (Macmillan, N.Y.), 4th edition, 1924
BERDYAEV, N.   *Origin of Russian Communism* (Bles), 1937

CECIL, Lord Hugh. *Conservatism* (Home University Library), 1912

CHASE, E. P., VALEUR, R., and BUELL, R. L. *Democratic Governments of Europe* (Nelson), 1935

CORWIN, E. S. *The [American] Constitution and What it Means To-day* (Oxford University Press), 1946

GORDON, A. S. *Our Parliament*, 3rd edition (Hansard Society), 1948

HOBHOUSE, L. T. *Liberalism* (Home University Library), 1929

LASKI, H. J. *The American Democracy* (Allen and Unwin), 1948

MIDDLETON, W. L. *The French Political System* (Benn), 1932

MUIR, Ramsay. *How Britain is Governed* (Constable), 1937

OGG, F. A. *European Governments and Politics* (Macmillan, N.Y.), 1939

SMELLIE, K. B. *The American Federal System* (Williams and Norgate), 1928

SOLTAU, R. H. *French Parties and Politics* (Oxford University Press), 1930

THOMSON, D. *The Democratic Ideal in France and England* (Cambridge University Press), 1940

WEBB, S. and B. *Soviet Communism* (Longmans), 1935

IV. WORKS ON PARTICULAR TOPICS

A. On the Problem of Freedom

ACTON, Lord. *Lectures on the History of Freedom* (Macmillan), 1907

BURNHAM, J. *The Machiavellians, Defenders of Freedom* (Putnam), 1943

COBBAN, A. J. *Dictatorship* (Cape), 1939

FORD, G. S. *Dictatorship in the Modern World* (University of Minnesota Press), 1939

FROMM, E. *The Fear of Freedom* (Kegan Paul), 1942

JAEGER, M. *Liberty v. Equality* (Nelson Discussion Books), 1943

LASKI, H. J. *Liberty in the Modern State* (Faber and Faber), 1930

MARITAIN, J. *The Rights of Man and Natural Law* (Bles), 1944

MUIR, Ramsay. *Civilisation and Liberty* (Cape), 1940

ORTON, W. A. *The Liberal Tradition* (Yale University Press), 1945

POWICKE, Sir F. M. *History, Freedom and Religion* (Oxford University Press), 1938

SCHERGER, J. L. *The Evolution of Modern Liberty* (Longmans, N.Y.), 1904

TAWNEY, R. H. *Equality* (Allen and Unwin), 1931

WOOTTON, Barbara. *Freedom under Planning* (Allen and Unwin), 1945

B. Morals and Politics

CARRITT, E. F. *Ethical and Political Thinking* (Oxford University Press), 1947

CROCE, B. *Politics and Morals* (Allen and Unwin), 1936

DICKINSON, G. Lowes. *A Modern Symposium* (Dent), 1930

NIEBUHR, Reinhold. *Moral Man and Immoral Society* (Scribner), 1933

—— *The Nature and Destiny of Man* (Nisbet), Vol. I, 1946, Vol. II, 1948

STAPLETON, L. *Justice and World Society* (Oxford University Press), 1944

WELDON, T. D. *States and Morals* (Murray), 1946

C. *Psychology and Politics*

KOHN, H. *Force or Reason?* (Oxford University Press), 1937

LEBON, G. *The Crowd, A Study in Collective Psychology* (T. Fisher Unwin), 1896

MURCHISON, C. *Social Psychology, The Psychology of Political Determination* (Clark University Press), 1929

ORTEGA Y GASSETT, J. *The Revolt of the Masses* (Allen and Unwin), 1932

RUSSELL, B. *Power* (Arnold), 1938

SMELLIE, K. B. *Reason in Politics* (Duckworth), 1939

WALLAS, Graham. *The Great Society* (Macmillan), 1914

—— *Human Nature and Politics* (Constable), 1914

WHITEHEAD, T. N. *Leadership in a Free Society* (Oxford University Press), 1937

D. *Economics and Politics*

BORKENAU, F. *Socialism, National or International?* (Routledge), 1942

BURNHAM, J. *The Managerial Revolution* (Putnam), 1943

COLE, G. D. H. *Some Relations between Political and Economic Thought* (Macmillan), 1934

LIPPMANN, W. *The Good Society* (Allen and Unwin), 1937

LEWIS, W. A. *Principles of Economic Planning* (Dobson), 1949

MERRIAM, C. E. *The Role of Politics in Social Change* (Chicago University Press), 1936

SHAW, G. B. *Everybody's Political What's What?* (Constable), 1944

—— *The Intelligent Woman's Guide to Socialism, Capitalism, Sovietism and Fascism* (Constable), 1928

TAWNEY, R. H. *The Sickness of an Acquisitive Society* (Allen and Unwin), 1920

E. *Geography and Politics*

MACKINDER, Sir H. *Democratic Ideals and Reality* (Constable), 1919

MOODIE, A. E. *The Geography Behind Politics* (Hutchinson), 1949

V. ORIGINAL TEXTS

The scope of this book does not allow of any treatment of the evolution of ideas concerning the State and Politics. Students should try, however, to read one of the following books, which give a brief and simple sketch of this evolution:

BURNS, C. D. *Political Ideals* (Oxford University Press), 1931

CROSSMAN, R. H. S. *Government and the Governed* (Christopher), 1939

Useful selections from the chief authors will be found in:

GETTELL, R. G. *Readings in Political Science* (Ginn, Boston), 1911

SAIT, E. C. and FOSTER, M. B. *Masters of Political Thought* (Harrap), Vol. I, 1942, Vol. II, 1947

But all students should endeavour to read at least two or three of the following works, which are indicated in their chronological order:

PLATO.   *The Republic*
ARISTOTLE.   *The Politics*
AUGUSTINE.   *The City of God*
AQUINAS.   *The Government of Princes*
DANTE.   *On Monarchy*
MACHIAVELLI.   *The Prince*
BODIN.   *The Republic*
MORE.   *The Utopia*
HOBBES.   *Leviathan*
LOCKE.   *Second Treatise on Civil Government*
MONTESQUIEU.   *The Spirit of the Laws*
ROUSSEAU.   *The Social Contract*
BURKE.   *Reflections on the French Revolution*
HEGEL.   *Lectures on the Philosophy of History*
MARX and ENGELS.   *The Communist Manifesto*
MILL.   *Essay on Liberty*